The Valley's Legends and Legacies IV

The Valley's
Legends & Legacies IV

By Catherine Morison Rehart

Word
Dancer
Press

Clovis, California

Printed in the United States of America

Published by
Quill Driver Books/Word Dancer Press, Inc.
8386 N. Madsen
Clovis, CA 93611
559-322-5917
800-497-4909
QuillDriverBooks.com

Word Dancer Press books may be purchased for edu-
cational, fund-raising, business or promotional use. Please
contact Special Markets, Quill Driver Books/Word Dancer
Press, Inc. at the above address or phone number.

Quill Driver Books/Word Dancer Press, Inc.
Project Cadre:
Doris Hall, Stephen Blake Mettee

ISBN 1-884995-21-7

First printing November 2001
Second printing November 2003

Rehart, Catherine Morison, 1940-
    The valley's legends & legacies IV/ by Catherine Morison Rehart.
          p. cm.
    Scripts of the KMJ radio program, The valley's legends & legacies.
    ISBN 1-884995-21-7 (pbk.)
    1. Fresno County (Calif.)--History--Anecdotes. 2. Fresno County
    (Calif.)--Biography--Anecdotes. 3. San Joaquin Valley (Calif.)-
    -History--Anecdotes. 4. San Joaquin Valley (Calif.)--Biography--Anecdotes.
    I. Valley's legends and legacies (radio program)
    II. Title.
    F868.F8R44   2002
    979.4'82--dc21   CIP

Front cover photo shows Clovis Cole, who gave his name to the
Valley town of Clovis, stands next to the smoke stack. (See page 236)

With love to my forever friend
Jan
and to all my other Heaton School kindergarten classmates
especially
Dee Dee, Jayne Ann, Jeanne, Jim S., Jim M.,
& Charles B. (aka "Chico Charlie")
"Our strong bands will ne'er be broken!"

With love and gratitude to Dodie & Ron Tanner

IN MEMORIAM
William Reid "Scotty" Morison
my cherished father
and
Maynard Munger, James M. Malloch,
David L. Greenberg, & James G. Dowling
his close friends who stand tall in my remembrance
as men of integrity

Contents

Contents

Contents

Contents

Contents

Contents

Foreword

History is the DNA of the American culture. It ties together all people and their actions into a collection of facts that entertain, inform, and teach. History's moments of joy, blood, war, discovery, and creation mold us—they make us what we are and help us define the path we must take into the future. On that path we set the guidelines for a future that remembers the mistakes of years gone by and reveres the triumphs of old—from both we learn valuable lessons.

In our fertile valley, where I was born, we find the great history of gold, of farming, the Civil War, the American Indian, the Westward migration, and the towns that now flourish from seeds planted long ago. Cathy Rehart has studied those "seeds" and embraced this valley—a valley so often ridiculed in the national media. A valley that truly does feed the planet and is often overlooked for its importance in today's world.

Yet, in order for us to evolve into a region that so many on earth unknowingly depend upon, we had to have come from somewhere special!

These chronicles, *The Valley's Legends & Legacies*, define the "somewhere" and take us right down to the very fiber of the first settlers who took the green of the valley and made it greener.

Enjoy yet another sojourn to the small but significant corners of our valley's history.

—Ray Appleton

Preface

E ach time I begin a new chapter in the stories of our valley, I do so with eager anticipation, always wondering where the journey will lead. Every nook and cranny of this valley and its foothills are rich with history—the quest is never dull. Sometimes it is frustrating, often exciting, occasionally nostalgic, but always fascinating.

As I worked on the stories that are contained in this volume, an important milestone was celebrated—the twentieth century became the twenty-first. I decided to find out how the people of our valley celebrated the turning of the last century. I wondered what they were thinking and doing—how they were living their lives. What great events occurred in 1901? Were there any similarities between that time and 2001? One historic irony to me was that the electric fan, the only air-conditioning device available to homeowners in 1901, was the very gadget that homeowners rushed out to buy to get them through the energy crisis during the hot summer of 2001. History does sometimes repeat itself.

On this journey, I spent hours sitting in front of the microfilm machine in the California History Room of the Fresno County Library reading 1900 and 1901 newspapers. I was amazed at all that happened during those years. You will read about those events in this book.

My journey also took me far beyond the microfilm machine and far beyond Fresno. In this book you will read about people and events in Sanger, Grangeville, Clovis, Hanford, Academy, Millerton, Bowles, Fowler, Madera, Dos Palos, Biola, and Centerville. These explorations have allowed me to experience yet again the interesting diversity and beauty of our valley.

One of Fresno's great strengths is its wealth of distinctive ethnic cultures. I hope to eventually explore them all. In this book, you will read about the Volga Germans, the Italian, and the African-American communities.

I also have had the opportunity to meet the owners of some of Fresno's oldest businesses. Their stories are part of this book.

As always the journey has provided not only revelations that beg for a great deal of reflection, but also ones that contain a lot of humor. History, after all, is just a chronicle of everyday life and, as such, is a record of joys as well as sorrows. A sense of the ridiculous can be an important tool for any historian—at least it is for this one. As I read the newspapers of 1900-1901, I became very aware of—and quite mesmerized by—the ads placed in the Republican by W. Parker Lyon. I felt the need to share two of them with you in the last story. For this reason, this book ends on a slightly ridiculous, but I hope rather uplifting, note. As one old saying goes, "Always leave them laughing."

Cathy Rehart

Acknowledgments

In the course of writing this book, I have met and visited with wonderfully generous people. Harold, Morris, Richard, and Merlene Samuelian, Robert Schoettler, Koula Skofis, Jeannie Adkins, Dolph "Bud" Ruschhaupt, Ted Rusmore, Brian Ziegler, and my cousins Mary Helen McKay and Oliver Pickford graciously allowed me to interview them and provided marvelous stories for this book. Dave and Tom Schoettler not only told me the history of their family business, but also gave me a tour of their tire retreading plant. Bill Kratt, Doug Wilson, and Walter Harpain shared stories of their respective businesses and allowed me to borrow photographs. Jack Brase talked to me about the history of the San Joaquin Power Club and shared photographs. Thank you many times over.

I will always cherish the memory of a morning spent talking with Frank Caglia and his daughter Sally Caglia Martinez. He shared stories of his life, his family, the village in Italy where he was born, and his reverence for St. Elia. Hours spent in such company are a blessing—I thank you with all my heart.

Johnna Meisner wins the prize for gathering folks together! She organized two incredible afternoons at the American Historical Society of Germans from Russia Museum. The first was a large group of Fresnans who grew up in "Roosiantown." The second was comprised of the descendents of the Germans who settled Biola. On both occasions, my pencil and my tape recorder worked mightily as I listened to an incredible outpouring of memories and stories.

To top it off, Johnna invited me to watch berrock making at the Cross Church—an amazing and delicious experience. My gratitude to my new friend Johnna and to all those who came to share knows no bounds. Also thank you to Diana Bell who gave me a tour of the German museum and archive.

An amazing surprise came out of the Biola meeting. Seated across the table from me were two delightful people who had journeyed all the way from Manteca to be there. Byron and Nila Eisner brought pictures to share with me. As I opened the packet, I was amazed at what it contained. Nila, the granddaughter of Charles Owen and a grandniece of Clovis Cole, had brought family photographs. They were treasures that Nila generously has allowed me to use for this book. A short time later they returned to Fresno and invited me to their daughter Karen's home to visit with a cousin, Harvey Owen. An incredible afternoon was spent talking about the Cole and Owen families and listening to Harvey's reminiscences. A simple, "thank you" is a tremendous understatement for the gratitude I feel. I am also grateful for the new friendships that emerge after such an afternoon.

James R. Walton, president of the Sanger Historical Society, gave me a marvelous and informative tour of the Sanger Depot Museum. Peg Bos and Ron Sundquist extended me the courtesy of allowing me to linger at the Clovis Big Dry Creek Museum and answered all my many questions. Thank you so much. Also, my gratitude to Tom Flores for a marvelous phone interview and to Jim Gonzales for providing information on the Tom Flores Foundation.

I traveled to Fowler for a delightful morning with Pauline Blayney and Jean Pereira of the Fowler Improvement Association. We perused scrapbooks and photographs as I listened to the telling me the history of their club that Pauline's great-grandmother founded. A tour of Fowler with Jean followed. A marvelous morning—many thanks.

Although I have traveled by the Dos Palos turn-off of Highway 152 all my life, I had never visited that city. Now, thanks to Dan Sniffin, I have. We left Fresno early one morning and traveled to Dos Palos. A delicious lunch at the home of his relatives Betty and Bud Wooten was preceded by an informative session with Bud on the history of Dos Palos. After lunch, they took me on a tour of the city, including a stop at the office of the Dos Palos Sun newspaper to see an old acquaintance, publisher Bruce Pankratz. Then we headed for South Dos Palos and a rather scary, but enjoyable, ride along the levees to see the famous duck clubs of the west side. Thank you for a most memorable day.

A very special thank-you to Detective Todd Frazier of the Fresno Police Department for sharing information regarding the department's history. Thanks also to Lieutenant John Fries for your assistance. Whenever I need help regarding Fresno street names, I call local expert Ken Hohmann who never fails to have the proper answer. When I need help regarding the history of water, Selma, or Fowler, I call my dear friend Randy McFarland who not only provides the answers but also regales me with a great story or two. Thank you both.

I truly can't imagine life without the Fresno County Free Library's California History and Genealogy Room. Supervising Librarian Ray Silvia presides over a group of intelligent, well-versed, humorous, and generous staff persons who always have time to help. My gratitude to Bill Secrest, Sr., Bill Secrest, Jr., and Melissa Scroggins for answering my endless questions and for making the many hours I spend there at the microfilm machines enjoyable as well as profitable.

Also, many thanks to Mabel Wilson and her staff at the Fresno Bee Library for all your assistance. I am deeply grateful to Joyce Hall of the Kings County Museum at Burris Park for allowing me to use the marvelous photo of Kenzie Whitten "Blackhorse" Jones.

To my dear friend and superlative editor, Bobbye Temple, my warmest thanks. Also, my gratitude to Doris Hall for typesetting this book and for applying her excellent editing skills as well.

Also to publisher Steve Mettee and all his staff at Quill Driver Books/Word Dancer Press, my heartfelt thanks.

"The Valley's Legends & Legacies" would not have been possible without the vision of KMJ general manager and vice president Al Smith. The program was his idea and it is he who breathes life into the scripts everyday. My deepest gratitude to Al and to KMJ Program Director John Broeske for asking me to begin writing these scripts eleven years ago and for your incredible support ever since. The more I delve into our local history, the more this program continues to be a real "labor of love."

Many thanks to Ray Appleton for writing the Foreword for this book and for your interest and concern regarding the preservation of our local history.

To Robert Wilson, owner of Fresno Lincoln-Mercury and long-time sponsor of "The Valley's Legends & Legacies," my heartfelt thanks for your support and belief in this program.

As always, my deepest gratitude goes to those who tune in to KMJ to listen to the tales of our valley, to the readers of the Legends books, and to all those who send me your comments and story ideas. Your enthusiasm and observations are very much appreciated. Your encouragement inspires me to keep searching out new stories in this fascinating historical journey.

CMR

The Valley's Legends and Legacies IV

The year was 1943. The war was raging in Europe and in the Pacific. Many of Fresno's sons and fathers had left to fight for their country. It was a time of fear, hope, loneliness, and struggle—yet the country was united in the cause of freedom.

For three Fresno families, August 19, 1943, was a day of pride in their sons' dedication to serve their country. On this day, as it did on many days for other Fresno men, the *Fresno Bee* published an account of their achievements.

Kenneth T. Craycroft, a member of one of Fresno's early families and formerly the general manager of Craycroft Brick Company, had been called to active duty in the United States Army in 1940. He quickly rose through the ranks and, in January of 1943, was appointed provost marshal of the Southern California sector. On August 5, 1943, he was promoted to the rank of lieutenant colonel.

Gordon P. Davis, who had been working with his father in the cattle business after graduating from Fresno State College, had spent his first year of service in the armored field artillery branch of the United States Army. He received his promotion to first lieutenant.

Another Fresno man, Milo Popovich, had trained as a pilot and earned his license under the civilian pilot training program. Popovich, a graduate of Hastings Law School in San Francisco and a special legal investigator for the district attorney's office, received greetings in the mail from Uncle Sam ordering him to report to the Presidio of Monterey on August 30, 1943. Here he was to finish the qualifications needed for Army civilian pilot service. It was reported that, after his final examinations, he would be assigned for duty.

The list of Fresno's men who served in World War II was long indeed. As they left to serve their country, their family's hearts were fearful, yet filled with pride. Their dedication and service is another rich legacy for this community as the tales of our valley unfold.

A Mountain Journey on an April Day

As the traveler leaves Fresno and journeys east on Highway 180, he leaves the bustling urban environment behind and finds himself slipping into a more tranquil scene. Soon, lovely old trees line the two-lane road and the traveler realizes he has reached Centerville. The historic Odd Fellows building on his left reminds him that this is one of the oldest towns in the Central Valley...the scene of more than one encounter between canal builder Moses Church and cattleman Yank Hazelton's men. The road curves and the traveler drives over a bridge, with the waters of the Kings River churning and rushing noisily beneath. The road dips slightly as the traveler reaches Minkler. Soon, the tall eucalyptus trees are replaced by citrus groves. The traveler begins his ascent into the foothills.

The climb into the mountains is steep, but affords breathtaking views. The traveler stops at the first overlook so he can look back over the valley. He can see Campbell Mountain in the distance. In early April, white popcorn flowers, golden poppies and yellow fiddleneck carpet the hillsides. Blue lupine, growing in thickets, dots the landscape, cascading among the crevices in the rocks. From this vantage point, our valley still seems like a world untouched by man.

Proceeding on his journey, the traveler wends his way upward. He passes through the community of Squaw Valley, so named because of a footprint. It seems that near this settlement there is a depression in a granite rock that looks as if it were made by a woman's moccasin. The footprint carries the Indian name of Wootona, which means woman's foot. The footprint points into this small valley nestled in the hills, thus indicating that this area is woman's land. According to legend, if anyone puts his foot into this print, he will die.

Continuing upward, the road curves, following the outline of the mountains. Signs along the highway point the way to Wonder Valley and Dunlap. Pausing for a few minutes at Clingan's Junction for a cup of coffee, the traveler then starts his trip once more, crossing into Tulare County and heading into the Sequoia National Forest and the entrance to the Kings Canyon National Park.

Just when it seemed as if nothing else could have survived from the old town of Millerton, a driving trip through Selma proved that premise wrong. A turn in the road takes the traveler to the corner of Mill and Keith streets. There, beside the steps of one of Selma's oldest houses, sit two granite pillars.

The house was built in the 1880s and is an example of Eastlake architecture. It was constructed by an Englishman with the surname of Sheets. It was later purchased by Frank Dusy, a pioneer cattle and sheep man. It was in this house that he died in 1898.

Sometime between 1874, when the county seat was moved from Millerton to Fresno, and his death, Dusy brought the two granite pillars to Selma. They had graced Fresno County's first courthouse at Millerton. Why he brought them is a mystery, but, perhaps, he just wanted to preserve them. Legend says that his reasons were sentimental ones.

The pillars stand about four feet high and are made up of three parts. The tops and bases are made of granite that came from the quarries at Raymond in Madera County. The center posts are a conglomerate of fossilized seashells that probably came from near Coalinga. At the front and center of each post is a decorative element consisting of four scalloped edges.

The casual visitor to Selma might drive right by this house, noticing only its Victorian elements, so well do these pillars seem rooted to their site. A second glance might give the visitor pause. Perhaps they do seem a little out of sync with their environment. After all, few Victorian homes have granite pillars attached to their front steps. Even if they are a little incongruous, how nice that these elements of our first county courthouse have been preserved. In these times when we are so quick to throw away parts of our history, it is a nice surprise to turn a corner in Selma and see these pieces of history living on.

From 1998 to 2000, we celebrated the sesquicentennial, the 150th anniversary of the discovery of gold in California and the events leading up to statehood. It is important for the citizens of Fresno and Madera counties to remember that, although gold was discovered near Sacramento, the Gold Rush happened here, too.

Before the railroad came down the Central Valley, before the first colony farm was sold by a developer, before the first canal was built to bring water to irrigate crops, before the first heads of cattle were pastured near the foothills, gold was discovered on the San Joaquin River. As early as 1849, it was whispered about that a gold pan and determination could make a man rich in the rivers of what would become Fresno County. Soon the foothill and lower mountain areas were alive with miners trying their luck, living along the rivers and tributaries and in mining camps with such colorful names as Poison Switch, String Town, and Grub Gulch. Many struck it rich. One historian, writing of this period some thirty years later, said that millions of dollars worth of gold was extracted from the foothills of the Fresno area. Gold dust rather than coins became the medium of exchange.

In 1865 a notice was published in the *Fresno Times* at Millerton listing gold dust rates. Pure San Joaquin River or Bar dust was worth $15.50 an ounce; Fine Gold Gulch, Long Gulch and Cottonwood dust, $14 per ounce; Coarse Gold Gulch dust, $16.60; Big Dry Creek dust, $16.50; Sycamore Creek dust, if free from quicksilver and not mixed with other dust, $17.50; Fresno River dust, taken out above McKeown's store, $15.50; below McKeown's store—no price given. The notice was signed by the merchants of Millerton, who also pledged not to accept or pay out anything that did not equal the value of United States gold and silver coins.

Without a doubt, it was gold that brought the first real prosperity to the area.

On May 19, 1983, fourteen ladies arrived at the Tea Room of the Y.W.C.A., housed in the historic Einstein Home. It was a sad day because the Emma Miller Study Club was meeting for the last time.

Who was Emma Miller? She was a woman of keen intelligence who had received her education in the study of the classics and literature. She had a reading knowledge of Greek and Latin, but Shakespeare was her forte. She and her husband settled in Sanger in 1888 and moved to Fresno in 1891. She was the force behind the establishment of the leading women's study clubs in Fresno and nearby towns.

In 1925, Blanche Wagner organized the Emma Miller Study Club in honor of this woman who more than any other person had inspired the women of the new city of Fresno to expand their horizons. The women of this growing frontier town had been consumed with the day-to-day business of caring for their families. Emma Miller inspired them to feed their minds and souls through a study of literature. The club was a fitting tribute to a great lady.

The club's membership was limited to twenty-five. Their mission was simple: "The object shall be the general improvement." The motto was also concise. *Non Palma Sine Labore* (No Victory Without Labor).

For fifty-eight years the members met twice each month to hear speakers, book reviews, and dramatic readings. The members prided themselves on keeping their cultural standards on a par with what Emma Miller would wish. By 1983, the membership had dwindled to a stalwart few, many of whom were unable to attend meetings due to age and illness. Twenty-three names were on the roster but the average attendance had dropped to ten at each meeting and they were not able to attract younger members. It was also harder to obtain good speakers. The decision was made to disband. The only consolation was the feeling that Emma Miller would approve their decision. It would not be fair to the memory of Emma Miller to continue unless her standards could be maintained.

And, so, the final meeting was held in a fitting historical place.

Dr. and Mrs. W. P. Miller. Emma Miller was the driving force behind the formation of women's study clubs in Fresno. *Courtesy of Mary Helen McKay.*

Lunch was served, pictures were taken, and memories were shared. The ladies went home and the Emma Miller Study Club faded into history.

Frank Latta.
Courtesy Bear State Books.

Frank Latta, one of the foremost authorities on the Indians of the Central Valley, published more than a dozen books on valley history. He was born near the mouth of Orestimba Creek in Stanislaus County on September 18, 1892. His father was a Cumberland Presbyterian minister and his mother was a school-teacher. His passion for history developed when he was asked by his grammar school teacher to collect the history of the school. In completing this assignment, he interviewed a pioneer, James Hitchcock, who had come to California before gold was discovered and had countless tales to tell, including being scalped at the hands of Indians as he journeyed to California on one of the first wagon trains to cross the Sierra.

During his career as a writer and historian, Latta interviewed well over 1,700 pioneers and collected thousands of stories. He felt lucky to have had the opportunity to do this because so many of the earliest settlers were still alive and remembered how things were in the beginning. He wrote more 3,000 newspaper stories, magazine articles, and books—an incredible publishing effort. One of his more controversial books dealt with the life of Joaquin

Murrieta. In it, he refutes the idea that Murrieta was killed at the hands of Captain Love in the area of Cantua Creek. The book was the culmination of sixty years of research.

His *Handbook of Yokuts Indians* is regarded as the definitive study of the Yokuts in the Central Valley. A fascinating book, it details all one might wish to know about the Indians of our area.

Author Frank Latta will long be remembered by those who, like him, are captivated by the rich history of our Central Valley. His lifework remains as an important legacy to us all.

It is a while since we have recorded some of the more vexing of life's trials as we pursue our chronicles of life in our Central Valley. Indeed, some of the most pleasurable activities available to us have their flip side, so to speak. How many of us have gone for a walk in the country on a beautiful summer day and have returned only to find nasty, prickly, pesky, tiny bur-like bits of weeds in our stockings? The same little bits of evil can be found clumped in the hair of the family dog after a frolic in some tall grass or weeds at the garden's edge. Just try to remove them— they take on a life of their own, clinging to the fabric or pet hair with a persistence that elicits howls of pain from Fido and much cursing from Fido's master. The only help for it is to resort to the use of scissors. The result is a major dent in Fido's haircut and, perhaps, a ruined pair of stockings. Have you ever wondered what these little demons are and where they come from?

According to a book titled *Weeds of California,* these pests come from the sandbur weed. Sandburs love the warm climate of our valley and grow luxuriantly just about everywhere. They do not discriminate; indeed, they share their wealth with everyone. The sandbur's growth pattern is sometimes erect. Other times it grows in a spreading fashion along the ground. It also floats in water. The weed has spikelets that have at their base a seedpod that, as it matures, becomes a dense, hairy bur with strong spines. These spines are so strong they can penetrate shoe leather. The seeds germinate within the bur. Each plant can produce almost a thousand seeds in a rather speedy amount of time.

So the next time Fido comes in with burs in his fur, you can blame the sandbur weed. When trouble comes into your life, it's always nice to be able to call it by name.

Over the years, our valley has experienced floods and earthquakes, but, thankfully, not the plagues and pestilence that have hit other parts of the world. However, we do have one scourge that has caused many among us to resort to tearing of hair and gnashing of teeth—it is called Bermuda grass. Its name conjures up visions of the lovely, balmy Caribbean island for which it is named. Indeed, it is native to the warmer climes of the Old World.

Bermuda grass came to the warm inland valley of California for use as a pasture crop. It also was planted along canal banks where it served the important purpose of binding the soil so it would not erode. People began planting it as a lawn in their yards. It survived drought and alkali. That made it seem perfect for the Central Valley. Soon, however, it was found this perennial survived almost everything else as well. It produced runners and rootstocks that spread rapidly, not just on the surface of the soil, but underneath as well. The roots grabbed onto the soil and held on for dear life not content with merely creating a grassy lawn, but spilling over into flower beds and rock gardens. Merrily they grew, taking over everything in their path. Just try to get rid of them. Grab onto those rootstocks and runners and pull as hard as you can and see who wins the war—it probably won't be you.

Another amazing feature of this pesky weed is how it has managed to spread its influence everywhere. Its seeds are borne by wind and water. They can be found tucked away in commercial seed packets in the form of impurities—hiding away where they don't belong. They can be found in hay, in livestock feed, and are dragged from one place to another by cultivating machines. You may decide to plant an exotic grass in your yard. Soon patches of Bermuda grass will appear. The struggle begins. It will go on for years. Only the hardiest and most determined of souls will stay the course. For most of us, it's just easier to plant the darned stuff in the beginning and let the weed have its way. A legend of the valley in its own special way, Bermuda grass will probably outlive us all.

In the early 1890s, Fresno High School classes were held at the White School located on the site of the present-day Memorial Auditorium. The rooms were spartan with wooden floors, plain walls, blackboards, and windows that were opened in the hot weather to catch any breeze that might exist. The only unusual feature in the classroom was a wooden platform—about two to three inches higher than the rest of the room—that held the teacher's desk and chair.

On the day our story took place, it was very, very hot. There was no such thing as air-conditioning—all one could do was pray for a slight breeze to stir the air. The girls wore cotton dresses, but with high necks, long sleeves and long skirts, as befit the fashion of the time. The boys wore shirts and long pants. The afternoon heat seemed to be increasing by the minute. It did not help, of course, that the teacher, who was rather overweight, droned on and on about a subject that had failed to capture the interest of the class—the Trojan War. This same group of students had been studying avoirdupois weight in their math class and, somehow, math teacher Chester Harvey Rowell had made that subject more interesting.

All at once, one of the students noticed something fascinating. The teacher had become so involved with his subject that he was leaning back in his chair. The back legs of the chair had moved and were now balanced precariously on the edge of the platform. Notes began to circulate throughout the room. Soon, all eyes were on the chair legs. The teacher, noticing that his audience seemed engrossed, waxed ever more eloquently about the great Trojan horse and the trick that was about to play itself out on the Trojan people. No one dared to breathe—one fraction of an inch was all that separated the teacher from disaster—all it would take was one more tiny motion.

Then it happened. The teacher raised his arm to declare the treachery of the soldiers in the horse and the chair crashed down off the platform—teacher and all. In the moment of silence that followed, a lone voice was heard to exclaim, "Rather than the fall of Troy, we have just witnessed the fall of avoirdupois!"

During the years of the Civil War, Fresno County was a Confederate stronghold. The county's earliest newspaper, the *Fresno Times,* published first at Visalia and then at Millerton, espoused the Southern cause. Many people were afraid to say openly that they supported the Union. One of the few early settlers who was a Union supporter, William Hazelton, was given the nickname "Yank." Sentiments ran so high that the Union felt it necessary to reactivate Fort Miller to hold the area. As Colonel Olney and his troops crossed the Chowchilla River, then the northern boundary of Fresno County, on their way to open the fort, Olney commanded his men to load their muskets because they were entering enemy territory.

After the war was over, many Southerners came to Fresno County seeking a new life. Many others who had fought for the Union came from the midwest. They found a common purpose in their new locale. Dr. Chester Rowell had served in the Union Army. He fought at the Battle of Shiloh. Dr. Thomas R. Meux was at Shiloh, too, serving as an assistant surgeon for the Confederate Army. Yet, they both served their new community of Fresno with distinction, treating the sick and participating in building a strong foundation for the future of their city.

Today, the issues of the Civil War still fascinate many. In the spring of 1990, a group of people, primarily members of the Rotary Club of Fresno, started meeting once a month to discuss the issues of the war. A year later they were joined by another group which had been meeting at California State University, Fresno. In October of 1991, they formed a single group. In October of 1992, they organized with the name of San Joaquin Valley Civil War Round Table.

The Round Table meets once a month to listen to programs relating to Civil War history. They sponsor trips to historic sites and support the preservation of battle sites. Each year, many of their members participate in the annual Civil War Revisited at Kearney Park. Fascinated by the history of the period, the members of the San Joaquin Valley Civil War Round Table continue to review the issues and events of that period and, in so doing, keep history alive.

One of the benefits of living in our great Central Valley is the close proximity of both the ocean and the mountains. When summer's heat gets unbearable, those who can take advantage of this geographical bonanza pack their bags and head for the hills or the seashore. In the later part of the nineteenth century, when ocean breezes beckoned, Fresnans journeyed either to Pacific Grove or to Santa Cruz.

Santa Cruz became a tourist attraction as early as 1865. In this year John Liebrandt and several others built public bathhouses near the mouth of the San Lorenzo River. They advertised the health benefits of bathing in the ocean's salt water to attract tourists. The bathhouses were used, for a fee of course, as places in which to change clothes. Soon concessions opened nearby.

Around the turn of the century, promoter Fred W. Swanton drafted a plan for a casino and boardwalk patterned after similar facilities at Coney Island in New York. The casino opened in 1904, only to burn down two years later. In 1907, it was rebuilt from plans drawn by William H. Weeks. The boardwalk opened at the same time.

To celebrate the opening, a grand ball was held. The Royal Hawaiian Orchestra and three brass bands played for the festivities. President Theodore Roosevelt sent his congratulations.

A year later the first ride, the L. A. Thompson Scenic Railway, opened. In 1911, a merry-go-round with seventy hand-carved horses made by well-known Danish woodcarver Charles I. D. Looff made its debut. The carousel's original 342-pipe Ruth band organ, which was built in 1894, still provides the music as the riders go round and round. For many, the music of the carousel drew them to the boardwalk, calling out in its singular way that fun was in store for all who came.

In 1924, the Giant Dipper Roller Coaster was added. It provided thrills for those hearty souls who loved a taste of excitement. Today, the dipper and the carousel have attained national landmark status and are the centerpieces of the boardwalk.

For those who grew up spending many summer days at the beach at Santa Cruz, the music of the carousel still rings in our ears—a sort of siren's call promising fun and thrills to all who venture to the boardwalk. Those days of fun and frolic have been enjoyed by generations of Fresnans for over ninety years.

B rilliant, high-strung, well-educated, Chester Harvey Rowell burst onto the editorial pages of his uncle's newspaper, the *Fresno Morning Republican*, like a comet casting light on the darker side of life in the pioneer town of Fresno. In 1898, he came at the invitation of his uncle and namesake, Dr. Chester Rowell, who wanted him to take over the newspaper. It had a low subscriber list and was nine thousand dollars in debt. This posed a challenge for a man who had absolutely no background in journalism.

Rowell was born in Bloomington, Illinois. His father, Jonathan Rowell, was an attorney and later served in Congress. Young Chester liked school and tackled learning with a vigor and enthusiasm that, coupled with his brilliant mind, allowed him to finish school ahead of his classmates. He had total recall and picked up languages easily. By the time he reached adulthood he was fluent in twenty-one languages and dialects. After graduating from the University of Michigan, he went to graduate school in Germany, but did not complete his degree. He taught at a small college in Kansas for one year. In 1896, he came to Fresno to teach German and mathematics at Fresno High School. The students found him fascinating, but, because he paced the floor, gestured constantly, and never seemed able to sit still, they privately called him "Wiggily Chet."

When he took over the *Republican* in 1898, politics in Fresno was still dominated by the saloon bosses who were deep into gambling and prostitution. Conditions were ripe for change, but no one had come along with the vision and necessary influence to clean up the town. Rowell took on the task. Through his editorials he waged an all-out campaign for reform. He stood firm in the face of many local business people who felt that reform would be bad for the town. He spearheaded the drive for a new city charter, which finally was voted in 1900. This, and the election of an honest man, undertaker L. O. Stephens, who became Fresno's first strong mayor, marked the beginning of a new era for Fresno.

In 1910, Rowell and others founded the Lincoln-Roosevelt League that began as a populist movement in the Republican Party and soon became the Progressive Party. It was this party that nominated Hiram Johnson for governor of California. In 1912, Johnson was elected to that office. With this election, the railroad's stranglehold over government at all levels was broken. Rowell's editorials in the *Republican* contributed to this outcome.

By now the *Republican* was one of the major newspapers in California. When it was sold, in 1920, its value had definitely increased. It had 35,000 subscribers. The selling price was one million dollars. The brilliant editor had certainly surpassed his uncle's dream.

Chester H. Rowell and his wife moved to Berkeley, California. From 1932 to 1935, Rowell served as the editor of the *San Francisco Chronicle*, taking the ferry across San Francisco Bay each day to get to work. In 1936, he stepped down as editor and became a columnist for the *Chronicle*. Illness forced him to retire in 1947. He died a year later.

Rowell's significant contributions to the reform movement aimed at making changes in Fresno's governmental structure at the beginning of the twentieth century are well worth remembering. Later, his passion for reform helped pave the way for political change statewide. Chester Harvey Rowell's legacy is also contained in the large body of his written material—mostly in the form of editorials in the *Republican*—that still exists on microfilm. Many of his opinions and musings seem as timely today as when they were written. They are a fascinating "must read" for anyone interested in local history.

A Magical Place for Children

One of Fresno's treasures is a place in Roeding Park where storybooks come alive—where children of all ages can leave the modern world behind and slip into an enchanted world of make-believe. As soon as he steps inside the Magical Gateway that marks the entrance to Storyland, the visitor enters an enchanted garden shrouded in trees and foliage. Following a well-marked path, he first meets the caterpillar from *Alice in Wonderland*, who is sitting high up on a mushroom welcoming him. Continuing on the path, he visits many storybook settings and characters such as the House of the Three Bears, Gulliver's Pirate Ship, King Arthur's Birthday Castle, Hansel and Gretel and the Wicked Witch, and the 100 Acre Wood where Winnie-the-Pooh and his hunny pot can be found high up in a tree. As he visits each place, he follows the path that wends its way through this delightful setting. In doing so, he sometimes has to walk over small bridges that allow him to cross the stream that winds and splashes through the gardens.

In the center of Storyland is the Children's Chapel. On the back of each pew is a quotation from the scriptures of the Christian, Mohammedan, Hebrew, Zoroastrian, Buddhist, Confucian, or Muslim faith. The windows of the chapel have drawings of animals from Noah's Ark.

Storyland opened in May of 1962. It was the dream of many people to create this magical place for children where literature would come to life. It was through a community-wide effort by local businesses, private citizens, and local artists that the dream became a reality. In 1994, Storyland joined with Playland to become part of Rotary Storyland and Playland.

As the visitor leaves this land of enchantment and returns to the real world, he remembers what he read on a sign as he began his journey. For those who created this place "No profit has been sought. No credit desired. Just the happiness of children of all ages who enjoy this Storyland of Fresno."

Christmas at the Meux Home

One of the warmest and brightest of Fresno's holiday events centers around a restored Victorian family home in an area of Fresno known for its most prominent landmark, St. John's Cathedral. Built in 1889, this home boasted continuous occupancy by the family of Dr. Thomas R. Meux for eighty-one years. Purchased by the City of Fresno in 1970, the home is now listed in the National Register of Historic Places.

Always a treat to visit, at Christmas time the Meux Home becomes a feast for the eyes, ears, and heart. Here, one visits a time in our history when life was conducted at a slower pace and when Christmas was celebrated with a certain pageantry and style that, in our modern fast-paced world, is often overlooked.

From the moment you step over the threshold of the front door, you are aware of entering a more richly textured world. Music fills the entry as carolers sing the carols of Christmas. The scents of potpourri and evergreens quietly spin their magic, transporting you to another time. Everywhere you look you see a Victorian Christmas in all its grandeur—greens bedecked with red ribbons, trees decorated with period ornaments and toys, a dining table lavishly set for the traditional dinner, plum pudding waiting in the kitchen for its grand entrance, and stockings hung on the mantelpiece. As you tour the home, you truly feel as if you are participating in a family event.

Perhaps this is because the Meux Home has a special tradition. Each year, in late November, a tree trimming party is held. The volunteers and members of the Meux family gather together for an evening of decorating the many trees in the house. The Meux family shares memories of past Christmases celebrated there.

For those who visit this grand old home at Christmas, the sense of family is evident in every nook and cranny. It reaches out to embrace all who enter. When you leave, it is with a quiet sense of joy in your heart.

A Compiler of History

On the shelves of the California History Room at the main branch of the Fresno County Free Library can be found a two-volume set of books that is an invaluable aid to local historians. Written by Paul Vandor in 1919, they chronicle the early history of our Central Valley and contain hundreds of biographies of early pioneers. So prized is this set of books that those who own it give it pride of place in their private libraries.

Who was Paul Vandor? What was his background? He was a newspaperman, working in San Francisco as assistant city editor of the *Call*, a reporter on the *Chronicle* and the *Examiner*, and as drama critic for the *Golden Era*. He was a charter member of the San Francisco Press Club. He moved to Fresno, where he was the editor of the *Democrat* and a news writer on the *Evening Expositor*, the *Fresno Republican*, and the *Fresno Herald*. That was his professional life; his parental background was far more fascinating.

Vandor's father, Joseph, was an exiled Hungarian nobleman who, after coming to the United States in 1849, served for a short time in a Wisconsin regiment during the early part of the Civil War. He later was appointed American consul at Papeete, the main city on the island of Tahiti. Vandor's mother, Pauline, was a direct descendant of Major von Knobelsdorf, the royal architect of Frederick the Great. Joseph Vandor lost his properties in the ill-fated Hungarian revolution of 1849.

Paul Vandor was born in Milwaukee in 1858, the eldest of three children. His early years were spent in Tahiti. One of his memories was of a native uprising that was quelled only when his father hoisted the Stars and Stripes up the mast of a Tahitian schooner. Vandor was thrown to the deck of the ship to escape the barrage of bullets the natives fired before the flag was raised.

Instead of writing his own story, Vandor collected the stories of the early settlers of our valley, adding greatly to the knowledge of the history of Fresno County. His legacy is appreciated by all those who turn to his work.

Paul Vandor was the author of what many consider to be the definitive history of Fresno County. A newspaperman by profession, he served as assistant city editor of the *San Francisco Call* and as editor of the *Fresno Democrat* as well as holding reporting positions with the *San Francisco Chronicle* and *Examiner* and the *Fresno Morning Republican*. His deep love for and knowledge of California history led to the monumental work that is his legacy.

The Special Bells of Christmas

Each holiday has special sights and sounds that make it unique. This is especially true at Christmas—that most resplendent of seasons—when we are treated to rich colors and textures, sparkling lights, and glorious music. Amid all this there is a sound that seems to transcend even the traffic noises as it wafts its way through the cold, crisp air to remind us that Christmas is a time for giving. The sound comes from a little bell rung by a Salvation Army soldier or volunteer standing next to a large kettle. That little bell helps us to remember that there are many less fortunate people in our community who need our help.

How did this Christmas tradition begin? In December of 1891, Salvation Army Captain Joseph McFee wanted to give the poor people of San Francisco a free Christmas dinner. But how he would pay for the food? Then he remembered that when he was a sailor in Liverpool, England, a large pot that someone called "Simpson's Pot" was used to collect donations. He got permission to place such a pot where the ferry boats from Oakland docked—at the foot of Market Street. He placed it so it could be seen by everyone who came on and off the ferry. He placed another pot inside the waiting room. It was a success. The money was collected and the poor had a real Christmas dinner.

The tradition begun that year quickly spread throughout the country. Someone ringing a bell would stand next to a kettle to attract the attention of passers-by. Today the collected moneys provide Thanksgiving and Christmas dinners for over three million people—the poor, the ill, inmates of jails and other institutions—the people society tends to forget. Indeed, kettles and bell ringers can be found in Korea, Japan, Chile, and throughout Europe.

On March 14, 1890, the Fresno Citadel Corps of the Salvation Army was opened under the leadership of Captain Minnie Grace Tully. For over a hundred and ten years they have worked with the needy of the Fresno community. Again this Christmas season, their bells will be heard reminding us that this is the season of giving.

One of downtown Fresno's most historic neighborhoods centers around Holy Trinity Armenian Apostolic Church. Popularly known as "Armenian Town," its residents were primarily Armenian immigrants who came to the San Joaquin Valley because of persecution in their homeland. They chose the Fresno area because the climate was similar to that in Armenia. This neighborhood where William Saroyan was born developed just after the turn of the century and, at one time, included three churches, two bakeries and an Armenian newspaper. The two bakeries, Valley Bakery and Hye Quality Bakery, are still operating in the neighborhood.

Over the years, the neighborhood has changed dramatically. The building of a freeway and encroaching commercial development has meant the loss of many of the residences. However, a few remain. One of them is the subject of this story.

Located just a block from Valley Bakery, the Hoonanian home was built in 1900. The single-story residence is an example of the Queen Anne-Eastlake Victorian style which was once seen throughout the downtown residential areas. The home is being restored by its present owner who, in the renovation process, has uncovered some of the spindle-work on the front of the house.

The name of the original owner is unknown, but the family of Richard Hoonanian lived in the home from 1920 to 1976. Mr. Hoonanian was born in Armenia in 1882 and came to Fresno in 1902. His wife, Nectar, was also a native of Armenia. They were the parents of two sons, Deran and Carl, and a daughter, Dickey. Mr. Hoonanian owned the Chicago Tailors on Tulare Street.

Unlike many of the historic homes that have been lost to our city, the Hoonanian home stands as a reminder of a neighborhood that is almost gone and of a people who have enriched beyond measure the city they chose to call home.

The Home of John C. Hewitt

The area just north of Community Hospital is one of the few places in Fresno where one can still find Victorian homes which date from before the turn of the century. This was once a strong middle-class neighborhood. Today, it is a neighborhood in transition as it faces the threat of encroaching development and the construction of a major medical center.

One of the homes on North Diana Street was built in 1890 by John C. Hewitt. A native of Atlanta, Georgia, Mr. Hewitt served his country in the Mexican War. The lure of the gold fields brought him to California in the early 1850s, but he soon turned to farming as a way to earn a living. His ranching operation consisted of 640 acres located on Big Dry Creek.

He married Mary Morgan in 1880. She was a widow and the mother of J. D. Morgan, the last city marshal of Fresno and the first police chief of our city under the new city charter in 1900. It was J. D. Morgan who was shot by bandit Chris Evans the night he escaped from jail. Morgan survived the shooting.

John Hewitt sold his ranch shortly after his marriage and built the home for his family on Diana Street. The charming one-story wood framed house has two gables in the front that are decorated in Victorian Eastlake style. The porch across the front of the house is held up by four turned wood posts with jigsaw brackets. Other ornate gingerbread and spindles decorate the front of this home in typical Victorian style. Five years after the home was built in 1890, the Santa Fe Railroad laid track built right down the middle of Diana Street, changing the character of the area.

Although the Hewitt home has been divided into apartments, it still stands and is a charming reminder of an earlier time in the history of Fresno.

One colorful figure in the early history of Fresno County was Jesse Morrow. Hearing the news of the discovery of gold in California, he left his home in Star County, Ohio, to journey across the plains. In Salt Lake City, he joined up with a party of twenty-one men and began the trek to California following a southern route. When they arrived in Inyo County, Morrow and four others left the party and headed out on their own, traveling north through the mountains. After three weeks and suffering near starvation, they reached French's Ranch on the north side of the Tejon Pass. Continuing on, they reached the Kern River and met up with a party that included Dr. Lewis Leach. On January 20, 1851, they arrived at Woodville just after an Indian massacre had taken place. They buried fourteen corpses that day. Members of the party took turns guarding the camp while the others slept. They killed wild animals for food. They arrived many days later at Millerton.

Jesse Morrow spent the next few years mining gold at Fine Gold Gulch and on the San Joaquin River. For a time he ran a ferry at Millerton. Then he headed to Los Angeles and started in the cattle business. A year later he drove 1,100 head of cattle to the San Joaquin River and then settled into the cattle and sheep business at a ranch on the Kings River. He became one of the wealthiest men in the area.

Morrow had other irons in the fire, too. He operated a four-horse stage line that ran between Centerville and Fresno every day. It was taken over by Clark Stevens around 1877. Morrow also owned a flour mill in Centerville. Like many others, he moved to Fresno Station, establishing himself as a prominent businessman. He took over a hotel, the Henry House, and, in 1877, renamed it the Morrow House. Jesse Morrow died in 1897. He was one of the county's earliest pioneers and well worth noting in our legends of the valley.

A New Year—A New Auditorium

New Year's Eve of 1936 was a celebration unlike any the city of Fresno had ever seen. It was the height of the Great Depression, but, in 1933, the citizens of this community had pledged themselves to support a $375,000 bond issue to build an auditorium. The building was complete and now the people of Fresno were going to participate in the city's first community celebration of the arrival of the New Year.

A parade through the streets of downtown Fresno heralded the beginning of the event. The Fresno State College Band, wearing their new blue and red uniforms with Drum Major Betty Lou Knapp at the head, led the way. It was followed by decorated cars carrying Mayor Zeke Leymel, the city commissioners, the board of supervisors, and other dignitaries. Floats, marching bands, mummers, clowns, decorated automobiles, drill teams, and a drum and bugle corps entertained the bystanders. Marchers, some dressed in hundred-year-old native costumes, paid tribute to Fresno's ethnic diversity. The Native Sons and Daughters' float depicted a scene of pioneers crossing the plains. The Sciots drill team with electric lights on their shoes won the sweepstakes award. It was the most spectacular parade Fresno had ever witnessed.

After the parade, five thousand people crowded into the Memorial Auditorium for the public dedication ceremonies. A massed band of two hundred musicians struck up "Stars and Stripes Forever." The front seats were reserved for one hundred twenty-five pioneers; people who had lived in Fresno more than fifty-one years. In his dedicatory address, attorney M. E. Griffith noted that this building would be a memorial to those who have served our country and to those who have laid the foundation for our city—our veterans and our pioneers. After the dedication, Sherman Dix and his orchestra played for hundreds of people who danced in the New Year. It was an incredible beginning to the year 1937—an evening long to be remembered.

Our stories of the valley have told of the arrival of the fig in Central California. We talked of the experiments of Gustav Eisen that resulted in the knowledge that to propagate the Smyrna fig one must pollinate its flowers with a Capri moth. The result was the Calimyrna fig. We found out that George C. Roeding also learned of this and taught Melcon Markarian who, in turn, taught Jesse Clayton Forkner this important lesson. We have traced J. C. Forkner's incredible feat of taming the hogwallow lands and turning them into a paradise of fig orchards and homes. And, we explored the development of the Old Fig Garden area by Wylie Giffen and J. C. Forkner. OK, now that we have the figs, there are two questions we might ask: "Where did they come from?" "Now that we have them, except to eat them right off the tree, of what use are they?"

The history of the fig is the stuff of romance. The fig makes its first appearance in the Book of Genesis. Although, in this case, it is the leaf that is important because it is used as wearing apparel—some say that, perhaps, the tree of life was a fig tree. The first figs were found in an area stretching from Turkey to northern India. Caravans took the fig to other parts of the Middle East. Pictures of figs were found in Egyptian pyramids. Homer and Plato's writings contain references to the fig. The Roman god Bacchus considered the fig to be sacred; indeed, it was used in religious ceremonies. In 1882, fig cuttings were brought to our valley.

According to the California Dried Fig Advisory Board, figs contain a high quantity of important minerals and are an excellent energy source. Aside from eating them right off the tree, figs may be dried, stewed, pickled, or made into jam. Figs can be added to salads, breads, and puddings. Figs can be used in waffles, coffee cakes, cookies, pies, and compotes. And, what would Christmas be without a Figgy Pudding? Indeed, not just another fruit, the fig has added a delicious and romantic component to life in our great Central Valley.

J. W. Beall was born on the one hundred sixty-acre farm his grandfather, Zephaniah, had taken up from the government in Ripley County, Indiana. The year was 1849. The nearest trading town and steamboat landing was Aurora and it was here that J. W., as a young boy, saw steamboats for the first time. He attended district schools and later entered Moore's Hill College. He became a teacher and taught school for several years. In August of 1874, he headed west to California, settling first in San Francisco and then, in 1876, moving to Fresno. He married Martha Hutchings and, in 1877, moved to the Temperance Colony that had been formed by Moses J. Church. He became involved with the affairs of that area, served on the board of trustees, and became a director in the M. J. Church Canal Company. He and Moses Church became close friends. A strong Seventh-day Adventist like his partner, Church, Mr. Beall was a strong advocate of temperance and used neither coffee nor liquor.

As the years progressed Beall became involved in real estate, purchasing 680 acres of land where present-day Riverdale is located. He also purchased numerous parcels of land in other sections of Fresno County that he developed and sold for a profit. He was also involved in farming—mostly alfalfa, although he was an orchardist and vineyardist as well. In the 1893 financial crash, he lost the fortune he had made. He managed to recover and pay off all his debts.

Mr. and Mrs. Beall had a unique connection to two important figures in American history. Through his mother, Elizabeth Hallowell Hancock, J. W. Beall was a direct descendant of John Hancock, the first signer of the Declaration of Independence. Martha Beall was a direct descendant of George Wythe, who was the last man to sign the Declaration of Independence—an interesting footnote to history in the tales of our valley.

One feature of the issues of the *Fresno Bee* in the 1920s, 1930s, and 1940s was the cartoons drawn by Art V. Buel. His pen and ink sketches of the great, near great, and not so great figures of Fresno public life graced the pages of the *Bee*. His signature, BUEL, in block letters, usually appeared in the lower left hand corner of his work. Who was this man whose name became well known among the readers of the *Bee*?

Art Buel was born in San Jose, California, on February 6, 1877. When he was a young boy, he spent hours sketching his family and friends, but, except for a few private art lessons, received no formal training. In 1897, he headed for Alaska where a gold rush was underway. Not finding any gold for himself, he picked up his pen. He worked for newspapers in Dawson and Nome, drawing the first newspaper cartoons of the Yukon—signing it with a sketch of a malamute dog. This signature became well known throughout the area. He counted among his friends the legendary Klondike Kate and Jack London. He left Alaska and followed the gold trail to Goldfield and Tonopah, Nevada, in 1905. In newspapers there, the signature sketch of the dog was replaced by a prospector's burro.

In 1911, he came back to California to work for the *Sacramento Bee*, thus beginning his long relationship with the McClatchy newspapers. He came to Fresno in 1922.

Illustrating was not his only interest. While in Alaska, he stepped into the ring as an amateur prizefighter. This did not last very long, but long enough, as he stated, "to have the daylights beaten out of me by Stanley Long, an English heavyweight who was visiting in the Klondike."

Art Buel died in 1952, four years after retiring from the *Fresno Bee*. A man of strong opinions, his sometimes gruff exterior masked a warm, sympathetic personality. His sketches captured the personalities of the newsworthy figures of Fresno and were a staple of the *Fresno Bee* for three decades.

The Viking Bell

In the courtyard of the First Baptist Church complex at 1400 East Saginaw Way an interesting bell can be seen. Imbedded in the concrete planter below it, and providing a link to the past, is the cornerstone from the congregation's former red brick church at the corner of Merced and N streets. The visitor may wonder what significance the bell has and what role it has played in the history of this church.

The Viking Bell, for so this bell is named, carries a date of 1874. It first saw duty on a ship called the *S. S. Viking*. The *S. S. Viking* was wrecked off the coast of the Falcon Islands. Later it was salvaged by Lloyds of London. In keeping with salvage law, the British Admiralty ordered that the salvaged items be placed in storage. During World War I, the United States and Britain exchanged some important materials. The bell was part of this trade. It was placed on a United States troop ship and served on that vessel until the end of the war. Then the ship was dismantled. Once again, the bell had to be moved. This time, it was given to the U. S. Shipping Board for safekeeping. A gentleman named Gilbert Curtiss requested permission to obtain the bell. Permission was granted and the bell was given to him. He brought the Viking Bell to California and gave it to his daughter, Hazel Curtiss Adams, who placed it in the garden of her home in Pismo Beach.

For many years, Hazel Adams listened quite regularly to the radio broadcast of the services of Fresno's First Baptist Church. In 1963, the minister of the First Baptist Church, the Reverend Bernie G. Osterhouse, and his wife visited Mrs. Adams at her Pismo Beach home. She told them the story of the Viking Bell and offered it to them. They brought it back to Fresno.

For many years the Viking Bell was rung eleven times every Sunday morning at 10:45 to call people to worship. The Viking Bell is quiet now, but still holds a special place in the church garden and in the hearts of the congregation.

A Little Boy's Dream

The tales of our valley have told of men of great vision, but this tale concerns a legendary figure in our valley whose story quite literally begins with a dream. One day a little peasant boy in Germany was tending pigs and calves. His name was Heinrich Alfred Kreiser. He fell asleep in the grass and dreamed that he saw huge herds of cattle with a Double H mark on their left hips—something he had never seen in Germany. He was awakened by a calf nudging him. He never forgot the dream.

He came to New York and met a German shoe salesman named Henry Miller. Mr. Miller had a non-transferable ticket to California that he could not use. Heinrich Kreiser bought the ticket from Miller for a reduced price. To use it, he had to use Miller's name—so he became Henry Miller. Using his new name he went to San Francisco, arriving with six dollars in his pocket. He worked in a butcher's shop and saved his money. Dissatisfied with the quality of available beef, he decided that he wanted to produce beef of a higher quality.

Henry Miller left for the San Joaquin Valley. The year was 1851. Riding on horseback, he crossed the Coast Range Mountains. As he started his descent into the valley, he saw tremendous numbers of cattle spread out across the plain—all bearing the Double H mark—just like he had seen in his dream. He met with Henry Hildreth, the owner of the ranch, who was willing to sell. The deal was made.

Miller returned to San Francisco and visited cattleman Charles Lux, his competitor for the San Francisco market. The two decided to form a partnership. Their personalities complemented one another—whatever talent one lacked, the other possessed. It was a winning combination. They agreed to buy, but never to sell, land. Their holdings would grow over the years to such an extent that after Miller's death in 1916, it was said that their holdings covered 22,717 square miles of California, Arizona, Oregon, and Nevada. Their wealth was calculated at over thirty-one million dollars. The German peasant boy's dream had become a reality.

A Memorial for "Blackhorse" Jones

Dotted throughout the countryside of our great Central Valley are small towns and hamlets—each with its own distinctive personality, with its own unique reason for existence and, usually, with its own final resting place. These small cemeteries often are fascinating places to visit and offer the visitor a glimpse into the history of these communities and some of the eccentric characters who have lived in them.

A visit to the Grangeville Cemetery in the town of Armona is a case in point. Traveling south on Fourteenth Avenue southwest of Hanford, the traveler turns into the tree-shaded park. Gravestones of varying sizes dot the landscape. Civil War veterans, pioneers and more recent residents of the area are all entombed here. Walking among the headstones, the traveler recognizes the names of some of the victims of the tragedy at Mussel Slough. As he reaches the westernmost section of the cemetery, he sees a memorial that is so unusual, so incredibly unique, that he stands and gazes in wonderment. He has just come fact-to-face with the grave of Kenzie Whitten "Blackhorse" Jones.

"Blackhorse" Jones, an inventor and rancher, lived on Las Garzasas Creek twenty-five miles south of Huron. Initially, he ranged 15,000 sheep, but later turned to breeding cattle and horses. He owned a huge ox named "Big Dick" who accompanied him on travels, pulling one of his inventions—a house trailer. Some twenty years before his death in 1909, Jones began building his own burial vault in the Grangeville Cemetery. Although roughhewn, it symbolizes his time on this earth from the cradle to the grave. The cement base of the long monument symbolizes the cradle—the beginning of life; atop the cradle is a boat—symbolizing his journey through life; and, at the head is a tall stone marker—symbolic of life's end. All around this are cairns in memory of his parents and his family. His coffin, which he made and tried out for size, now contains his remains and rests within the cradle of the memorial. An interesting viewing experience and well worth a visit to this quiet corner of Kings County.

Kenzie Whitten "Blackhorse" Jones, holding the oar that will power his journey through life and beyond, stands on the grave that he built for his remains in the Grangeville Cemetery. The child is unidentified.
Courtesy of the Kings County Museum at Burris Park.

The Sanger Depot Museum

Nestled amid huge trees in the middle of Sanger's Civic Center is a large yellow and brown structure. Built in 1887, this building originally was situated next to the Southern Pacific Railroad tracks that ran between Fresno and Porterville. It is the Sanger Depot, the oldest building in Sanger.

By the mid-1970s, the railroad no longer needed the depot and offered it for sale to anyone who would move it. The John Tenney family purchased it for $2,500 and offered it to the newly formed Sanger Historical Society if it would pay to have it moved. The society accepted the depot and, in 1977, moved it to land which is owned by the Sanger Unified School District, but is in the heart of the Civic Center. The task of restoring, rewiring, updating plumbing, and adding sprinklers to the building was completed in the early 1980s. The Sanger Historical Society opened its museum in the depot in 1984.

Pioneer Sanger druggist Oscar A. Brehler often accepted Indian baskets in trade for medicine. By the end of his long career he had acquired one of the finest Yokuts and Western Mono basket collections in the United States. He placed them in the custody of Ted Barr, Sr., with one stipulation—the formation of a non-profit group to display them. Eventually, half the collection went to the Discovery Center in Fresno and half to the Sanger Depot Museum. The baskets were inventoried by representatives from the National Park Service who also designed the exhibit. Baskets used for a variety of purposes—for cradling babies, storing food, cooking, carrying heavy loads and playing games—can be seen in the exhibit.

The front room of the museum houses a replica of the Brehler Block that stood on Seventh Street. A bank, general store, post office, bakery, and the office of the *Sanger Herald* contain many artifacts that came from the original businesses. Because Sanger is the gateway to the Nation's Christmas Tree celebration each year, it has the distinction of being called the "Christmas Tree City." A Christmas tree donated by the Rotary Club of Sanger, decorated with ornaments from every country that has Rotary clubs, is on permanent display. The museum also has a pioneer room featuring photos of many of Sanger's early families.

The Domoto Room, the original baggage/freight room, contains a detailed diorama created by artist Joan Aller. It depicts the lumber companies in the mountains, the city of Sanger, and a model of the Hume-Sanger Flume that was the longest flume in the world. Also featured are photos of the building and operation of the flume.

A visit to Sanger is not complete without a tour of the Sanger Depot Museum. Here, the visitor learns first-hand the history and development of the "Nation's Christmas Tree City."

The Festival of Saint Elia

There is a hill in southern Italy called Mustafa. In the sixteenth century, following the conquest of Albania, immigrants from that country found their way to Italy and settled in Maschito, a small village on Mustafa. Farming was the principal occupation of the people of Maschito. One year the area suffered a terrible drought. The people of Maschito prayed to Saint Elia (Elijah the prophet) for help. The rains came and the land was able to produce crops once more. Saint Elia became the protector of the village. In his honor a festival was celebrated each year.

Early in the twentieth century a number of the families from Maschito settled in Fresno because the terrain reminded them of home. They settled in West Fresno in a several block area bounded by A and F streets. Saint Alphonsus Catholic Church became their religious home. A niche in the church held a statue of Saint Elia.

In September of 1910, the first Fresno festival of Saint Elia was held. As the years went by it grew to include a vaudeville show on Thursday and Friday nights; a torchlight parade to the Italian Entertainment Park on Kearney Boulevard where dinner, dancing, and a carnival were held on Saturday evening; and a Sunday morning Mass in honor of Saint Elia at Saint Alphonsus Church followed by a procession in which the statue of the saint was carried by members of one of the families. The festival ended Sunday evening at the Italian Entertainment Park with midget auto races, a band concert and a huge fireworks display.

After ninety years, the families from the old Italian neighborhood continue to gather to honor the prophet whose life has inspired their dreams and comforted their souls. As the procession forms and family groups with several generations represented gather to march, they are reminded once again of their rich cultural heritage that includes a deep devotion to faith and to family.

John S. Eastwood

There are many things one takes for granted in our twenty-first century world. A simple touch of a key turns on a computer, a flip of a switch lights a room, and a light tap on a touch pad turns on an oven. Seldom when doing these simple tasks does one consider where the electricity comes from to provide these conveniences—one just assumes the electricity will be there.

Of all the names one thinks of in the history of electricity in our valley—Wishon, Kerckhoff, Huntington, Balch—one name is rarely mentioned. Yet it was the genius and vision of this man, John S. Eastwood, that paved the way for the projects that provide hydroelectric power for our valley.

John Eastwood was born in Minnesota in 1857. He inherited a family interest in engineering and, after graduating from State Normal School at Mankato, was hired to work on the extension of the Minneapolis and St. Louis Railroad's line to the Pacific. He came to Fresno in 1883 with his bride, started an engineering business, and, after the city was incorporated in 1885, became Fresno's first city engineer. He still kept his private business going. Among his clients was the Fresno Flume and Irrigation Company owned by Charles Shaver and Lewis Swift. His trips to the Shaver Mill provided him the opportunity to study the terrain. The rushing waters of the San Joaquin River cascading into a deep canyon piqued his interest. He envisioned how that force of nature could be harnessed to create electricity.

Those who heard his plan were skeptical. One man, however, was not. John Seymore, the president and major stockholder of the Fresno Water Company, joined forces with him. In 1895, they formed the San Joaquin Electric Company. Using Eastwood's plans they built a powerhouse on the north fork of the San Joaquin River where the rapid descent of the river would power their turbines and generate electric power. Their project worked. Fresno, thirty-seven miles away, received electricity through their transmission line which, at the time, was the longest in the world. Four years later, the Fresno Gas and Electric Company filed riparian water claims, cutting off their water supply. Eastman's company went bankrupt. His story, however, does not end here.

Joseph Sanger, Jr.

With the opening of a post office on June 26, 1888, the newest community in Fresno County was officially open for business. It was named for Joseph Sanger, Jr. Who was this man and why was this town given his name?

Joseph Sanger was born in Watertown, Massachusetts, to a distinguished family who could claim that several generations of ancestors had lived in Massachusetts since leaving England. His mother died when she was only twenty years old. His father re-married and it was his step-mother who raised him. He had a quiet demeanor, strong principles, and many loyal friends. He married Susan Webster Smith of Compton, New Hampshire, and began working in his father's contracting business in Watertown. Among their projects were several churches and Watertown's town hall. Sanger was very interested in Masonry and served as a past master of his lodge.

Joseph Sanger's brother-in-law was the manager of a branch of the New York Central Railroad. He urged Sanger to become part of railroading. Sanger moved his family to Indiana and entered the railroad business. Shortly after that he became ill and remained an invalid until his death in 1899.

In spite of his illness, he served as national secretary of the Railroad Yardmasters Association. In 1887, he attended the organization's annual convention in San Francisco. While there, he was told by Southern Pacific Railroad officials that they were going to name a new town on their latest rail line for him. Unfortunately, he never had the opportunity to visit the town named in his honor.

Sanger's daughter, Alice, did get reports of the town's progress from friends who traveled through the area. Alice B. Sanger had a distinguished career of her own. She began her career working in the law office of General Benjamin Harrison and, when he became president, she became the first woman clerk in the White House.

As the nineteenth century drew to a close, Fresnans were not overly concerned about the beginning of a new century. The newspapers did not mention the end of an era or embarking on a new frontier in the final months of 1899. Perhaps it was because the city was still so young and its residents had yet to feel a sense of history about their place; or, perhaps it was because many Fresnans had blazed their way to a new frontier so recently that, in comparison, starting a new century was just one more step forward, and a fairly easy one at that. The only mention of the new century can be found in an editorial in the *Fresno Morning Republican* on December 31, 1899. In it Chester Harvey Rowell points out that the new century did not truly begin until January 1, 1901—just as ours did not begin until January 1, 2001.

This is what Rowell had to say: "Today, for the last time in history, we write our date beginning with '18.' The oldest man who writes that date, never wrote a current date with '17,' and the youngest will not live to write a '20.' It is one of those changes which stretch beyond the span of human life. It is a little change, a new scratch with the pen, a new syllable, a new cog in the counting machine, and yet it is a great one, so great that there is no greater. It is a greatness of the imagination, to be sure, for there is no substantial fact corresponding the change of number...mathematically and chronologically [the twentieth century] begins a year hence, but it is not the...chronological fact that counts...After all, are not dates the most important facts in life and history. Whether a man was born to write—"16,' or '17.' or '18,' or '19' determines the manner of man he was and the kind of world into which he was born."

Rowell's words ring as true today as they did then except for the fact that life expectancy has increased. There just might be a few people among us who wrote the beginning of a date with a 19 and will live to write a 21. Such is the nature of progress.

A Vision Realized

Intrigued by the Sierra terrain, John Eastwood began to venture further into the rugged mountains. Even before his San Joaquin Electric Company went into receivership in 1899, Eastwood set out exploring. Accompanied only by a burro loaded with supplies, he walked through the Sierra wilderness searching for possibilities—for rapid falls in the river, for canyons, and for places where water could be stored. He knew future hydroelectric projects depended on that. He had learned that lesson the hard way. His trips were a success. He found what he was looking for and came away with a vision and a plan.

In 1902, he organized a survey party that headed up the mountains from Shaver Lake. When they returned a month later, it was with a preliminary plan to build dams and reservoirs with connecting tunnels to carry water that could be dropped down the mountains again and again. Powerhouses would be built to harness the electricity thus created. He wrote to William G. Kerckhoff who, in partnership with A. C. Balch, had bought Eastwood's defunct company. Kerckhoff saw the possibilities. He hired Eastwood to do a concrete plan and prepare designs. For three years, Eastwood worked. When finished, the scope of Eastwood's plan was mindboggling. Not only did it plan for the building of dams and the creation of a number of lakes, but it also called for the building of a tunnel through Kaiser Ridge, a barrier of solid granite almost eleven miles wide. Big Creek was the main site of his hydroelectric plan. When the project began nine years later, it was an engineering achievement second only to the building of the Panama Canal. When completed in 1920, three lakes, six dams, eight tunnels, five powerhouses, and 248 miles of transmission lines brought electric power to the valley and to Southern California.

Eastwood had received stock for his efforts, but another company was hired to do the project. Unfortunately, costs were high and, as the project developed, assessments were made against his stock. Eastwood came out of the situation was nothing except, according to Gene Rose in *Reflections of Shaver Lake*, "the satisfaction that he had engineered the most ambitious hydroelectric project ever conceived by one man."

An apocryphal story is sometimes told that the Southern Pacific Railroad wanted its new branch rail line between Fresno and Porterville to go through Centerville, but those who owned land in the Centerville area were uncooperative and declined to give land for a right-of-way and a depot. So, the railroad had to look for another site for a station and chose land closer to Fresno. Whether this story is true or not doesn't really matter. What does matter is that the rail line was completed, a depot was built, and, on July 1, 1888, trains began to run. In anticipation of this event, settlers actually began to arrive earlier that year. On June 26, 1888, the post office opened—a new town officially was born, the town of Sanger.

Named for Joseph Sanger, Jr., who was the secretary of the national Railroad Yardmasters Association, the new town began to grow. Lots had been offered for sale in May. By mid-July a hotel, restaurant, livery stable, blacksmith shops, a saloon, lumberyard, butcher shop, and general store were open for customers. The town also boasted three doctors and an office where one could purchase real estate and insurance.

A year later, in 1889, successful negotations with the owners of the Kings River Lumber Company and community leaders assured the residents of Sanger that their town would be the terminus of the flume that was being built from the foothill community of Millwood and also the site of a large lumber finishing plant. By the fall of 1889, the fifty-four-mile flume, the longest in the world, was completed. The town held a gala celebration. Hundreds of people turned out. After listening to the required speeches, they feasted on, among other things, three entire bulls, ten sheep, and three hundred loaves of bread.

Sanger prospered. It was incorporated in July 1911. Because of its proximity to the major highways leading to Kings Canyon and Sequoia national parks, it has been given the designation of the "Nation's Christmas Tree City."

Free Evangelical Lutheran Church

On March 15, 1892, the Evangelical Lutheran Cross Church was organized in Fresno with the Reverend Jacob Legler as the minister. The eighty-five members were immigrants of German descent who came from the Volga River colonies in Russia. Services were held in the parsonage. Three years later, a church was built on F Street for $1,077.80. The congregation grew as more immigrants came to Fresno. It soon became evident that a new, larger building was needed. In 1915, the second church was dedicated. This imposing brick structure, which stood in the heart of the Volga-German neighborhood at F and San Diego streets, had six white columns in front and was capped by a large square bell tower.

In 1947, a decision was made to build an overpass on Highway 99. The church lay in the path of this project. After consulting with Star House Movers of Los Angeles to determine the feasibility, it was decided to move the church building to a site at Los Angeles and E streets two blocks away. The move was undertaken with much interest by everyone in Fresno. The sight of the 1,800-ton brick structure being moved on rollers to the new location caught the imagination of the community. The move was completed and the church was rededicated on April 25, 1948. It still was in the heart of the neighborhood once known as "Roosian Town" and served its members for many years.

In 1965, the members of the church voted to sell their historic church. Many members had moved away from the neighborhood and relocated in Fresno's newer areas. The congregation bought property at the corner of Palm and Gettysburg avenues and built a new church designed by local architect Allen Lew. The church was completed and the first service was held there on May 5, 1968.

When the congregation moved to the new church one very special element of the old church went with them. The historic altar made the trip from West Fresno to the new church on Palm Avenue where it continues to play its important role in the life of the Free Evangelical Lutheran Cross Church and Fresno's Volga German community.

The Free Evangelical Lutheran Cross Church, with the parsonage next door, at the time of its completion in 1915. It was located at F and San Diego streets.
Courtesy of American Historical Society of Germans from Russia Museum.

Berrocks by the Thousand

On a cool May morning in the year 2000, the delicious aroma of onions, cabbage, and roast beef drew the visitor into the social hall of Fresno's Free Evangelical Lutheran Cross Church. Upon entering, the visitor was met with an astonishing sight—scores of men and women manning stations around the room, kneading, chopping, shredding, grinding, cooking, packing and, at the same time, visiting, laughing, and enjoying the fellowship that comes from working together for a common goal. On this particular day and the day to follow, these good people would make 14,500 berrocks in a series of production lines that would delight the most serious efficiency expert.

When faced with paying off the debt for their new church building, member Ray Schwabenland and other members came up with an idea. Let's make berrocks and sell them at a country fair! Members were invited to join the work party, but they had to bring a bag lunch—no one could eat a berrock—they all had to be sold! The debt was paid in record time—due in no small part to berrock sales.

The church's first berrock making session in 1966 was held at McLane High School. Every step was done by hand. Two thousand berrocks were made. Each year the number of workers and the number of berrocks grew. Every penny of profit made went to pay for the new church building. Before the loan came due, the debt was paid off. By that time, however, the berrock making had become an important tradition for Fresno's German community so the sessions continued—three times during the year. A few machines have been added to help the process. Eighty-nine-year-old Rose Bier has worked every year since 1966—her job is still to oversee the kneading of the dough.

Watching the operation, the visitor is fascinated. The dough rises, then is cut and kneaded into small balls. As each tray is filled it is carried to the next station. There it is put into a tortilla machine and rolled into flat circles. Many hands work to place the filling of cooked and ground meat, onions, and cabbage on each circle, fold the dough over, and press it closed. Then it goes to the kitchen to be baked. The kitchen is a hub of activity, too, with people overseeing the chopping, shredding, grinding, and cooking. Even the minister is working—cutting cabbage and joking with the crew. As the finished berrocks are wheeled from the kitchen and placed on cooling racks, someone changes the total on the tote board. By 10:20 a.m., 2,500 berrocks are done. That evening when the last berrock is finished, Rose will hit her bread board with a knife and a shout will go up. Finished 'til the next session!

Many of these workers also go to the Edison Social Club in early October to make berrocks for the Oktoberfest held each year by the American Historical Society of Germans from Russia. The scene is much the same—serious cooking, visiting, and laughter— all for a good cause. And, along the way, new traditions are made as the old ways are preserved.

To Dare or Not to Dare

Many fascinating stories can be told of the early pioneers and why they came to Fresno. But, one wonders, how many pioneers came to Fresno on a dare?

John Robert Cameron McKay was born in Churchville, Nova Scotia, on December 17, 1867. He learned the art of blacksmithing from his father, Issac McKay, who, like his father before him, practiced that trade. After J. R. received his apprenticeship at age sixteen, his father gave him a Bible and his blessing and sent him into the world to seek his fortune. McKay traveled to Boston where he worked as a blacksmith for four years. Then he found work as a horse car driver, but the winter was so cold, the horse car lines were shut down.

McKay met a man named Charles Telfer who spoke glowingly of a place called Fresno, California, where the sun shone and the land bore fruits of all kinds. Telfer had some first-hand knowledge of Fresno because his cousin, George Freeman, had a ranch there. McKay was out of work and not sure when he could get another job. On a whim, Telfer dared him to take a chance and buy a train ticket to Fresno. McKay took him up on the dare. Telfer did such a good job of convincing McKay that he decided to join him. The two men arrived in Fresno in 1889. Freeman gave them a job pruning grape vines on his Elm Avenue ranch. McKay had never seen a grape vine before, but was delighted to have a job. He worked hard and, like a true Scot, saved what money he could.

After two months, J. R. McKay decided to return to his trade. James Porteous hired him as a blacksmith at his Fresno Agricultural Works. A few months later, McKay purchased a shop on I (now Broadway) Street owned by Creba & Son. He made horse shoeing a specialty. He later purchased the Dexter Stables on I Street and formed a partnership with H. W. Wilbur. It was the most modern business of its kind in turn-of-the-century Fresno. The young Scotsman had become a successful businessman. He had come a long way from his roots in Nova Scotia—all because he had the courage to accept a dare.

The interior of the modern Dexter Stables circa 1900. Note the hayloft with horse stalls below. The man is unidentified. *Courtesy of Mary Helen McKay.*

The frame house in Churchville, Pictou County, Nova Scotia, where J. R. McKay and most of his eight siblings were born. McKay's great-great grandfather John Robertson built the first house in Churchville in 1784. A memorial cairn was erected in Robertson's honor during a Churchville gathering of his descendants in 1934. *Courtesy of Mary Helen McKay.*

A Thanksgiving Day, 1919, gathering of the McKay family at the Pickford home at Wishon and Cambridge avenues. Back row, left to right: Ernest Pickford, Ada Pickford, J. R. McKay, Kate McKay, W. R. McKay, Belle McKay, Loverne McKay, Henry McKay. Center: May McKay and J. M. McKay. Front row: Bill McKay, Mary Helen McKay, Oliver Pickford and Catherine McKay.
Courtesy of Mary Helen McKay.

Many of our early Fresno pioneers found they liked Fresno and the opportunities afforded in the growing community, so they urged other members of their families whom they had left behind to come to the new town.

The J. R. McKay family was no exception. After leaving Nova Scotia and traveling to Fresno by way of Boston, J. R. McKay had purchased the Dexter Stables on I (now Broadway) Street. He sent for the girl he left behind, Belle Ellen McDonald, to come to Fresno. They were married just after her arrival in November 1891. He then sent for two of his brothers, James Martland and William

Roderick, to join them in Fresno. A third brother, Colin Henry, had left home to seek his fortune in the copper mines of British Columbia. All four brothers had learned blacksmithing from their father, Issac McKay. Five sisters remained at home with their parents in Nova Scotia. One of the sisters, Sarah Christina, Ada for short, was more adventurous than the others. She decided to come west to join her brothers and arrived in Fresno in the mid-1890s.

Ada first took music lessons and then entered Heald's College in 1896. She decided business wasn't her forte and enrolled in nurse's training at the Burnett Sanitarium. She graduated in 1902, with the first class of nurses to receive certificates, was hired by Dr. William Maupin, and worked in his office for a number of years.

Ada McKay's two year business course was not a waste of time. She met another business student, Loverne Kinsley. They became best friends. Ada decided Loverne would be perfect for her brother Henry, who was in British Columbia. She wrote a long letter to her brother telling him all about the lovely girl who had become her friend. She enclosed a photo of Loverne. Henry read the letter, looked at the picture, packed his bag, and got on the first train to Fresno. Ada introduced Henry to Loverne. Henry established himself in business and courted Loverne for six years. In late April 1906, the day after the San Francisco earthquake, Henry proposed to Loverne. They married three weeks later. It was a happy marriage that lasted until his death in 1949.

Best friends who were soon to be sisters-in-law, Loverne Kinsley and Ada McKay. While enjoying a day of shopping and lunch in downtown Fresno, the two girls decided to pose for these pictures in a photo booth in one of I (now Fulton) Street's stores.
Author's collection.

On July 27, 1899, just ten years after the founding of Sanger, the Sanger Union High School district was formed. Two months later, on September 10, twenty young people gathered in a room in the Sanger Opera House and formally enrolled as students in a brand new school—Sanger Union High School. Their teacher's name was A. C. Olney.

For two years, the Opera House served as the site for classes while a proper school was built at Date and Dewitt avenues. In November 1901, the one-story white frame building with a bell tower was dedicated. The first class of eight graduates proudly received their diplomas in 1903. As the school grew, more teachers were added to the faculty. In 1914, a two-story brick building was erected just east of the white frame schoolhouse. In 1928, it was enlarged to house additional classrooms and an auditorium. Six massive ionic pillars were added to the front of the brick building giving it a true classical appearance befitting a house of learning. In 1954, the Apache became the school's mascot.

Over the years, many additions were made to the campus, including a gymnasium and the Tom Flores Stadium. In 1957, a major renovation project was undertaken which resulted in demolishing parts of the 1928 brick building and constructing several new buildings to accommodate the school's one thousand students.

Although Sanger High School has always had a fine athletics program—turning out players like Pete Beiden and Tom Flores—it has gained recognition in other areas as well. On a 1988 visit to the San Joaquin Valley, presidential candidate George Bush praised Sanger High's Naval Junior Reserve Officers Training Corps, pointing out that they had more graduates in the United States Naval Academy than any other high school in the country. In that same year Sanger High was named one of the top ten schools in California by the state's Department of Education. In 1996, it was named a California Distinguished School.

As Sanger High School celebrated its centennial in 1999, its students looked back with pride on their school's achievements and looked forward to beginning the new century in a new modern campus at Annadale and Bethel avenues. Here, Apache pride and spirit will continue to play a role in the tales of our valley.

One of Sanger's favorite sons is a man who grew up in Sanger, attended schools in Sanger, graduated from Sanger High School, and went on to remarkable achievements on the football field.

In his youth, his parents never had to urge him to go to school. He loved school. They encouraged him to find his passion and follow his dream. When he entered Sanger High School in 1950, he was a reserved young man, tall and easy-going, with a natural talent for athletics. He played baseball, basketball and football, but it was on the football field where his gifts were most evident. He began as a quarterback for the Apaches (the Sanger High team) and found his passion quickly—it was football. He had other interests, too. He played in the band and was active in student government.

After graduating from Sanger High School in 1954, our young man entered Fresno Junior College (now Fresno Community College) and continued playing sports. Two years later, he transferred to the College of the Pacific (now University of the Pacific) in Stockton on an academic scholarship and played football and baseball. In his last year at COP he was chosen to play in the East-West Shrine game. After a stint in the Canadian Football League, he signed with the Oakland Raiders in 1960. After distinguishing himself on the playing field with the Raiders, he signed with the Buffalo Bills and then with the Kansas City Chiefs.

He eventually turned his sights to coaching football rather than playing it. He served as assistant coach for the Buffalo Bills for one season. Then he returned to his old team, the Oakland Raiders. After serving as receiving coach and assistant coach, he became the Raiders head coach. He is one of only two people in National Football League history who have the distinction of having earned a Super Bowl ring as player, assistant coach and head coach.

Today, Tom Flores broadcasts for Oakland Raider football. In the year 2000, he was honored as one of the twenty-five greatest Central Valley athletes of the twentieth century. He has not forgotten his hometown of Sanger, where he got his start. He returns home often and sponsors activities that raise money for the Tom Flores Youth Foundation which he founded to benefit the young people of Sanger.

In 1982, Sanger native Tom Flores decided he wanted to give something back to the community where he had received his early education and taken the beginning steps that led him to an outstanding career in football. He valued the lessons he had learned in Sanger, but remembered seeing many of his friends drop out of school. He knew that a good education was the key to a successful life and decided that he wanted to do something to help the young people of Sanger.

After sharing his ideas with a group of his former classmates from Sanger High School, Flores organized the non-profit Tom Flores Youth Foundation using $80,000 out of his own pocket as seed money. The foundation benefits young people from kindergarten through eighth grade. It targets the areas of science, fine arts and athletics, thereby helping to enrich the subjects that are needed to provide a well-rounded educational experience. In addition, the foundation provides help in special circumstances.

Two events—a golf tournament and a wine tasting—are held each year to benefit the Tom Flores Youth Foundation. In its first twelve years the foundation raised $320,000 to benefit the young people of the Sanger Unified School District. To assist the work of the foundation, Adobe Systems Incorporated donated $80,000 worth of software which has been installed into the school district's computer system. This has enabled students to improve their knowledge in a wide range of subject areas.

With the support of the Sanger community and its citizens, the Tom Flores Youth Foundation board of directors, its team of volunteers, and Mr. Flores himself, are dedicated to continuing their mission for many years to come—to make sure every young person in Sanger has the opportunity to receive the best education possible and to have the tools necessary to fulfill his or her potential and dreams.

The Electric Motor Shop

In 1913, buildings in downtown Fresno were still predominately Victorian in style. It would be another year before the first skyscraper would be built. It was an election year and temperance was the major issue both locally and nationally. Mayor Alva Snow, a man of intelligence and vision, won reelection. The city was moving forward and needed businesses that would meet the demands that presented.

In 1913, Edmund and Mary Jane Elzea opened Central State Electric at Fulton and Kern streets. They soon changed the name to Electric Motor Shop. A growing city needed businesses like theirs that could service the new machines that were being developed.

Frank Caglia, who was born in the village of Maschito, Italy, came through Ellis Island with his family and then to Fresno where he settled and became active in Fresno's Italian community. In 1929, the Elzeas hired sixteen-year-old Caglia as a bookkeeper. As the business grew, Caglia had the opportunity to learn all phases of the operation. In 1954, he became the owner. As the years progressed, the business moved to Fulton and Monterey streets and expanded to keep up with the latest technological advances.

Frank Caglia and his late wife Florence were involved in projects that brought great benefit to Fresno. They purchased and restored the historic Pantages Theatre (now Warnor's Center for the Performing Arts) and the Welcome to Fresno sign on Van Ness Avenue. They also gave the historic Vartanian block to Poverello House. In the late 1980s, Frank received the Leon S. Peters Award and the Pope John XXIII Award.

Today, the Electric Motor Shop not only offers a full range of contracting services for electrical design and engineering, expert technicians, and a huge inventory of equipment and supplies; but, with three generations of the Caglia family working together, it is also a family business in the truest sense. The Electric Motor Shop—an important part of our valley since 1913.

The historic Fresno County Courthouse and its park as it appeared six years before the turn of the twentieth century. Courthouse Park has always been the setting for important public gatherings.
R.W. Riggs photo. Author's collection.

On January 1, 1900, when the nineteenth century began to ebb into history and the twentieth century loomed on the horizon, the citizens of Fresno did not mark the event with public ceremonies. They certainly made up for it on July 4, 1900, when the nation's birthday was celebrated with all the pomp, patriotism, panache, and just plain fun that the city fathers could dream up.

When daybreak came all was in readiness. The lawns of Courthouse Park were well manicured. Businesses were decorated with bunting and streamers. Light standards held flags that fluttered in the breeze of the early summer morning. Trains arrived bringing carloads of revelers from valley towns. By nine o'clock the streets were lined with people awaiting the first event—a parade. At ten o'clock, City Marshal J. D. Morgan and a detail of policemen stepped out with gusto as the leaders of the line of march that began at H and Tulare streets and wended its way through the streets of downtown. They were followed by bands, floats, and dignitaries of all kinds including carriages carrying veterans of the Civil War.

At the close of the parade, everyone walked to Courthouse Park for the rest of the day's events. A band concert featuring patriotic music played by the Raisin City Band lasted until two o'clock. Following the reading of the Declaration of Independence by George Cosgrave, a choir of school children sang. The park was filled to capacity with noisy celebrants. But, when Miles Wallace began his eloquent patriotic oration, his voice soared above the din—silencing everyone. His stirring words filled many a breast with nationalistic pride.

The evening began with two more band concerts. As darkness fell, the Courthouse was illuminated with hundreds of electric lights, making a colorful backdrop to the vaudeville show that began at 8 p.m. The day's festivities ended with a wildly jubilant carnival parade. Yes, indeed, Fresno's Fourth of July 1900 celebration was truly unforgettable.

Courthouse Park in its infancy. This photo, taken in the late 1870s, shows numerous trees, a water tank, and the original Courthouse—all surrounded by a white fence. The four men are unidentified. *Courtesy of Robert M. Wash.*

King Willie I and His Carnival Parade

The Fourth of July festivities in 1900 were capped off by a grand carnival parade. It had been a day of nonstop celebration—except for a morning parade it had all been centered in Courthouse Park. Now, at nine in the evening, a parade to end all parades was due to begin. An assemblage of masked revelers unlike any Fresno had seen before was lined up on Fresno Street between H and K (now Van Ness Avenue) streets. Now they would wend their way through the streets of Fresno presided over by King Willie I—who was none other than W. Parker Lyon. Among the cast of characters were female impersonators riding in open carriages, grotesquely fat men on horseback, burlesque figures of all kinds riding on horses or mules, comic characters sporting huge mustaches—it was an event more befitting Mardi Gras than the Fourth of July.

In the days before the event, the *Fresno Morning Republican* ran articles and letters from the public wondering if the proposed parade was appropriate. "Will it be Wicked?" one headline asked. Prayers were offered up against the carnival—a rather odd circumstance in a city that was just beginning to close its saloons for a few hours after two o'clock in the morning. However, Fresno was becoming a city of many churches and reform was definitely an issue in the new century.

W. Parker Lyon answered the critics in a letter printed in the *Republican's* July 3, 1900, edition. He said, "Today we celebrate the Declaration of Independence. The Blue and the Gray mingle together bound by ties of friendship. A few words to my unruly subjects the 'knockers.' Why not quit knocking and save your clubs for the rabbit drives? Why not stay at home. You will not be missed and you may spoil the pleasure of someone's evening…by your grumbling." Lyon said the carnival was for the purpose of fun and foolishness—a brief escape from life's harsh realities.

The carnival parade took place. Much merriment was enjoyed by all. It was a Fourth of July that will long be remembered in the legends of our valley.

Alva E. Snow

Mayor Alva Snow's administration was noted for honesty, but the reformers felt he was not aggressive enough in his efforts to tackle the ongoing issue of the saloons.
Reprinted from Fresno County Centennial Almanac.

The year 1913 was a remarkable one for Fresno. In April, the voters elected Alva E. Snow to the office of mayor. After the May 23, 1912, death of Dr. Chester Rowell, Fresno's mayor, Snow had been appointed to fill out the doctor's term. By electing Snow in his own right, the voters had retained in office a man who was not only intelligent, but honest and capable. They also elected a board of trustees who were well-qualified to serve. One of the major campaign issues was temperance—the "wet" versus "dry" controversy. It was apparent that the saloon owners were still a major force in Fresno, The citizens voted to allow saloons to stay open and assumed the sale of liquor would be regulated.

Who was Alva Snow? His ancestors Nicholas Snow and Constance Hopkins came from England on the *Mayflower* and married at Plymouth in 1627. Their descendants continued to live in Plymouth County and to be active in the public affairs of that area. It was there that Alva Snow was born in 1860. He was educated in local schools, graduated from Tufts College, and entered Harvard Law School. After completing his education, he was admitted to the bar in Massachusetts in 1889. He came west to San Francisco and practiced law in the firm of Herman & Soto for fifteen months. In January of 1891, he moved to Fresno.

The new city of Fresno, just six years old, offered opportunities for an intelligent, ambitious young man. After practicing law on his own for two years, he became a deputy district attorney. In one celebrated case he obtained the conviction of train robber Chris Evans. In 1894, he ran for the office of Fresno County District

Attorney and won—the first Republican to do so. He served for four years and then returned to private practice. In 1909, he was elected to the city board of trustees and then became mayor. During Snow's tenure, the skyline of downtown Fresno underwent major changes. Numerous high-rise buildings went up on Fulton Street indicating a city on the move.

Although in many ways Alva Snow served his city well, his efforts to control the saloons were not adequate in the eyes of many reformers. Snow decided not to seek reelection and, after serving his four-year term, he returned to his large private practice. Alva E. Snow died in 1935.

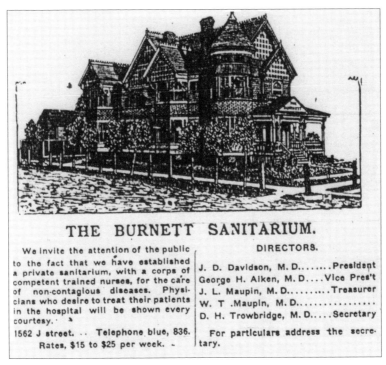

This ad for the Burnett Sanitarium appeared in the *Fresno Morning Republican* on December 16, 1900.

In the mid-1890s, a large thirty-room boarding house stood at the southeast corner of Fulton and Calaveras streets. Operated by Mrs. Celia Burnett, the establishment was very successful.

In 1897, Mrs. Burnett was approached by five doctors, J. D. Davidson, J. L. Maupin, W. T. Maupin, George Aiken, and Dwight Trowbridge, Sr., who had an interesting idea. They wanted to form a private hospital. Would she like to join with them and allow her home to become the new hospital. She said, "Yes." The new facility opened that same year and was called the Burnett Sanitarium. Three years later, on May 16, 1900, the hospital was incorporated. A training school for nurses began—the first class graduated in 1902.

The hospital filled a real need in the community. By 1905, more space was needed. A new, larger facility was built on the corner of Fresno and S streets. Eleven years later, a new building—this one five stories high—was built at the same location. It was one of the most modern hospitals on the West Coast.

Over the years, the increased health needs of the growing community were reflected in the tremendous growth of the hospital. In 1945, Burnett Sanitarium was sold and became Fresno Community Hospital. A new hospital was built at Fresno and R streets in 1959, and in 1972 a ten-story tower was added. Following mergers with Clovis Memorial Hospital and Sierra Hospital Foundation, the new corporation was called Community Hospitals of Central California. In 1996, another merger took place that resulted in the placement of the University Medical Center and its clinics under the management of Community Hospitals. In 1997, due to the expanding scope and services offered, the name was changed to Community Health Systems.

Today, Community Health Systems looks forward to the development of the nearby campus for the Central California Regional Medical Network and to continuing its mission of bringing excellent health care to the people of the valley. It has come a long way from its start in Mrs. Burnett's thirty-room boarding house.

In this 1931 photo, a neon sign featuring a majorette is loaded on the truck and ready to be installed.
Courtesy of Bill Kratt.

When you drive by a theater or business with an eye-catching, dramatic neon sign, do you ever wonder how it was made and by whom? Maybe not, but it may be of interest to know that there is a company in Fresno that has been making neon signs since 1932.

In the early 1920s, John McKenzie started a sign company in San Pedro, California. He made only painted signs, but was fascinated with the electric and neon signs that were becoming popular throughout the state and wanted to start creating them. During a visit to Fresno, he realized that there was only one sign company in the city. He decided there was potential for another sign business, so he moved to Fresno in 1930 and opened his own business—Neon-Lite Sign Company. Two years later, he changed the company's name to Fresno Neon Sign Company.

The business was a success. There was such a demand for neon signs that McKenzie and his staff were kept very busy. McKenzie's son Donald became involved in the business and when John died of cancer in 1956, Donald took over the company. In 1982, Bill Kratt, a company foreman, became a junior partner. When Donald McKenzie retired in 1985, Kratt became the president of the corporation and the owner.

The process of creating a neon sign requires skill. First the framework is built; then it is skinned or covered; the pattern for the sign is drawn and placed on a bench top; the neon tubing is then blown and formed into the shape on the pattern. Then the tube is filled with filament in different colors and filled with neon or argon gas. There are only three glass benders in Fresno who are trained in this process. Usually today, lexon and plastic tubing are used along with the latest cutting-edge computer and digital-imaging technology for sign design and fabrication.

Fresno Neon Sign Company not only creates neon signs, it repairs them. One of Bill Kratt's memories is of repairing the sign on one of Fresno's tallest buildings—the Security Bank on Fulton Street. He and his partner tied ropes around their waists and leaned way out over the edge of the roof of the building. They would take the neon off, take it in to be repaired and then bring it back and reinstall it. He said that they would always make this particular job the last one of the day. By the time they were finished, they needed to go home and unwind!

Whether it is the Leilani Restaurant sign or the Clovis Gateway sign that still welcomes people or the business signs that once brought color to such downtown businesses as Hart's, Rodder's and the Hotel Fresno, Fresno Neon Sign Company has been lighting up the valley for many years and plans to keep creating the eye-catching electric signs that have graced our valley since 1932.

Night scene of Hart's Restaurant on Tulare Street. Note the neon clock sign.
Courtesy of Bill Kratt.

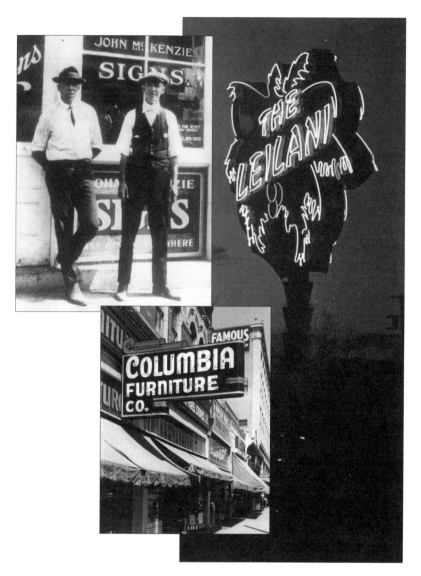

Clockwise from top left:
    In this 1926 photo, John McKenzie (right) stands in front of his San Pedro sign store. The Leilani sign has been a familiar sight on Blackstone Avenue in Fresno for years. The Chicago Furniture sign heralds the store at the corner of Van Ness and Tuolumne.
Photos courtesy of Bill Kratt.

A Parish for Saint Alphonsus

Traveling west on Fresno Street, the traveler passes B and A streets, makes a right turn onto Kearney Boulevard and enters a neighborhood of tree lined streets and large dwellings. At the centerpiece of this historic area is a large, stately church with twin bell towers. Built in 1908, this church is named Saint Alphonsus for the founder of the Congregation of the Most Holy Redeemer—the order of Redemptorist Brothers.

In the early years of the twentieth century, Bishop Thomas J. Conaty of the Monterey-Los Angeles diocese wanted to establish a parish and mission center in Fresno. On December 8, 1908, Father Henry Weber accepted the bishop's offer in the name of the Redemptorists. Saint Alphonsus became the second Catholic parish in Fresno and the first Redemptorist house and parish in California.

The parish originally stretched over a vast area—from the Southern Pacific railroad tracks on the east to Caruthers, Mendota, and Tranquillity on the west. Two city blocks were purchased on Kearney Boulevard. A small frame church was built at the back of the parcel on the corner of Trinity and Oleander streets. The first Mass was celebrated on June 13, 1909, in the new building. By November of that year a rectory was built.

The parish grew to such an extent that a larger church—the present church—was built in 1914. Many of the parishioners were immigrants—the majority were Italian, but Mexican, Portuguese, Basque, and Slavs were also residents of the area. One of the challenges was to effectively serve the needs of a diverse parish where many languages were spoken. The Redemptorist Brothers solved this problem by learning the languages so they could preach sermons and counsel their congregation in their native tongues. The church also became the setting for many festivals the immigrants brought from their homelands.

Since 1908, Saint Alphonsus Parish has been home to many residents of West Fresno and the west side of Fresno County. It has played an important role in the history of our valley.

The Second Baptist Church of Fresno

The year 1888 was an important year for Fresno's African American community. On March 31 of that year, the Reverend Edward Lindsay brought his wife and six children from North Carolina and settled in Fresno. Finding no Baptist church in West Fresno, Rev. Lindsay gathered together a group of families that held prayer meetings in each others homes. In August, the Reverend H. G. DeWitt of the First Baptist Church helped the group organize the Ebenezer Baptist Church. There were ten charter members. Rev. Lindsay was elected the first pastor.

Ten years later, in 1898, the Reverend Timothy Smith was called to be the new pastor. He embarked on a program to build a church. After the church was completed, however, the members lost the property. They had never been given a deed. They filed a lawsuit, but lost. Disheartened, Rev. Timothy Smith left. A new pastor, the Reverend S. A. Smith, was called to serve the congregation.

Rev. Smith brought renewed vigor to his flock. Property was purchased at Merced and F streets. Services were held in a building on the property. The members banded together and, through prayer and hard work, they raised the money to pay off the mortgage. The church was incorporated and the name was changed to the Second Baptist Church.

Over the years the membership continued to grow. Other ministers were called to serve the congregation. A fire destroyed their church; but, once again, the congregation banded together and, in time, a new church was built.

In the early 1950s, five acres at the corner of Jensen and Fig avenues was purchased as a site for the present church building. The first services were held in the new church on July 26, 1953.

Today, the congregation of the Second Baptist Church continues to play an important role not only among the African American community of Fresno, but also among the community as a whole. Its history, dating back more than a hundred years, is Fresno's history and is an integral part of the tales of our valley.

Mugerdich Samuelian in his Mariposa Street store.
Courtesy of Richard and Merlene Samuelian.

For many Fresnans one word, "Sam's," has been synony-mous with fine leather goods for as long as anyone can remember. Since 1917, Fresnans have depended on Sam's for shoe repair and, more recently, for purchasing quality luggage and leather items.

In 1912, Mugerdich Samuelian immigrated to Fresno from Ar-menia and lived with his sister, who had arrived earlier, in a house in the 500 block of L Street just south of Ventura Avenue. Mugerdich's (everyone called him "Sam") first job was buying fruit from nearby farmers and pushing it in a cart to sell at the Free Market on Fresno Street. In 1915, he began working in Mr. Rosenburg's shoe repair store at 1047 Fulton Street in the Grand Central Hotel building. He learned the business thoroughly. Dur-ing this period something else life-changing happened—he married a young woman he met at the First Armenian Presbyterian Church, Dovey Johnson. Then, in 1917, Mr. Rosenburg died. Sam bought the business from Mrs. Rosenburg and changed the name to Sam's Re-Nu-All. From his store, Sam watched the Security Bank building being built.

These were good years for Sam and Dovey. Three boys, Morris, Harold, and Richard, were born to the couple. When the boys were old enough, they helped in the store. Morris remembers roller skating with his brother Harold from Lowell Elementary School to the store after school. Their father wanted them to learn the business, but he also wanted them nearby so he could keep a watchful eye on them. They started as delivery boys. They would deliver, on foot, the newly repaired shoes to customers and shoe stores all over Fresno. Later, Richard made deliveries on a motor scooter. Harold remembers delivering shoes to a building at 1050 H Street. When he opened the door a long flight of stairs went to the rooms above. He climbed the stairs and gave the shoes to the lady in charge. When his father found out, he made sure that any future deliveries to H Street were made by one of the older men.

In the early 1930s Sam moved the store around the corner to 1940 Mariposa Street. During World War II, all three Samuelian boys left Fresno either to go into the service or, in the case of Morris, to Southern California to work at Lockheed.

During the war supplies were hard to get. Sam made his own glue from crepe soles. Because shoes were rationed, Sam suddenly saw his repair business increasing to an overwhelming extent—he was having trouble keeping up with the demand. He wrote to the older boys asking them if they wanted to return to the business after the war was over. They said, "Yes." After the war, the boys came home. Morris and Harold went to work for their father. Richard went to Fresno State College and graduated with a degree in engineering. After working at Valley Foundry designing machinery, he went back to FSC, took business courses and returned to the family business.

After the war, Sam began to expand the business by adding luggage and leather goods. However, shoe repair was still the fo-

Mr. & Mrs. Morris Samuelian, Mugerdich Samuelian, San
Joaquin Valley Junior Miss, and Dovey Samuelian.
Courtesy of Richard and Merlene Samuelian.

cus of the business. One service Sam still provided was going to
shoe stores to pick up shoes that needed repairing and returning
them when they were finished.

In 1964, Sam retired. He had had a wonderful career. He was
proud of the workmanship he brought to his craft. He won certificates of merit for superior workmanship at both the Chicago and
New York world fairs. In the mid-1950s, Sam's also became part
of the National Luggage Dealers Association—an affiliation that
remains to this day.

The city tore down the Grand Central Hotel when the Fulton

and Mariposa malls were being built. The sons decided to move the store to 1017 Fulton Mall next to the Bank of America. The business now featured an even larger selection of luggage, attache cases and a variety of leather goods in addition to offering shoe repair. The business grew steadily until Fashion Fair opened. Then, like so many businesses downtown, it began to decline. In 1986, Richard opened a second store on Blackstone Avenue. It became Sam's Luggage North.

Morris retired in 1982 and Harold in 1987. In 1991, Richard closed the downtown store. Today, his wife, Merlene, manages the store on North Blackstone. Although the location has changed, the quality shoe repair component of the business that Mugerdich Samuelian started so many years ago is still very much a part of a business that has played its own unique role in the history of our valley.

Lyon's Beribboned Gavel

The ladies of the Fresno chapter of the Women's Christian Temperance Union had other things on their minds one September day in 1905. Their mayor, W. Parker Lyon, did not have a gavel. Sadly, the mayor had only a bung starter to use as the official tool to call the trustees' meetings to order. Now, bung starters have their role in life; indeed, they are quite useful for plugging holes in barrels and kegs, but they tend to diminish the authority of the office of mayor when used at public meetings. The ladies wanted to provide a symbol of authority that Fresno's mayor could pound with pride.

The ladies went to a local planing mill and ordered a specially turned out gavel. Then the wooden gavel was taken to an engraver so that an appropriate message could be emblazoned on its surface. Then the sturdy gavel was tied ever so beautifully with a white ribbon—the symbol of the W.C.T.U. With this accomplished, the ladies waited with great excitement for the next meeting of the Fresno Board of Trustees.

On the evening of September 5, 1905, the meeting of the board of trustees was called to order by Mayor Lyon. After he banged the bung starter and asked for a reading of the minutes of the last meeting, he noticed all the ladies in the audience and asked that the ladies be allowed to speak first. Mrs. Mary Fletcher Norwood rose to introduce Mrs. Robert Ballagh, president of the Fresno chapter. Mrs. Ballagh addressed Mayor Lyon by saying that her organization, which supported the cause of prohibition, was in hearty sympathy with his administration and hoped the gavel would always "be used to wield justice in the interest of righteousness, justice, mercy, and temperance... ." Mrs. Norwood then placed the beribboned gavel in Lyon's hands.

Lyon, who had come into office with the support of the saloon interests, said with a perfectly straight face, "I thank you ladies very much. I am afraid some of you have been under a misapprehension with regard to my attitude upon these matters. In fact, I'm told that when I was invited to speak before the W.C.T.U. convention, some of the ladies feared I should not be in proper condition to address the visitors. Now, while I am not a Prohibitionist, I wish to assure you that I have not drunk a drop since July 29, 1899." There were smiles all around. The bung starter was retired and the temperance gavel took its place in the tales of our valley.

The Fly-swatting Campaign of 1914

The spring of 1914 saw Fresnans focused on a major campaign to beautify their city. Indeed, a City Beautiful Committee had been formed to promote and oversee all the projects necessary to carry out their mandate. Their ultimate goal was to make Fresno a spotless town. One week—from April 20 to 26—was set aside as the official "clean-up week." During this week, homeowners and business people alike were urged to clean up unsightly spots in their yards and around their shops. Sidewalks should be swept and washed and litter should be placed in the proper receptacles, they were told. This, however, was not enough. There was another matter that needed to be made known to the public—the threat to the public health posed by the common housefly. And so it was that the fly-swatting campaign of 1914 was launched.

Fresnans were invited to come to the Empire Theater on April 18-21 to view a film on the life cycle of the fly from egg to maturity. The film was shown both in the afternoon and evening on four consecutive days so everyone who was interested might attend. The public was warned that the film was graphic in its depiction of the fly and its habitat. Originally made to educate the public about the prevention and spread of tuberculosis, the film showed the fourteen-day life-span of the fly, including its ability to multiply rapidly.

At 8:30 each evening, immediately following the showing of the film, Mr. Henry N. Creger, who devoted his life to the study of the fly and its habits, presented a learned lecture on Mr. and Mrs. Fly and their offspring. His talk focused on the disease-spreading aspects of the insect and impressed upon his audience the need to swat the little pests—NOW. Mr. Creger's talk ended with the admonition that more people succumb to the typhoid germ carried by the fly each year than were killed in the Spanish-American War. Fresnans left the theater armed with new knowledge about germs and, with fly-swatters held high, made ready to wipe out the common pest wherever they found it and to make their city a more beautiful and healthier place in which to live.

A Horsewhipping in Hanford

On the afternoon of April 10, 1914, the lodgers at Hanford's Hotel Artesia were treated to quite a spectacle. It began just after the Reverend E. J. Bulgin, an evangelist who conducted meetings in the valley, checked into the hotel. Rev. Bulgin decided to take a walk and enjoy the sunshine. He had not gone far when a young woman, who had just checked into the same hotel, approached him and asked him to go riding with her. He politely declined. Later, she met him again, repeated the invitation and, once again, was turned down.

The clergyman had been warned that an attempt might be made to entrap him. He called his friend, the Reverend Loomis, to join him in his hotel room. When Rev. Loomis arrived, Bulgin insisted he hide in the closet so that, if the girl came to his door, he would be a witness to the conversation. They waited three hours until they heard the girl's voice in the hall telling a man about her attempts to entice Bulgin. She swore that, although she had failed so far; she would not fail again.

Suddenly, the door to Bulgin's room flew open. The girl came rushing up to him and said she wanted to show him a good time. Bulgin backed up and threw open the closet door. Loomis jumped out. The girl ran for the door, but Loomis got there first and barred the exit. He pressed a buzzer to call the porter. The porter arrived. The girl fled through the door, down the stairs and out to the street where a horse and buggy were waiting. Loomis was close behind. She jumped into the buggy and grabbed the reins and whip. Loomis grabbed the bridle. The girl began to whip the minister—lashing him about the head and face. He dropped the bridle. She fled in the buggy. The sheriff was called. Two deputies on motorcycles chased her for five miles before they caught up with her. By this time, she was in such a frenzy, she was no longer thinking clearly. She grabbed the horsewhip and began to use it on the lawmen. When they got her to jail they put her in a cell and let her cool down before they tried to talk to her. It seems the old saying was true on that April day in Hanford: "Hell hath no fury like a woman scorned!"

A Crusade Comes to Town

An Adventist tent meeting is being held in a field bordered by O, Mariposa, P, and Tulare streets in 1884. Since 1874, evangelists and other religious groups have held tent meetings in Courthouse Park and in vacant lots in downtown Fresno.
R.W. Riggs photo. Author's collection.

From the earliest days of Fresno's history, evangelists have made a point of stopping here on their way through the valley—probably due, in part, to Fresno's reputation as a "wide-open" town. Their tent meetings usually were attended by a large number of people—this was a fertile area for those who preached redemption.

None of them, however, had the impact that was felt during the month of July 1958, when Billy Graham came to Fresno to bring his message of God's salvation to the people of the Central Valley. Graham's evangelistic career began in 1949. Since then, The Southern Baptist minister had brought his message to large crowds in Asia, Europe, and some of America's largest cities. He was arriving in Fresno on July 12, 1958, and anticipation was high.

For months the Central Valley Billy Graham Crusade Committee had been busy. Advertising and publicity were carefully planned. A contract was signed with Fresno State College for the use of Ratcliffe Stadium for the meetings. Churches throughout the Valley were contacted and were planning to send members.

Counselors completed their training and the choir began to practice. By July 12, all was in readiness.

At the first night's meeting, Billy Graham strode to the podium, Bible in hand, and faced the crowd of over 20,000 people. As he spoke, he seemed to focus on each person in attendance. His lithe, tall body, piercing blue eyes, and thick shock of blond hair seemed to heighten the magnetism of this personality.

On the second and final night of the Billy Graham Crusade of 1958, 26,500 people from all over the Central Valley filled Ratcliffe Stadium. They left with changed hearts and with the hope that Billy Graham would return for a longer crusade in the future.

The Reverend Billy Graham at the time of his crusade in Fresno in 1962. The inscription on this photo reads, "To My Beloved Friend Scotty Morison. God's Blessing Always, Billy Graham."
Author's collection.

Billy Graham Returns

After the successful Billy Graham Crusade of 1958, the many people who had worked hard to ensure its success were anxious for Graham to return. They continued to work toward that goal and were rewarded by Graham's decision to return to Fresno from July 15-22, 1962. This time, the organization ran even more smoothly. Churches from all over the valley made plans to charter buses to bring their members to Fresno. The Santa Fe Railroad provide a special train on three nights of the crusade to bring people from Bakersfield, Shafter, Wasco and Hanford to Fresno and return them to their cities after the evening meetings ended. The anticipation and excitement were evident everywhere.

On the night of Sunday, July 15, 1962, the bleachers of Ratcliffe Stadium filled with people. A choir of 4,000 voices filled the warm summer night with glorious song. Billy Graham preached eloquently and meaningfully, his Gospel message reverberating from the highest point in the stadium.

Cliff and Bernice Ruby arrived late that evening and sat on the cool grass of the stadium's football field. Cliff remembers looking up at Graham and thinking how sincere and dedicated he was—delivering a simple message in a straightforward way.

At the Wednesday night service, famed blues singer Ethel Waters sang "His Eye Is on the Sparrow." The crowd, normally subdued, applauded wildly.

On the final night, Sunday, July 22, a record crowd of 28,000 packed Ratcliffe Stadium. Before Billy Graham spoke, the choir rose to sing. This time their song was one fraught with meaning for W. R. "Scotty" Morison, who served as chairman of both the 1958 and the 1962 Fresno crusades. Morison, a native of Glasgow, Scotland, was sitting next to Graham on the platform. He smiled broadly as he heard the choir begin to sing his favorite hymn—the "Twenty-third Psalm" set to the metrical tune "Crimond." The choir had been secretly practicing so they could surprise and honor him. It was a moment he never forgot.

The Central California Billy Graham Crusade of 1962 drew 172,200 people from all over the Central Valley. For those who attended, it was an experience they never forgot either.

The Burglar with Nine Lives

There's an old saying that cats have nine lives. There was a burglar in Fowler who just might have proven that some human beings do, too.

On a Thursday afternoon in September 1905, someone overheard a conversation between two men about plans for a robbery that night at Nance & Delahanty's Saloon on Front Street. Just as in the game of gossip, word of the planned burglary spread like wildfire. Within an hour the whole town of Fowler knew about the upcoming event and citizens were making plans to be there to witness the festivities. Meanwhile, Delahanty was making sure that his guns were clean and that he had plenty of ammunition. Constable Al Mason and Deputy Constable Asa Wilkins also made sure their guns were in order and, by early evening, made their way to the saloon. Others joined the fun, giving the saloon the appearance of an armed camp.

By the time darkness had settled over Fowler, everyone was ready. Suddenly, there was a rapping noise on the front window. Then it stopped. Evidently the burglar thought he had made too much noise and made his way to the back of the saloon. This was not a good plan. As soon as he got to the rear of the building he saw Delahanty leveling a shotgun at his head. "Throw up your hands!" Delahanty shouted. The burglar yelled back, "I'll be darned if I will!" He turned around and started off on a dead run. Delahanty fired two loads of buckshot at him, but still the man continued to run.

Deputy Constable Wilkins came running to help Delahanty. He began to fire at the fleeing burglar. The man dropped to his knees, got up and kept running. Wilkins kept firing. Each shot only made the burglar run faster. He disappeared into the night without a trace.

The next day two things were apparent: the fence behind Delahanty's saloon was so full of large buckshot holes it resembled a lacework cloth; and, the burglar who didn't get a chance to burgle had—like the proverbial cat—lived to see another day—one that hopefully would see him mend his ways, if not Delahanty's fence, in the continuing saga of our valley.

The Green Bush Spring Revisited

An earlier story was told about how the town of Fresno Station got its name from a green bush that was mistaken for an ash tree. Fresno is the Spanish word for ash tree. Next to the green bush was a spring of flowing water. Antelope, deer, wild horses, and elk used the spring as a watering hole. Later, cattle and sheep drank its pure, cold water. It became known as the Green Bush Spring. There is an addendum to the story.

In the 1950s and early 1960s, Sam's Re-Nu-All, a quality shoe repair store, was located at 1928 Mariposa Street. Right after World War II, Mugerdich "Sam" Samuelian added luggage to his store inventory. He converted the basement into display space for the new items. This worked very well except that, when there was heavy rain, water would seep the basement. One day in the early 1960s, there was more water than usual. Sam's son, Harold Samuelian, decided to try to find out where the water was coming from. He traced the path of the water to an open pipe just under the sidewalk, but the pipe didn't seem to lead anywhere.

Harold called the Fresno Water Department. They came out, put a cap on the pipe, and tore up the alley to inspect the lines. All they found out from all their efforts was that the water didn't come from city pipes. They had no idea about the source of the water. Finally, someone from the Fresno Historical Society determined that the source was the Green Bush Spring—it was still there, happily bubbling away under the basement of Sam's store.

In 1964, a plaque commemorating the Green Bush Spring was placed on the Mariposa Mall by the Jim Savage Chapter of E Clampus Vitus. An ash tree was planted appropriately next to it. Today, visitors to the Mariposa Mall can read the plaque and see the ash tree that continues to grow and flourish as a symbol of the naming of Fresno in the year 1872.

The Bells of the Cross Church

Church bells play an important role in the life of every community—whether large or small. Not only do they call the worshipper to services, they often ring the hour—pealing loudly to let all within listening range know what time it is. Their chiming often lifts the spirit or comforts the weary. On festive occasions, their wild tolling quickens the step and heightens anticipation. When a death occurs, their mournful tolling pierces to the very core of the grief-stricken heart. Such is the role of the church bell. And, so it was for the church bells in the neighborhood in West Fresno called "Roosian Town."

The centerpiece of that historic neighborhood was the Free Evangelical Lutheran Cross Church which, after it was moved from its original site in 1948, stood at the corner of Los Angeles and E streets. The church still stands, but now serves another congregation. The church has an impressive, square bell tower in which are housed two sets of bells—a big one and a small one. These bells were purchased in England at great expense. Their pealing caught the attention of those within the neighborhood, not only because of their beautiful sound, but because these bells had another purpose—they were used to communicate news to all within earshot.

The bells of the church would toll solemnly nine times to tell of the death of an old person; if a young person or young adult died, six slow rings would be heard; and if a child died, only the small bell would toll in three slow rings. When people heard both bells ringing joyously, they knew it was to announce a happy event—either a wedding or the birth of a child.

When the Free Evangelical Lutheran Cross Church built a new building on Palm Avenue, the bells had to be left behind. The neighbors in the new location made it a condition of allowing the church to be built at the new site. The bells may still ring in the old church, but no longer is their peal used to signal life's passages. And with their silence, another piece of Fresno's history becomes only a distant memory.

The Case of the Missing Light Globes

Christmas is normally the happiest of seasons. Joy seems to pervade the air. Tasks seem easier, steps seem lighter—the very business of living seems to take on a magical quality. Unfortunately, in December of 1900, there was one man in Fresno who was not happy.

Charles Elmore, the janitor in Fresno County's Courthouse had a problem. Electric light globes in the building kept disappearing—especially those in Judge Webb's courtroom. Every morning Elmore placed new globes in the empty light fixtures; the next morning they were gone. Then, one morning, he went into Judge Webb's courtroom and was amazed at the sight that greeted him. There, standing on a ladder calming unscrewing globes and putting them in his coat pocket, was a young man about twenty-five years old.

Charles Elmore yelled at him. The young man descended the ladder quickly and ran out of the courtroom. Elmore gave chase. The young man was faster than Elmore and made it out the front door ahead of him. Elmore was not far behind. The two men ran down the courthouse steps and through Courthouse Park. The young man headed for Fresno Street. Dodging horses and carriages, he sprinted across Fresno Street to the Blackhawk Stables that stood at the corner of Fresno and L streets. Elmore was getting winded and made the mistake of stopping to catch his breath.

By this time the man was running down L Street. A man on a bicycle who had been watching the proceedings started to give chase. Elmore, furious by this time, was determined to catch the man himself and asked if he could borrow the bike. This was a fine thought, but Elmore was so upset that when he tried to mount the bicycle, he found he couldn't. He tried again, got on the vehicle and promptly fell off. By this time, the robber and the light globes were far away, leaving in their wake a thoroughly distraught and humiliated janitor—one who probably would rather not be recorded in the tales of our valley.

Christmas in Fresno in 1900 was a memorable one. One century was ending and other was just about to begin. It was a time of reflection and anticipation. One hundred plus years later, Fresnans are experiencing the same feelings. They are also experiencing the same headache—shopping for those special gifts for family and friends. Some things never change.

In December of 1900, the *Fresno Morning Republican* was filled with advertising that called out to those who had not completed their Christmas gift list. The Red Front, a general merchandise store, claimed to have the "largest and most complete…apparel for men and boys in this city." It was featuring all wool suits and overcoats for $6.60, $8.50, $10.00 and $12.50. Three-piece suits for boys ages three to eight years were offered for $1.50 to $4.00. It advertised ladies' leather footwear for $1.00 a pair and boasted that they were "of [a] quality remarkable for their cheapness."

If a carriage was what one had in mind, Fresno Agricultural Works was offering discounts below the wholesale price. A small buggy for that special someone was a memorable gift, indeed.

Louis Einstein & Company's large advertisement let the public know that they were preparing for the largest business week in their history. They had extra staff on hand so they could ensure their customers not only high quality service in the store, but also the speedy delivery of all their parcels. On Friday, Saturday and Monday—December 21, 22 and 24—Einstein's was promoting a complete "Electric Illumination of our Window Displays." Another special promotion was offered only on December 24. On this day more than six thousand fine ladies' handkerchiefs were going to be on sale—ranging in price from seven to seventeen cents each.

The prices may have changed. The names of the stores may have changed. The quality of service may have changed. One thing has not changed—the excitement and joy this special season always brings.

The Christmas That Ushered in a New Century

The Christmas season of 1900 was a glorious one for most Fresnans. Shoppers kept the store keepers happy. Ministers polished their sermons while their choirs practiced diligently. Celebrations were being planned everywhere. A feeling of happiness seemed to spread through the city.

Kirk Elementary School presented a Christmas program on Friday, December 21. The school was festively decorated and the children had covered the blackboards with drawings. The program was opened by the principal, Dr. Melchonian. The students then presented recitations and songs. Similar presentations took place at the Huron and Lone Star schools.

The Barton Opera House scheduled two special shows. On Christmas night Gorton's Minstrels trod the boards with jokes, dancing, and songs. On December 26, George W. Lederer's comic opera, "The Belle of New York," entertained theatergoers for one night only. The show received rave reviews the next day. A good time seemed to be had by everyone.

Churches were the busiest of all. Since Christmas was on a Tuesday, most churches held to the tradition of holding Christmas services on the Sunday before Christmas, December 23. Two local churches, Saint John's Catholic Church and Saint James' Episcopal Church, decided to hold their services on Christmas Day. On Christmas afternoon, Saint John's held a children's Sunday school service in their school building at Mariposa and R streets. An appearance by Santa Claus and a Christmas tableau were the highlights of the event.

Ever mindful of the less fortunate, Fresno's Salvation Army Corps fed between two hundred fifty and three hundred people. Many of them were families with small children. Santa made an appearance here, too, with gifts for the children.

All in all, Fresno's last Christmas season of the nineteenth century was memorable for all concerned—and has been duly recorded in the legends of our valley.

A New Century Begins

During the month of December 1900, the anticipation of the new century that would begin on New Year's Eve was uppermost on everyone's mind. The pages of the *Fresno Morning Republican* for that month were dotted with stories and thoughts about the promise the new century held. One article says, "On [December 31] at twelve o'clock the nineteenth century will come to a close and the twentieth century, with all its great possibilities in all the walks of life, will be ushered in...this year there is more than the usual reason for sitting up to see the old out and the new one in."

A number of worship services were planned. Saint John's Catholic Church held a High Mass. Before midnight on New Year's Eve, the congregation filled the church. At the stroke of midnight, the procession entered the church, the bells were rung and the choir sang, "Gloria in Excelsis Deo." The First Presbyterian Church and the First Baptist Church held a joint "end of the century watch meeting." It began at eight o'clock at the First Baptist Church and lasted until midnight. The Reverend Thomas Boyd of the Presbyterian Church preached a sermon on, "Looking Backward." Baptist minister the Reverend Arthur Polk Brown spoke on, "Looking Forward—What Brings the New Century to Me." The Baptist Young People's Union gave literary, musical and social programs during the later hours of the meeting.

The Christian Church young people's society of Christian Endeavor hosted a New Year's Eve gathering at the church beginning at 8:30 p.m. An hour long program began at 9, followed by refreshments. At 11:30 p.m. a watch party began which lasted into the New Year.

Social events also were scheduled; but, for many Fresnans, the dawning of the twentieth century was a time to gather with friends in a worshipful setting to reflect on the past and to greet the future with hope—a future that for them seemed bright with promise.

A Secret Christmas Wedding

Planning a wedding involves many things. Choosing a date, selecting a place, preparing a guest list, planning a menu, and deciding on the proper music are just a few of the tasks that the bride and groom and, usually the bride's mother, have to take up. Add secrecy into the mix, and you have a situation ripe with a host of possibilities from headaches to surprises to just plain fun. So it was on Christmas Day 1900, when a few friends of James Porteous and Jennie Ritchie gathered at the Ritchie home at Church and Cherry avenues to witness their marriage.

Both James Porteous and Jennie Ritchie were born in Scotland. Porteous arrived in Fresno in 1874 and founded a very successful business—Fresno Agricultural Works. They were both members of the First Presbyterian Church. Although they planned to be married in a quiet, private manner at the Ritchie home, they certainly wanted their minister to perform the service. And thereby hangs a tale.

The streets of Fresno were usually quiet on Christmas Day. Someone noticed that the Rev. Thomas Boyd of the First Presbyterian Church was driving his buggy through town and heading for the country. This was unusual to say the least. Someone else noticed his arrival at the Ritchie place. Now the phone lines began to hum. The bridal couple were very popular in the community and had been courting for some time. It wasn't hard for the callers to put two and two together.

The popular honeymoon trip in 1900 was to go by train to Southern California. When James and Jennie Porteous waved goodbye to their family and journeyed by horse and carriage to the Southern Pacific depot, they were sure they had pulled off a successful secret wedding. Imagine their surprise when they arrived at the depot and were greeted by thirty happy friends who threw rice on the newlyweds and waved them happily on their way as they boarded the train and began their life together.

New Year's Eve 1900

Although many Fresnans celebrated the dawning of the twentieth century in church, many did not. Well over two hundred revelers donned costumes and masks, ordered carriages, and made their way to Fresno's Armory Hall for the volunteer firemen's thirteenth annual masquerade ball.

The ballroom of the Armory Hall was brightened by the red uniforms of the fifty or more firemen present. As the guests made their way into the party, they were greeted by the delightful music of Reitz's orchestra. The grand march opened the evening's festivities with true pomp and panache—the costumes of the marchers creating a panoply of hues and patterns that, as the waltz began, swirled round and round creating slashes of color of dizzying intensity.

As the evening progressed, prizes were awarded for outstanding costumes. Miss Ely won ten dollars for being the best dressed woman. Miss Farmer won the second prize in that category—a jardiniere stand donated by W. Parker Lyon. C. Hobson won ten dollars as the best dressed man. H. Lawrence, who came in second, won a toilet and shaving kit from Radin & Kamp. Many other prizes were given in various categories.

Several people arrived in costumes that showed a sense of humor rather than style. Herb Smith was completedly encased in a huge zinc dinner pail and, according to the *Fresno Morning Republican*, "made an interesting appearance." Will Holden came as a hobo, dressed in all the rags he could find. Evidently the ladies found this appealing, because he had plenty of dance partners all evening. Cora Hoen wore a dress and hat completely covered with cockleburs—it's safe to assume that her dance card was not filled.

During a reception later in the evening, the guests lifted their glasses to welcome in the New Year and the twentieth century and, in the wee hours of the morning, returned to their carriages and thence to their homes. The new century had arrived in Fresno.

The Honeymoon Caper

On Saturday evening, December 22, 1900, Miss Hannah Anderson and Mr. Victor Nelson were married. Following the ceremony, the bridal party, their families and friends went to the Grand Central Hotel where a lavish reception awaited them. During dinner, the couple said they were traveling to San Francisco for their honeymoon and were leaving on the train after the reception. At the appointed time, the carriage arrived and the couple left.

Before the departure of the happy couple, some of their close friends left for the Southern Pacific depot. Armed with rice, old slippers, and other items appropriate to the occasion, they arrived at the station in time to greet the couple. They waited and they waited and they waited. Twenty, then thirty minutes passed. The midnight train pulled into the station and still no sign of Mr. and Mrs. Nelson.

By this time the bridesmaids were shivering in their thin dresses. Where were the bride and groom? Maybe they entered a rail car unobserved and would come to a window as the train pulled out. One young man walked along the platform looking anxiously in each window. All at once he yelled, "Here they are!" Everyone rushed to the car's entrance and started throwing rice. With embarrassment they suddenly realized that they were pelting total strangers. Then, the blinds in one window were thrown open and a man's face appeared. Someone shouted, "That's Victor!" It wasn't Victor.

The train pulled out of the station. A very cold and unhappy group of young people was left in its wake. Their unhappiness was tempered by real concern for the newly married Nelsons. Where on earth had they gone? If they had noticed three men standing next to the depot laughing, they would have had their answer. The men had it on good authority from Grand Central Hotel owner Fulton G. Berry that the Nelsons' carriage ride through the streets of Fresno had been a ruse. The Nelsons were happily ensconced in their suite at the hotel. As all of Fresno knew, Berry loved a good practical joke better than just about anyone else.

Four members of the James Savage Chapter of E Clampus
Vitus dedicate a historic marker at Academy in 1968. Left to
right: Bill Atkins; Roy Gutner, the Noble Grand Humbug; Robert M. Wash; and Sidney Cruff.
Courtesy of Robert M. Wash.

With a career that ran the gamut from mule skinner to
valued member of the Fresno County Board of Supervisors, the life of Sidney L. Cruff was one of valued contributions
to the county and state he called home.

Sidney Cruff's life began on November 21, 1896, in Pocohontas,
Virginia. In 1900, his family traveled to the state of Washington
where they secured a homestead. After completing the seventh
grade, he left school and went to work. In 1915, he headed for
California. His first job as a mule skinner paid thirty dollars a
month. Early in 1917, after working in Tulare and Kings county
vineyards, he secured a job as a clerk and warehouseman for the
Southern Pacific Railroad. Near the end of World War I, he joined
the navy. After the war, he returned to his job at the railroad. In

1923, he became a laborer and tractor driver for the Fresno County road department—later becoming a welder and mechanic. In 1937, he became District 4's road superintendent.

In 1946, he ran for the county board of supervisors District 4 seat. He won easily. He held the post for twelve years, serving as chairman from 1951 to 1954. He was considered a man of wisdom and honesty who would fight determinedly to accomplish what was needed for the people in his district.

In 1961, Governor Edmund G. Brown appointed Sidney Cruff to the State Social Welfare Board. During his three years on that board his major accomplishment was ending the board's practice of making decisions privately before public hearings were held.

Sidney Cruff retired to his farm in 1964. He loved history and served as Grand Noble Humbug of the Jim Savage Chapter of E Clampus Vitus. He died in 1972. Just a week to the hour before his funeral, the "Clampers" honored him at a ceremony to dedicate a plaque marking the site of Fowler's Switch. Sidney Cruff left his family, friends, and the residents of the county he served so well a rich legacy—the knowledge that even a man from humble beginnings can accomplish important things for his community.

A Town Hall Forum for the Valley

On six Wednesday mornings each year, a large antique school bell rings loudly throughout Fresno's William Saroyan Theatre. It is no longer used to summon students to their studies, but rather to let the gathering of men and women know that it is time for the introduction of the latest distinguished speaker in the San Joaquin Valley Town Hall lecture series.

This long running organization traces its beginning to an interesting event. In 1937, Mrs. Cleo Aydelotte of Hanford attended a lecture in San Francisco hosted by the Town Hall Forum. She was so impressed she asked how one might go about establishing a similar group in the valley. She returned home, called together a group of women who shared her enthusiasm and, with the assistance of Dr. Albert Rappoport, the founder and director of Western Town Halls, Inc., they began to plan a lecture series. Their first series consisted of eleven lectures—six held in the morning and five in the evening. With Mrs. Guy Manson serving as chairman, the first lecture took place at Hardy's Theatre on January 10, 1938. Vicki Baum, the author of *Grand Hotel*, spoke on the topic, "Why Be Afraid?" The first series was a success. Town Hall was off and running. In 1945, it became an independent, non-profit forum. In 1961, it became San Joaquin Valley Town Hall, Inc.

What an adventure it has been! Some of the featured speakers have been: Drew Pearson, Max Lerner, Henry Kissinger, James Reston, Ogden Nash, Bennet Cerf, Jon Lindbergh, Margaret Mead, Agnes De Mille, Irving Stone, James Michener, Alex Haley and Maya Angelou. The Town Hall series has brought the finest speakers in journalism, literature, the arts, and government to the valley community.

Over the years, the membership has grown, the lecture site has moved and the number of lectures given each season has changed. The high cost of speakers' fees and the expenses involved in bringing speakers to Fresno now limits the number of lectures to six. One thing has remained constant—the enthusiasm with which the members of San Joaquin Valley Town Hall continue to work to bring interesting speakers to the Central Valley community.

William Rufus Nutting stands at the base of a giant Sequoia in the mountains of the Sierra Nevada. With him are Belle McKay and Mary Helen McKay.
Courtesy of Mary Helen McKay.

A date palm tree wrapped with the tent William Rufus Nutting devised to keep the roots warm during winter months. Mary Helen McKay stands at the door to the tent.
Courtesy of Mary Helen McKay.

A man of innate practical talents and wide-ranging interests coupled with the ability to envision far-reaching
schemes was born into one of New England's oldest families. His
ancestor John Nutting was the steward of John Winthrop's estate
in England. He came to the Massachusetts Bay Colony after
Winthrop had been named its governor.

William R. Nutting was born in Randolph, Vermont. While
going to school he worked with his father learning farming and
how to use wood and iron-working tools. After graduation from
the State Normal School of Vermont, he held a series of jobs in
reform schools throughout the state. The jobs involved organiz-
ing the shops in these schools which he did so skillfully that he
moved from one school to another with salary increases at each
new position.

In 1877, he headed for Boston and became involved in the new
field of electric power. He started a business that fitted homes with

electric lighters for gas burners. Four years later his business became the Boston Electric Company. He and one of his mechanics invented the nickel-plated push-button light switch. Then he turned his genius to transportation, creating electric rail systems in a number of Eastern cities that offered direct competition to the horse car lines. Next, he directed his talents toward agriculture.

Nutting came west in 1885 and, after writing a series of newspaper articles on farm mortgage loan programs and ways to organize fruit growers, he arrived in Fresno in 1891. He came to look at a parcel of alkali land southwest of Fresno to see if anything profitable could be grown on it. John S. Dole suggested Thompson Seedless grapes. The plantings came from William Thompson's original vines and resulted in a successful Thompson vineyard. In 1902, Nutting organized the American Vineyard Company and, in 1911, he chaired a committee that organized the California Associated Raisin Company.

Later, Nutting purchased acreage east of Fresno and began to propagate date palms. Because dates are usually grown successfully only in warmer climates, Nutting devised a tent that would encase the bottom part of the tree during the winter months. Inside was placed a kerosene lamp that kept the roots warm.

William Rufus Nutting was a Renaissance man of sorts—his vision, talents and wide-ranging interests had a lasting impact on the agriculture of our valley.

One of the many immigrant groups that made its way to Fresno in the 1880s was a group of German people from the Volga River colonies in Russia. In 1763, their ancestors left Germany to settle in Russia because Empress Catherine the Great promised them religious liberty, free land, exemption from military service and a degree of local self-government. When they arrived they found the land was undeveloped and plagued by marauding Tartar tribes. However, they developed the land, turning it into a rich agricultural area, and founded villages. They held fast to their German traditions and did not intermarry. After Catherine's death, Tsar Alexander I kept the pledges Catherine had made, but the next two tsars, Alexander II and Alexander III, began to take away some of their privileges.

As the situation deteriorated further, the German colonists began to leave. They looked toward America. Many settled in the Mid-west. One group who heard about the agriculturally rich Fresno area came west. On June 19, 1887, thirty-one men, women, and children arrived at the Southern Pacific depot in Fresno. The men were all farmers except one, who was a carpenter. Their brightly colored costumes and clean appearance made an impression on those who saw them. Three German businessmen, Mr. Zumkeller, Mr. Green and Mr. Goldstein, met them, helped them find food, lodgings, and work. Shortly after their arrival, an outbreak of measles killed seven of the children. Dr. Chester Rowell provided medical help and befriended the new arrivals.

They found jobs in agriculture and in various businesses in town. They saved their money and, eventually, were able to buy homes. Most of the Volga Germans settled south of California Avenue in an area that became known as "Roosian Town" or "German Town." They built a church, the Free Evangelical Lutheran Cross Church, which to these religious people became the centerpiece of their neighborhood.

Over the years, the descendants of the Volga German immigrants have taken their place proudly in the Fresno community. The areas of farming, government, education, and business have all benefited from their participation. In 1971, they opened a museum and are actively involved in the preservation of their culture. They provide another colorful piece in the rich tapestry that makes up the Fresno community.

On West Avenue, just north of Shields Avenue, is a building that was once a firehouse. Today, it is home to the Central California Chapter of the American Historical Society of Germans from Russia. It is a museum dedicated to the preservation of the history of the Volga German community in Fresno and the Central Valley. It also houses the only German-Russian genealogy research library on the West Coast.

Entering the museum, the visitor is struck by the large number of artifacts contained in the room. His eye first goes to a diorama of a colonist's farmyard in the Volga area of Russia. Created by Johanne Ehly Pekarck, it features a typical house, barn, outbuildings, and crops and gives the visitor a tangible image of life in the nineteenth century.

As the visitor continues his tour, he pauses to view a large collection of tools, many of them handmade, and several shoe stretchers that came from Wasemiller's Dry Goods and Shoe Store, one of the important businesses in West Fresno early in the twentieth century. Against one wall is a shoe bench—also from Wasemiller's. Inside a large glass case is a beautifully preserved white wedding dress that was worn by Maria Busick when she married Frederick Diel in Kukkus, Russia, in 1898. It is all hand stitched with insets of lace. One poignant reminder of the difficult and dangerous journey the Volga German pioneers made when they fled Russia is a pair of shoes worn by Catharine Heizenrader when she walked out of Russia in 1914.

The original pump organ from the Free Evangelical Lutheran Cross Church sits against another wall. Pictures of pioneers, the early Fresno churches of the German community, and pioneer businesses fill the walls.

One comes away from a visit to the Volga German museum with a deeper appreciation of the rich culture and significant contributions this important group of people has made to the Fresno area.

A German Neighborhood in West Fresno

One of the many ethnic groups who came to Fresno in the late nineteenth century were Germans from the Volga River area of Russia. The first ten families arrived in 1887. As they acquired jobs and homes, they told those they had left behind about the opportunities in Fresno. The result was that more of these industrious, hard-working people arrived in Fresno. The Volga Relief Society was created to help these immigrants learn English and find jobs.

The West Fresno area in which they settled became known as "Roosian Town" or "German Town." Bounded by Church and Fruit avenues and Mono and G streets, this neighborhood not only contained several churches, but was notable for its well-kept houses and clean, manicured yards.

One interesting feature of the homes could be found in the backyard. It was a small structure, separate from the house, that was called the *bachhaus* or summer kitchen. These structures, which allowed the cooking to be done in a building apart from the main house, thus keeping the main house clean, were common in Russia. In Fresno, with its hot summers, cooking in these summer kitchens had the added feature of helping to keep the main house cool.

The Volga German immigrants were deeply religious people. Several churches including the Free Evangelical Lutheran Cross Church, the Evangelical Zion Congregational Church, the Wartberg Evangelical Lutheran Church, and Saint Paul's Lutheran Church were built in the neighborhood. Some of the businesses were Laubaun & Sehr Dry Goods, Wasemiller's Dry Goods, Schamm & Steitz Used Car Dealers, Kinzel's Grocery, Rudy's Pharmacy, Nagels Market, and Reitz Cash Market. Jacob Nilmeier was the local doctor.

Today, the neighborhood once known as German Town has been divided by Highway 99. The families who once lived here have moved to other parts of Fresno. But, their memories remain of this once colorful part of West Fresno that had a pulse of life that was uniquely German.

An "Annual Banquet" for two hundred members of the newly formed San Joaquin Power Club took place on October 10, 1922. It was held in the Commercial Club located in the Holland Building (now the Crocker Anglo Bank Building) at the northwest corner of L and Fresno streets. The evening consisted of a seven-course dinner followed by the election of officers. The campaign for offices began on October 3 when the slate of officers was revealed by the nominating committee. Not everyone agreed with its selections, and several other names were put forth. Campaigning was spirited to say the least—the days before the election were filled with hi-jinks and good-humored muckraking—making working hours lots of fun. When the election was finally held following the banquet and the results totaled, Fred Pearson had been elected the club's first president.

With this first event a tradition was firmly established. Each year, the candidates for president of the club would campaign in the days leading up to the election. All sorts of pranks and spirited fun marked these campaigns. On the day of the banquet, a parade led by the Power Club Band would wend its way from the tenth floor down to the main lobby of the San Joaquin Light & Power Company building. The parade featured all the candidates and their campaign managers and gave them the opportunity to take their platforms to all the employees. Not a lot of work was accomplished on this day, and no one soon forgot the crazy slogans, costumes, skits, and merriment.

After that first year, the annual banquet was held in the huge room that encompassed almost the entire top floor of the San Joaquin Power Company building. It continued to be a lavish affair with formal dress and a dinner consisting of several courses. After dinner each candidate gave a short speech. The election was held and the winners were announced. The evening concluded with a dance and another year formally began for the members of the San Joaquin Power Club.

The annual banquet, in 1933, of the San Joaquin Power Club held on the top floor of the San Joaquin Light and Power Company building at Tuolumne and Fulton streets in downtown Fresno. Seated at the head table in the back of photo are: Vern Redman, Bob Martin, Jim Henslet, E. P. Smith, A. G. Wishon, Jr., Al Joy, A. G. Wishon, Sr., and Lee Duncan.

Courtesy of Jack Brase.

Large companies are often impersonal places to work. However, one large, local business that has a long history in Fresno found a way to make everyone who worked there feel like he or she was part of a family.

In 1921, about forty of the employees at San Joaquin Light & Power Company formed a council for the purpose of educating employees by discussing the many phases of the company's operation and the role that each played. Soon, the council found its focus had expanded to include social activities. This was so successful that, on April 25, 1922, the council was organized as the San Joaquin Power Club with temporary officers, a constitution, bylaws and a commitment to further expand the scope of social activities. At the club's first meeting plans were made for its first picnic and barbecue, which was held at Wards Oak Park on June 22, 1922. In October, the first officers were elected at a dinner meeting.

In 1924, a site was chosen on the shores of Bass Lake for a summer camp. Originally called "Cozy Cove," its name was later changed to "Emory Wishon Cove." As the years went by, a number of buildings were constructed there. The Cove was the scene of picnics and social events and was available for employees and their families during vacations.

In 1925, a Mutual Benefit Association was established to provide help for employees and their immediate families. During the Great Depression it provided medical insurance and financial loans to families in need.

The unique thing about the San Joaquin Power Club was that everyone who worked for San Joaquin Power Company—from the janitor to the president—was a member of the club. As the club developed, it created a sense of camaraderie among all the employees of the San Joaquin Power Company. They felt that they were more than just the people who worked for the company, they were part of a large family. This translated into a deep sense of loyalty and cooperation in the workplace and created happy memories that lasted long after retirement age was reached.

New Year's Day in the Morning

The *Fresno Morning Republican's* pages for January 1, 1901, are filled with snippets of fascinating information. In London, crowds of Scots stood outside Saint Paul's Cathedral at midnight on New Year's Eve singing "Auld Lang Syne" to usher in the new century. Also in London—at two o'clock in the afternoon (which was midnight in Australia)—the Lord Mayor hoisted the Australian flag as a sign that the Australian commonwealth was born.

In Fresno, many private parties had been held the night before. Two of them give some idea of the social life of the time. Three ladies, Mesdames Dr. Russell, Joe Summers, and Fred T. Moore, entertained their friends at the Kohler House. The chief amusement of the evening was card playing. The stroke of twelve o'clock was celebrated with due ceremony. Musical entertainment and light refreshments rounded out the evening.

One of the popular young ladies of the city, Ruby Olney, hosted a "Peanut Party" at her parents home. Vines of similax entwined with green ivy and pepper leaves decorated the entry hall, sitting room and parlor. As her guests arrived, they were asked to guess the number of peanuts in a large jar on the hall tree. Later, there was much merriment as the young people endeavored to walk across the parlor while balancing a peanut on the blade of a knife. Salted peanuts and dainty refreshments were enjoyed by the partygoers. Among those who welcomed in the twentieth century in such happy fellowship were Mary Meux, John Meux, Maud Helm, Blanche and Mae Pierce, and Earl Norton. An interesting footnote to this story is that their descendants still reside in Fresno and welcomed the twenty-first century here.

At midnight, impromptu music was punctuated by the noisy din of gunshots. Tule fog shrouded the city, prompting many to remark that the twentieth century arrived with its overcoat on.

David Cowan Sample

One of the earliest and most respected Fresno County pioneers was born at Lexington, Mississippi, on February 12, 1849. When he was a small child his father, Issac, died. His mother, Mary, was the daughter of Daniel Dulany, a large Mississippi landowner who had served as a colonel in the War of 1812.

After his father's death, the family moved to Cypress, his grandfather's plantation outside Lexington. The boy attended a private school until he was fifteen when he left to join a Confederate unit. He acted as a scout under General Nathan Bedford Forrest. He was then assigned to the Sixth Texas Cavalry, serving under Captain Scout until the end of the Civil War.

The Civil War brought devastation to many areas of the South. His family did not escape its effects. When he returned home to Cypress, he found the plantation in ruins. All the farm implements had been destroyed and the slaves and stock had disappeared. He worked as a clerk for one year. Then he returned to school and completed the final year of his education.

David Cowan Sample decided to set his sights on the West. He traveled with the families of Major Thomas P. Nelson and William Walter Shipp, their route to California taking them through the Isthmus of Panama. They settled first near Vacaville and then came to Big Dry Creek in 1868. He became a noted stockman in the area and planted lemon and orange groves.

In 1872, David Cowan Sample married Sallie Cole at Millerton. They became the parents of eleven children. Many of them would play important roles in the history of Fresno County.

Sample became interested in a number of Fresno businesses including the Fresno Meat Company, Fresno Flume and Irrigation Company, and the Fresno Abstract Company. In 1910, he and Sallie moved to Fresno. At the time of his death on January 14, 1929, David Cowan Sample was regarded as one of the most respected members of the community.

David Cowan Sample and his wife Sallie Cole Sample. Sallie was a daughter of pioneer William Temple Cole, whose story is told elsewhere in this book. Sample was a pioneer sheep man in the Academy area where some of his descendants still reside.

D.C. Sample.

Mrs Sallie Sample.

John Greenup Simpson

The lure of the West has called many a pioneer. Early in our country's history many men and women left the eastern seaboard in search of new prospects inland. Through the Cumberland Gap they came, onward into Kentucky and Tennessee, crossing the Mississippi River and settling the new states of Missouri and Arkansas. They struggled across the vast plains forging ever westward in their quest for new beginnings. For some it was the lure of gold that brought them finally to the fabled paradise of Alta California. So it was for the subject of our story.

John Greenup Simpson was born in Kentucky on October 22, 1829. He moved with his parents to Miller County, Missouri. It was here that he grew to manhood. A group of people desiring to go west was forming under the aegis of Governor Edwards. Simpson joined up. The group headed west across the plains with their ox teams. When they reached California, Simpson struck out for Mariposa to try his luck in the mines, but found he had better luck as a teamster operating from Fort Miller to Stockton and the mountains. He arrived in Big Dry Creek in 1852 and turned his attention to the stock business in partnership with J.N. Musick. When the partnership dissolved in 1861, he began to purchase land—eventually owning 7,000 acres in the Big Dry Creek area.

John Greenup Simpson became an influential citizen, serving as the first Fresno County tax collector, a member of the board of supervisors, and the superintendent of county schools. Always a supporter of education, he helped to build the Academy, the first secondary school in Fresno County. Simpson was a member of the Methodist Episcopal Church South and donated the land for the church at Academy, the oldest in Fresno County.

In 1859, Simpson married Sarah Baley. They had seven children, one of whom, Marvin, served in the California legislature. They and many of their descendants are buried in the cemetery at Academy overlooking the land they settled so long ago.

John Greenup
Simpson and his wife
Sarah Baley, a daughter of William Right
Baley and a niece of
Gillum Baley.

As the nineteenth century turned into the twentieth century the editor of the *Fresno Morning Republican*, Chester Harvey Rowell, provided editorials and commentaries that are worth looking at a century later. Rowell noted that it is a really imposing thing "to pass the line that bounds the centuries. Indeed, it is not imposing, unless you stop to think and thinking is a great deal of trouble. It is much easier to fill up on holiday punch and let it go at that." However, Rowell, being a thinker, could not let it go at that. He traced Western civilization from the birth of Christ to the present, focusing on the development of universal law under the Romans and tracing the evolution of the freedom that Americans take for granted. In Rowell's view, mankind had developed a character that was idealistic, fatalistic, yet admired aggressive behavior, and loved public order. It was this modern character, he said, that would be called upon to solve the problems of the twentieth century.

Rowell also listed a few of the thinkers of the time and their prophecies for the new century. David Starr Jordan, president of Stanford University, felt that biological science would focus on the study of heredity and life relations. Jordan did not think that any discoveries in the new century could be as revolutionary as the application of steam power. He stated that the major social problem of the twentieth century would be alcohol abuse which he felt would be successfully dealt with by "an uplifting of national character rather than through reforms by legislative enactment."

The Reverend J. K. McLean predicted a greater interdependence among the nations of the world, a greater spirit of tolerance of opinions, and a move from book learning to hands-on training in the field of education. French economist Paul Leroy Beaulieu saw a commercial union of continental Europe.

Rowell had one final thought. He predicted that within five years the horse would be replaced by the automobile. However, "in ten years time," he said, "the fashionable will be driving horses again simply for the distinction of being different from other people."

The tales of our valley have told of glittering opening nights at the Barton Opera House and the Pantages Theatre and of the famous artists who trod the boards in these establishments, but let's visit a theater of more recent vintage—one that continues to play a major role in the life of our community—the William Saroyan Theatre.

On October 14, 1966, a performance by the Fresno Philharmonic Orchestra opened the theater at the Fresno Convention Center complex. It was an exciting evening for all who attended and represented the culmination of the dreams and hard work of many people who made the new center a reality.

The next scheduled event in the new theater was a musical that had been a hit on Broadway—*Hello, Dolly!* The eight sold-out Fresno performances starred Ginger Rogers. Miss Rogers was a gracious lady and those who attended would never forget her charm and talent. She was gracious behind-the-scenes as well and thereby hangs a tale.

Hello, Dolly! played in August—Fresno's hottest month. Although the theater and dressing rooms were air-conditioned, Miss Rogers' heavy wigs and costumes were very hot and uncomfortable. Her manager asked Robert Schoettler, director of the Fresno Convention Center, if Miss Rogers' dressing room could have a room air-conditioner. Mr. Schoettler provided one immediately. Miss Rogers thanked him and said, "I wish I could do something nice for you." He told her that he would like to have some of his friends meet her. "Why don't you have them come into the Green Room after my performances?" she replied.

After each performance, Schoettler would gather fifteen or so members of his board of directors, government leaders, and people who had worked to bring the convention center complex together. Soon, the door would open and Miss Rogers would appear in her robe. With a dazzling smile she would say, "Mr. Schoettler, I'm so happy to see you!" She would give Bob Schoettler a kiss, greet his friends and then excuse herself so she could rest after her performance. Her graciousness would long be remembered by those she met and has been duly recorded in the tales of our valley.

Laura Alsip Winchell

E. C. Winchell   Laura C. Winchell

In the rough, gold mining camp of Millerton, Laura Winchell set a standard for education and manners that prepared the young people of the community for a more sophisticated life in the world beyond the gold fields.

The tales of our valley are not complete without recounting the lives of the incredible pioneer women who either alone or by their husbands' sides braved many hardships in order to lay the foundation for our county's greatness. It is the story of one such woman we tell here.

Laura Alsip was born on March 28, 1833, in Shepherdstown, Virginia, where her father was a planter and mill owner. Her family was not a stranger to hardship. Her grandfathers had fought in the Revolutionary War and her maternal grandfather also served in the War of 1812. Her father died when she was a child and her mother continued to run their plantation. Laura attended the Cincinnati Seminary, where she completed her education.

An older brother and sister of Laura Alsip's came to California after gold was discovered in 1848. Two years later, Laura and her mother decided to follow. After selling the plantation and freeing their slaves, they came west by way of the Isthmus of Panama. They first settled in Sacramento. Laura was hired as a teacher. She met and married a young lawyer named E. C. Winchell. In 1859, after their first child, Lilbourne, was born, they moved to Fort Miller. Three more children were born to the couple. Mr. Winchell was named the first county superintendent of public instruction. The first classroom in Fresno County was set up in the Winchell's dining room with Rebecca Baley, under the supervision of Laura Winchell, as the teacher. The school lasted for three months.

In 1861, the Winchells moved to a new home a half mile south of the fort. A school building was erected nearby. From 1864 to 1865, Laura Winchell taught classes for advanced as well as for primary students. She also opened her home for all kinds of social activities. Picnics, parties, and games were hosted by her for the benefit of the young people of the Millerton community. She also was a friend to the sick and needy. Her loving and self-sacrificing nature endeared her to everyone.

Laura Winchell's failing health caused the family to move to San Francisco. The earthquake and fire in 1906 hastened her decline and she died in 1908. In the wild gold mining camp of Millerton, Laura Alsip Winchell set a standard for good manners and provided knowledge to the young people of the area that they would not have received otherwise. Her contributions are worth remembering in the tales of our valley.

Schoettler Tire Inc.

In 1933, Hal Schoettler, an employee of Firestone Tire Company, and his wife, Loretta, moved to Fresno from Southern California. In 1937, Hal became the first general manager of Transstate Tire in Fresno. In 1947, he purchased a half interest in a small tire shop that Carroll Harrington had opened in Madera in 1934. Hal's brother Bob joined the firm and together the Schoettler brothers started to expand the company. When Harrington died in 1952, his share was purchased by the Schoettlers. A year later, they opened their first Fresno store at 1470 Blackstone Avenue. In 1961, Bob Schoettler left the family business to work for the Fresno Convention Bureau. Hal's sons, Tom and Dave, who started in the business when they were thirteen and fourteen years old, became the managers of the Fresno and Madera stores, respectively.

Before Highway 99 was rerouted and became a major freeway, travelers had to go through all the valley towns. Dave and Tom Schoettler remember many of the famous people who stopped at the family service station. Robert Mitchum, Clark Gable, Mickey Rooney, Earl Warren, and many others filled their cars with gas and parked them at Schoettler's. then walked the half block to the Fruit Basket to eat.

From those humble beginnings developed one of the largest commercial tire dealers in North America. Today, Schoettler Tire Inc. has twelve commercial tire stores between Bakersfield and Richmond. Seven of the locations are in Fresno and Madera counties.

Their new truck tire retreading plant in Fresno, which uses the latest computerized technology, is the most modern facility of its kind in the world. A visit to the plant allows the visitor to witness the process, which makes use of sophisticated equipment one doesn't usually associate with the tire business. First the tires are inspected. Unusable tires are sent to the recycler who cuts them up into small pieces that are used to make electricity. The tires that pass very rigid safety tests go through a series of steps from buffing off the old tread to adding new tread. The dust at the end of the buffing process is recycled—going to Southern California to be used in making other products. The finished tires are put into a curing chamber for an hour and a half, then labeled and checked again for safety. At a saving of 65 percent over the cost of a new tire, the retreads are used on trucks and buses throughout Northern California.

Today, Hal's sons, Tom and Dave, head the company. They both praise a loyal and dedicated work force for their success. All their children and many of their grandchildren work side-by-side with more than 220 employees. Schoettler Tire Inc. is still, at its heart, a family business—one that has served our Valley for many years.

Robert A. Schoettler

A visit to downtown Fresno often takes one past the Fresno Convention Center complex. Over the door of one building is written, "Robert A. Schoettler Conference Center." Behind that title is a story about a man and a vision.

Robert A. Schoettler was born in Los Angeles—the next to youngest of five children. When he was ten, the family moved to Fresno so his father could take over the management of the local Hoover vacuum cleaner store. He graduated from Fresno Tech High School and attended Fresno State College and the University of Tennessee. He married Gladys Farnsworth in December 1941 and, in June 1942, joined the United States Air Force. His unit left for England and he did not see his daughter, who was born in September 1942, until she was four years old. Schoettler's 94th bombardment group was stationed at Bury St. Edmund's, an airfield 130 miles north of London. Acting as a navigator, he flew seventeen missions—taking part in bombing raids over Berlin, Munich, Leipzig, and Bremen. After World War II was over, he was assigned to Templehoff Air Base in Berlin to serve out his tour of duty. When he returned to Fresno in 1947, he entered the family tire business.

In 1961, the revitalization program for Fresno's downtown included the creation of a convention center. A committee of the Fresno Chamber of Commerce was acting as the convention bureau. They were looking for a director to get a program started. Someone asked Schoettler, "Why don't you apply for the position of director of the Fresno Convention Bureau?" He interviewed for the position and was hired. Six months later, the bureau broke away from the chamber and became a separate entity. Schoettler had a vision of what the convention complex should be and wrote the plans. In 1963, a bond measure was put before the voters to finance the project. A majority of the voters approved, but not the two thirds necessary for passage. In the following year, a City and County Convention Center Authority was created. It was empowered to issue $8.5 million in revenue bonds to finance the project. In 1966, the Fresno Convention Center opened its doors for the first time. Schoettler's dream had been realized.

During Schoettler's tenure as director, the Fresno Convention

Center became an important setting not only for conventions, but also for the Fresno community's cultural, business, and sports events. Bob Schoettler retired as director of the Fresno Convention Center in 1985. Early in 1999, the Robert A. Schoettler Conference Center on M Street was named in honor of the man whose work and vision made the complex a reality.

By the year 1901, that venerable Fresno newspaper, the *Fresno Morning Republican*, had, besides its Fresno office and printing plant, an office at 230 to 234 Temple Court, New York City, and an office in the U.S. Express Building in Chicago. The paper could be purchased in San Francisco at Cooper's book store and at the news stand in the Palace Hotel. The newspaper had done its part in making Fresno known throughout the country.

The *Republican* had news stories and feature articles that covered a wide variety of subject matter—there was something for everyone. One column, in particular, was always worth a look. It was called "Local Brevities," and was a sort of catch-all for tidbits of every kind. It always could be found just below the weather report for the previous day.

On January 12, 1901, it was noted that Kutner-Goldstein's was stocking "Bayles' hand-made crackers for dainty lunches," the Hughes cafe was advertising dinner for seventy-five cents, the Hughes laundry was offering to beat and clean your carpet for an unspecified amount, and Prickett & Munderbach's store was selling strawberries, green chilies, tomatoes, and green peas. Another item reported that Mrs. C. J. Craycroft would host a meeting of the orphanage association at her home. A tragic note was that the body of Filipino soldier Harry Foin arrived on the midnight train and was taken to the home of his father, F. A. Foin. A funeral was going to be held the following day at the Catholic church.

One amazing tidbit was the theft of an overcoat from Herman Levy's store three days before. It seems the thief sold it to a Mr. Gaheroni for $7.50 who, in turn, sold it to someone else for $9.50. By the time the police located the coat, the trail of the thief had turned rather cold, indeed.

These tidbits from January 1901, giving us a glimpse of the daily life of our city so many years ago, are now duly noted in the tales of our valley.

One of the traditions of the Volga German community was the building of a Gebet Haus or Prayer House. It was often the forerunner of the founding of a church. So it was for the people of Biola. In 1918-1919, a small building only twenty-four by thirty feet in size was erected on land owned by the Schwabenland family. Two years later, it was moved to Biola and placed on land at F and Fifth streets.

Three times a week—Saturday evening, Sunday afternoon, and Wednesday evening—people gathered at the Prayer House to discuss the Bible. Those who attended these meetings were first generation Volga Germans from varying backgrounds in the Lutheran and Reformed traditions. Two women's groups were established during the 1920s—the Ladies Society and the Tabitha Society. The latter is still active today.

In 1925, the Biola Congregational Church was built just south of the Prayer House. It is the tallest building in Biola. The handsome white exterior features a portico held up by four substantial pillars. A Russian cupola topped with a cross caps the tall bell tower. On each of the four corners of the belfry is a white stand holding a globe—representing spreading the Gospel to the four corners of the world. The interior combines the Lutheran and Reformed traditions. The large elevated pulpit symbolizes that the heart of Reformed belief is the preached word. The altar and altar rail reflect the Lutheran tradition.

In the 1950s, the congregation needed more room for other structures on the property. Because of the treasured memories it held, the Prayer House was purchased by Walter and Lillian Salwasser and moved onto their land near the San Joaquin River.

In 1996, the Biola Congregational Church celebrated its seventy-fifth anniversary. It continues as an active, vital congregation to serve the needs of the Biola community.

Mr. Smith's Ear Goes to Court

On a cold January morning in 1901, the courtroom of Judge George E. Church was the setting for a trial that quickly took on all the characteristics of a comic opera. The room was filled to capacity with friends of both the victim and the defendant. Excited voices were quieted as the victim, Jim Smith, a highly respected bootblack, walked up to the front table with Deputy District Attorney Edwards and attorney S. J. Hinds. They were followed by defendant Samuel Chavrs, a porter, who was escorted to the front of the courtroom by his attorneys, Frank Short and M. K. Harris—two of the finest barristers in Fresno. The charge on this particular day was mayhem, a serious charge in the eyes of the law. Webster's dictionary defines mayhem as "the act of intentionally maiming a person." It seems that Jim Smith was missing a portion of his left ear and charged the defendant with biting it off during a fight.

After a jury was impaneled, the trial began in earnest. It was argued by both sides that the men were of upright character. Indeed, the defendant's pastor was on hand to attest to his integrity. The bootblack victim had quite literally rubbed the toes of Fresno society so everyone knew of his honesty. The deputy district attorney argued that to violate the sanctity of a man's body was a heinous crime. He paraded his client before the jury to show them the diminished ear. Unfortunately for the victim, the jury had trouble deciding which ear had been violated—they both looked rather large. If it was not for Exhibit A, which was the aforesaid portion of an ear floating in a jar of alcohol, it would be hard to know that a crime had taken place.

The lawyers waxed eloquent. It soon became apparent that the law was taking a back seat to emotions. The defense called star witnesses to the stand to show that, since the preliminary hearing, their testimony had improved with each retelling. By late morning the case went to the jury, which shortly returned to the courtroom with a verdict of "not guilty." The defendant, the victim and their friends went on their way. The jar containing part of Mr. Smith's ear was not as fortunate. It was given to Mr. Ewing, the clerk of the court, for safe-keeping.

Bibb Hall

The San Joaquin Power Club, an organization of the employees of the San Joaquin Light & Power Company, had developed a fine camp area at Wishon Cove in the Bass Lake area; but there was a need for a clubhouse in Fresno. A clubhouse committee was formed to take charge of this project.

An old warehouse building at the Herndon substation provided a solution. Through arrangements with division electric superintendent D. D. Smalley, the building was moved to a site at California and Orange avenues. Once the building was in place, the clubhouse committee members began enlarging the structure, installing a floor and painting the building. On May 21, 1943, their efforts were celebrated with the formal dedication of the Fresno Chapter Clubhouse during a "Nite Club Dinner Dance" event.

In 1947, the Pole Room was added to the clubhouse. The bar top and rail were made from square redwood poles which had been removed from a 1905 transmission line that extended from Powerhouse #1 to Powerhouse #3 near Auberry—part of the vast hydroelectric project in the mountains and rivers of the Sierra Nevada.

The Fresno Chapter Clubhouse was used for a variety of Power Club and company sponsored functions. It also was rented out to individuals and organizations who wanted to hold functions there. The rent provided funds for maintenance and improvements to the building and to subsidize the club's many social activities. In 1955, it was renamed Bibb Hall in honor of Bill Bibb, a member and past president, who gave many years of service to the club.

On September 19, 1973, a blaze that was the result of an attempted burglarly tore through Bibb Clubhouse, destroying it completely. Also lost were the trophy case filled with the Power Club's trophies and awards and the many historical artifacts, pictures, and memorabilia that adorned the walls of the Pole Room. The fire had an even more poignant effect. The clubhouse had been the glue that held the club together. With its demise, the San Joaquin Power Club lost heart. Although it still exists, it has never been the same.

This drawing of Bibb Hall, the clubhouse for the San Joaquin Power Club, was done by Aaron Clary, the club's president in 1962.
Courtesy of Jack Brase.

It Started with a Nickel

In early May of 1906, a new hotel opened in Fresno. Travelers had long complained that, although Fresno boasted many hotels, there was not a hostelry in the city that was modern and, most important, quiet. With the advent of the Sequoia Hotel that situation was remedied.

The four-story Sequoia Hotel was located on J (now Fulton) Street adjoining the Forsyth Building that filled the corner of J and Tulare streets. The entrance to the establishment was on Tulare Street through the main lobby of the Forsyth. Owner Charles J. Lindgren's hotel reflected elements of the Arts and Crafts movement so popular at the time. The furniture throughout the building was weathered oak in Mission style. Each room had a private bath, hot and cold running water, steam heat, and both gas and electric lights. Every room also boasted a telephone that was not only connected to the hotel switchboard, but also to the city telephone system. Travelers could arrange to be met at the train and conveyed to the hotel. Every conceivable convenience was available to the guests.

In 1912, lumber man Robert Kennedy purchased the building and built another Sequoia Hotel on Van Ness Avenue between Tulare and Kern streets. He connected his two hotels with a bridge across the alley at the second, third and fourth levels. Over the years the hotel saw a number of changes. In 1935, it underwent extensive remodeling and became home to George Mardikian's famed Omar Khayyam restaurant. In 1960, the hotel was sold to rancher Steve Pilibos. In 1962, it was torn down to make way for a modern building.

Although the Sequoia Hotel is now only a dim memory, let us for a moment remember Mrs. Bertha Nichol, the hotel's first guest in 1906. She was given a royal welcome and treated to a sumptuous banquet. The next day the *Fresno Morning Republican's* article bore the headline, "Sequoia Hotel Starts Business With a Nickel."

Coney Island Red Hots

Take a step inside a storefront on Tulare Street in downtown Fresno and a tantalizing aroma wafts through the air—for on the stove just waiting to tease the taste buds are hot dogs and chili and all the fixin's. They're ready to be served up and to satisfy the customers of the Coney Island just as they have for almost eighty years.

George Callas served the first Coney Island red hot on Thanksgiving Day 1923. It cost a nickel. A bowl of chili, the house specialty then as now, cost fifteen cents. In the years since, the eatery has been in three different locations, but always on the same block of Tulare Street between Fulton and Broadway streets.

Before he came to Fresno, George Callas emigrated to Spokane, Washington, from his native Greece. He worked as a cook, waiter, janitor, bookkeeper, and dishwasher. Then he worked for the railroad for nine years washing train engines and driving spikes. He also went to school nights to study English and became a United States citizen.

Over the years, Callas had four partners at the Coney Island including Pete Yiannopoulos and Dimitrios Kalomiris, who later sold his share to his son-in-law, Jim Grusis. Today, Grusis's daughter and son-in-law, Virginia and Amador Toscano, own and operate the restaurant.

When Callas opened the Coney Island on Thanksgiving Day 1923, the city was in the throes of the Roaring Twenties. The 1930s brought hard times for many and, on Sundays when the restaurant was closed, Callas and Kalomiris allowed their countrymen and friends to use the kitchen. The decades of the 1940s and 1950s were good years for downtown Fresno. It was the retail center of Fresno and the Coney Island prospered. The 1960s brought many changes as redevelopment and shopping malls in other parts of the city drew businesses outside the central core of the city. The Coney Island weathered these challenges. All was well until the year 2000 when a new project brought the real possibility of closure. What happened next will be told in another tale of our valley.

Claud Salmon and Harry D. "Ott" Wilson, on their Harley-Davidson motorcycles, in front of their motorcycle agency in 1919.
Courtesy of Doug Wilson.

For many years Fresnans who wanted to purchase a Harley Davidson motorcycle or to have one repaired looked to Harry D. "Ott" Wilson, the local Harley dealer from 1919 to 1955. He later sold most of the leading imported machines. This is his story.

Ott Wilson was born in Ohio. In 1910, after the death of his father, his family moved to the Rolinda area. He bought his first motorcycle from Ben Bresee, the local Harley dealer, in 1913. Soon he was working for Bresee at his 2323 Kern Street shop. In 1917, he was drafted into the army and sent to France, where he spent his tour of duty repairing the motorcycles that were used by the army in the roadless countryside. On his return, he went back to work for Bresee. Shortly afterward, Bresee was killed in a motor-

The top photograph taken in 1923 in front of the newly built Fresno High School on Echo Avenue, shows five of the County Cops (that later became the California Highway Patrol). Left to right: Heine Bush, unidentified man, Ed Carr, unidentified man, and Harry D. "Ott" Wilson.
Courtesy of Doug Wilson.

cycle race and Ott was asked to take over the Fresno dealership. Claud Salmon, who also had worked for Bresee, became Ott's partner. In 1919, they opened a new shop at 457 Broadway Street under the name Salmon & Wilson Motorcycles. Ten years later, Salmon moved to Oakland to become the Harley dealer there. Ott's business then became Wilson's Motorcycles.

The Fresno Police Department purchased its motorcycles from Wilson's. So, too, did the County Cops, who later became the California Highway Patrol, and the Fresno Bee carriers. Wilson's three wheelers were ridden not only by the delivery boys from Vista Pharmacy and other local pharmacies, but the local garages also used them to pick up and deliver cars. The tow bar on the front made them a natural for this purpose. During the 1920s and 1930s, a rite of passage for many young men was to ride their motorcycle up the old Tollhouse grade.

The Fresno State College stadium had a speedway track. From 1934-36, Ott Wilson with Lloyd "Sprouts" Elder, a Caruthers boy who became a world champion speedway racer, promoted motorcycle races there every Thursday night.

An unidentified woman, relaxing in a three-wheel Harley-Davidson from Bresee's Motorcycles, is sitting in front of the original Van Ness sign at the southern end of Van Ness Avenue. Note the rural nature of the area in the early 1910s. *Courtesy of Doug Wilson.*

During World War II, many of Ott's workers were drafted so his two sons, twelve-year old Doug and his younger brother Harry, nicknamed "Butch," began working with their dad after school. They began by learning to fix and rebuild the bicycles that also were sold in the shop. Then they graduated to learning all there was to know about motorcycles. Later, Doug's son, Robert, also worked in the business.

In 1968, Ott Wilson died. Doug and Harry continued to operate the business until 1989—seventy years after Ott first opened it—when Wilson's Motorcycles was sold to Pat Cody. As the Wilsons look back over their years in business the one thing they value most is that the customers became their friends. They rode together and socialized together. For them, Wilson's Motorcycles was truly a family business and is one that continues to be part of the tales of our valley.

The month of February is the time each year when our nation celebrates Black History month. It is a fitting time to remember the early African-American settlers of two Fresno County communities—Fowler and Bowles.

In the 1880s, Mr. and Mrs. Curby moved to Fowler from Charlotte, North Carolina. They brought their servants with them. Among their number were Julia Bell and her husband. At this time, the site of Fowler was still a wheat field. When the townsite was laid out, Julia Bell planted the first tree. She became very enthusiastic about the new town and wrote about it to all her friends in the East hoping they would resettle in Fowler. When she saved enough money she purchased a train ticket for her brother, Jordan Young, who used it to come west. She continued to save money and used it to buy real estate in the Fowler area.

Another Fowler settler, Reuben Wysinger, purchased a tract of land in partnership with two other gentlemen. Eventually, the land was divided between them. Wysinger and his wife worked hard to plant a peach orchard that would produce enough to make a living for their family. Wysinger held a day job and worked his farm after hours. After several years of determined effort, it became a well-paying ranch. Their perseverance paid off.

Mr. and Mrs. W. W. Eason, natives of Atlanta, Georgia, came to the Bowles area, just four miles from Fowler. Mrs. Eason worked as a laundress and Mr. Eason as a ranch hand. They saved their money and purchased a ranch which they planted in peaches and grapes. The proceeds from the ranch enabled them to purchase fifteen city lots in Fowler. Also farming in Bowles were William H. Boatman, Marshall Sutter, William Asken, Hayes Patrick, and John Maxey.

These early African-American settlers paved the way for those who followed and wrote their own unique chapter in the legends of our valley.

A Most Untactful Tack

Every profession has its difficulties, its shortcomings, and, yes, its dangers. So it was for one of Fresno's leading undertakers on a cold January afternoon in 1906.

For L. O. Stephens, 1905 had not been the best year of his life. After serving four years as Fresno's first real mayor under the City Charter of 1899, he had lost the 1905 election to W. Parker Lyon. It was a blow not only to his ego, but to the reform efforts that he had instituted. He had hoped that the year 1906 would be better, but the year had hardly begun and already bad luck struck yet again.

On January 3, Stephens was busy lining a coffin in the back room of his undertaking parlor. As was his habit he put a fair number of steel tacks in his mouth. With his hammer in one hand, he leaned over the coffin and grabbed the material with his other hand. What happened next was one of those moments of horror that every mortal has known when the very thing one hopes will never happen suddenly comes to pass. One of the tacks, determined to leave the rest of the pack, slipped to the back of Stephens' tongue and, without a moment's hesitation, began to make its way down his throat.

Stephens dropped the hammer and material and tried to cough. Then he tried to gulp and gulp again. The errant tack, however, continued on its way, happily journeying down Stephens' esophagus—it would not be dissuaded from its course. Then the unthinkable happened—the tack stopped halfway on its journey and threw its sharp point into Stephens' gullet, fully intending to stay there for all eternity.

Stephens hurried to Dr. Dwight Trowbridge's office. The good doctor administered a shot of cocaine down the offended esophagus, dislodged the untactful tack and gave it a good shove so it could complete its journey—one that will tactfully be left to the reader's imagination. Stephens left to finish his coffin-lining chores—this time leaving the tacks on the table while he worked.

Lilbourne Alsip Winchell

One of Fresno County's most honored pioneers was a man who not only wrote a definitive history of the county in 1933, but also made singular contributions to our knowledge of the alpine regions of the Sierra Nevada.

Born in Sacramento in 1855, Lilbourne Alsip Winchell witnessed one of the defining moments in early California history. In January 1863, when he was eight years old, he watched as Governor Leland Stanford climbed onto a wagonload of dirt and threw off the first shovelful, thereby inaugurating the Central Pacific Railroad.

Winchell's early education was provided by his parents, Judge Elisha Cotton Winchell and Laura Alsip Winchell. The family moved to Millerton in 1859 and then to Fresno Station in 1874. Winchell completed his education at San Francisco City College and at Heald's College. He served as a clerk in his father's law office and worked in various county offices. In 1883, he married Ernestine Miller.

It was Winchell's lifelong interest in geology and a love of nature and the outdoors that led to his exploration of the mountain areas. In 1879, he was one of a party of five who took the first mules and horses into the Tehipite Canyon. He took his camera and, along with Frank Dusy, created a visual record of the magnificent walls, domes, and crests of the Tehipite Valley. He also photographed other hitherto unseen alpine areas of the Sierra Nevada. Winchell created the first map of the High Sierra, naming the prominent features; he sketched a plat of the Central Valley, naming those features also. He was the first to climb Mount Goddard—a marker at the summit commemorates the event. His work led to an appointment with the United States Forest Service.

Lilbourne Alsip Winchell died in 1939 at the age of eighty-four. In his long life he had the singular opportunity to witness the development of Fresno County from his youth in the gold mining camp of Millerton to his adulthood in the modern, fast-growing city of Fresno. Along the way, he left significant contributions to his county—he is a true legend of our valley.

Any chronicle of the pioneer women of Fresno County would be incomplete without the mention of one of our great women of letters. She made her appearance on the county scene in 1881 when her family moved to Fresno. On September 7, 1883, she married into a prominent local family.

Ernestine Miller was born in New York state in 1866 to John and Phydella Roberts Miller. Her mother's family had lived in America since the Revolutionary War. Soon after the family settled in Fresno in 1881, she met Lilbourne A. Winchell, the son of Judge Elisha Cotton Winchell, who was employed as chief deputy in the assessor's office. They were married at the Oakland home of Winchell's aunt and uncle in 1883. Three children were born to the couple, who made their home at 1009 Echo Avenue.

The Winchells were active members of the Fresno Historical Society. Lilbourne served as vice-president of the organization and Ernestine was the society's curator for fifteen years. However, it is for her writing that Ernestine will be remembered.

For nine years she wrote feature articles for the *Fresno Morning Republican*. She also wrote articles for the *Ladies Home Journal* and for *Mothers Magazine*. She believed that women should pursue their intellectual development and wrote many articles for women. Also important were the stories she wrote of everyday life in Millerton and pioneer Fresno. She interviewed many of the people who played roles in the development of Fresno County. Her sketches preserve not only key events in our history, but the snippets of daily life that otherwise would have been lost. Her writings about the Indians of California are another important preservation legacy to her community.

Ernestine Miller Winchell was a woman of generous spirit, loyal to her friends, and one who was always conscientious in her duty to those in need. When she died on May 7, 1952, at the age of eighty-six, she was mourned by her friends and her community. For her written legacy of the early history of Fresno County she will long be remembered in the tales of our valley.

In 1903, in Brookline, Mississippi, a daughter named Beatrice Maurine was born to George and Anna Gray. They provided a good education for their daughter not only in academic subjects, but also in the cultural arts. Beatrice studied piano and played publicly for the first time in church at age eleven.

Later, Beatrice Gray entered Campbell College in Jackson, Mississippi. She graduated with a bachelor of arts degree and served on the faculty. During her years as a student she met and married Jesse Ewellingsworth Cooley. In 1931, they moved to Fresno. Together they opened the Central Valley's first Black mortuary on C Street and founded a Black history forum. Two children, Jesse, Jr. and Dorythea, were born to the couple.

Beatrice Cooley continued to expand her horizons by taking classes in education, psychology, and music at Fresno State College. She also pioneered by teaching classes in Black history for the Fresno Adult School.

She became well-known throughout the valley as a lecturer and social activist. Her work on a variety of boards, including the Fresno Women's Committee for Social Action, the National Council of Negro Women, the YWCA, Hinton Community Center, and the Carter Memorial African Methodist Episcopal Church, expanded her awareness of the needs of her people. In 1955, she was hired by the Fresno County Housing Authority. During her tenure with that organization, she assisted in creating health care projects for farm and migrant workers.

Perhaps her greatest achievement was the completion of the Kearney-Cooley Plaza development, a housing complex in West Fresno sponsored by the Carter Memorial Church of which she was a trustee. The complex was part of a housing program under the Federal Housing and Urban Development Agency. It was named in her honor.

Beatrice Maurine Gray Cooley died in February 1970. She left to her community a rich legacy of accomplishments that benefited the people of Fresno and the valley.

The Coney Island's Comeback

The Coney Island is one of the oldest restaurants in the city. Ever since 1923 the Coney Island has been serving up hot dogs and chili to Fresnans from the same block on Tulare Street between Broadway and Fulton streets. The owners of this establishment have witnessed the city's development from the Roaring Twenties to the dawning of a new millennium. The Coney Island had become such a part of the fabric of downtown Fresno that Fresnans took it for granted that they would always be able to come in for one of those hot dogs smothered in chili that they remembered from childhood.

Then something happened. The approach of the twenty-first century brought a new challenge to the Coney Island—the building of a baseball stadium adjacent to the corner of their block. Because of uncertainty over the outcome of negotiations between the city of Fresno and the stadium group, their business decreased and, when they realized they were going to lose their parking lot, owners Virginia and Amador Toscano announced that the Coney Island would close on September 29, 2000.

Word of the possible closure leaked out and quickly spread. The thought that Coney Island chilidogs might become part of history was more than Fresnans could bear. On September 29, people began lining up before the business opened. By noon, the line was so long it stretched down Tulare Street. Some customers had to wait up to two hours for their hot dogs, but they didn't seem to care. Fresnans turned out—not just to show their support, but to eat a record number of hot dogs and chili. The colorful hot dog establishment had not been forgotten. City leaders were impressed and, moved by the show of public support, they agreed to work out the parking problems.

For now, the Coney Island remains open and one of Fresno's cherished traditions. The chili, made from a secret family recipe, continues to simmer on the stove just as it has for almost eighty years—a delicious addition to the legends of our valley.

The Day the Lights Went Out

The agenda for the May 3, 1898, meeting of Fresno's board of trustees listed a number of items that might still be of interest today. One item, in particular, has a very contemporary ring to it—the price and availability of electricity.

On this particular day, the trustee of the Fifth Ward, Joseph Spinney, had been dominating all the discussions. He was not the mayor, although he had held that position for ten minutes on one memorable day, but he was the political boss of West Fresno. He had long been the major power force at City Hall. He usually carried out most of his operations behind-the-scenes, but, on this day, he was unusually vocal and allowed his controlling personality to be on public display.

It seems Spinney had just been informed that the city's electric bill for the month of April was higher than usual. It totaled $500. Spinney was not pleased. In fact, he was outraged. He spoke loudly about the sorry condition of the city's exchequer and the need for economy. He pointed out that at least $500 could be saved if the electric streetlights were not used until the autumn months. No conservation cutback efforts or rolling blackouts for him. "Turn them off!" he demanded. "It's the only way."

As might well be imagined, a heated discussion ensued, but to no avail. In this day before anyone had heard of a strong mayor, the political boss took matters into his own hands. Spinney moved that the streetlights be turned off during the summer. The motion was seconded by Trustee McVey. Someone asked when it would go into effect. "Right away," said Spinney, who ordered City Clerk Shanklin to notify the electric company and to see that the electricity was shut off immediately. And, that was that.

Blossoms by the Millions

One of the wondrous sights of our valley is visible to us for only a brief time each year. This visual feast begins to appear in late February and can last well into March—the timing is wholly dependent on the whims and pleasures of Mother Nature. When it begins to unfold it is imperative for residents and visitors alike to get in their cars, hop on their bikes, or saddle up their horses and head for the eastern part of Fresno County to see blossoms by the millions adorning the trees of our valley.

The Blossom Trail was so designated in 1989 by the collaborative efforts of the Fresno County Farm Bureau, Fresno City & County Convention & Visitors Bureau, and the Fresno Chamber of Commerce. They laid out the route for the trail. In reality, the blossoming fruit trees have been a part of valley life ever since the valley's first fruit tree was old enough to bear fruit…sometime in the early 1870s. However, valley residents often take their beauty for granted. The bureau's staff did us all a great favor by reminding us that a short drive into the country can make us aware, once again, of this spectacular springtime show.

Traveling east on Belmont Avenue from Fresno, continue to Academy Avenue, turn north and follow the trail signs that will guide you through the entire route. Other signs can be found along the way telling the traveler which tree fruit is featured in each orchard. White almond blossoms, white plum, pink apricot, white apple, and peach and nectarine blossoms which vary from light pink to deep red create sweeping swaths of color that seem to shimmer across the valley floor. In May, the citrus trees add another dimension—their white blossoms hold a deep, aromatic fragrance that penetrates the very heart of the warm valley air.

Springtime in our great Central Valley evokes enchantments of all kinds, but none holds more beautiful promise than the blossoms on the fruit trees of spring that will soon bear the deliciously edible fruits of summer.

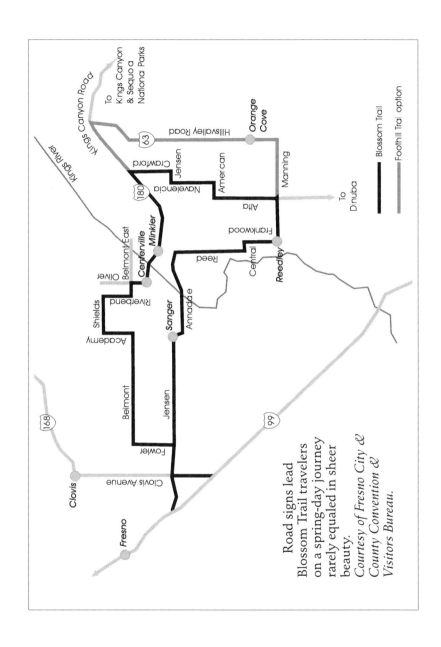

Road signs lead
Blossom Trail travelers
on a spring-day journey
rarely equaled in sheer
beauty.
Courtesy of Fresno City &
County Convention &
Visitors Bureau.

The Day Wendell Willkie Came to Town

Throughout Fresno's history Courthouse Park has been the scene of many historic gatherings, but on September 20, 1940, one of the largest crowds ever filled and then spilled over the park right onto the streets of Fresno. People began to assemble early in the morning—many coming from other parts of the Central Valley—to obtain one of the five thousand chairs that had been set up for their use. Many brought their lunch baskets and settled in for a memorable experience. Schools were closed so children could attend.

The day began with the arrival of a special train at the Southern Pacific depot. A man, his wife and son, members of the secret service, the press corps and several Fresnans who had boarded the train in Tulare, stepped off the train and into waiting cars. Showers of serpentine and paper rained down from the tall buildings onto the procession as it made its way along Mariposa Street, which was lined with throngs of people. The delegation arrived at Courthouse Park. The cars stopped. The crowd, which had swelled to twenty thousand, was hushed for a moment—then the car door opened and out stepped the man of the hour—Wendell Willkie— the Republican candidate for president of the United States. The crowd went wild as Willkie made his way to the park's bandstand. He mounted the steps, strode to the podium, and faced the crowd.

A few boos from the opposition could be heard, but they were soon drowned out as Willkie began to speak. The speech, which was broadcast live by KMJ Radio, was often interrupted by shouts of "We Want Willkie!" The candidate, who was running against the popular President Franklin D. Roosevelt, presented his case to the assembled gathering of valley residents. They listened and cheered and then, suddenly, it was time for the candidate to depart. He and his party left in their cars to board the train and continue their campaign trek throughout the country.

For those in the crowd that September day in 1940—the day Wendell Willkie came to town—it was a day to remember in the tales of our valley.

Wendell Willkie speaking to a crowd of Fresnans from the bandstand in Courthouse Park September 20, 1940.
Courtesy of Robert Wash.

Mr. Roeding's Streets

The subject of street names never ceases to fascinate. In this story, we learn about streets that were named to honor several members of one of Fresno's early families.

The family of Frederick Christian Roeding played a number of important roles in the history of Fresno County. These have been duly chronicled in other tales of our valley. What you may not know is that some of the streets you travel every day bear the names of his relatives.

Frederick Roeding was one of the members of the German Syndicate—the group of San Francisco-based investors who purchased all the land where Fresno is now located. The Central Pacific Railroad purchased land from the syndicate for a townsite. The members of the syndicate divided the rest of the land among them. Roeding ended up with eleven sections (7,040 acres) of land. His holdings northwest of Fresno included all the land between present-day Belmont and Olive avenues. When the city grew north, Roeding was asked to name several of the streets within his parcel.

Roeding had three children. His son, George, married Elizabeth Thorne. Elizabeth Street was named for her. Her father, Andrew Jackson Thorne, was the treasurer of Fresno County from 1874-84. Thorne Avenue was named for him. Elizabeth's twin sister was named Olivia—hence, Olive Avenue.

Roeding's daughters were not overlooked. Emma Roeding married Max Vagedes, so Roeding named one of the streets Vagedes Avenue. Likewise, Marie Roeding was married to Fred Weber. Weber Avenue honors this fact.

Mr. Roeding didn't fare as well as the rest of his family. He named a major street Roeding Boulevard. Later, the city renamed it Fruit Avenue with the exception of the large circle the street makes just west of the Belmont Avenue underpass on the east side of Roeding Park. This remained Roeding Boulevard, but there is not a single street sign in place to reflect this fact. Somehow, it just doesn't seem fair.

Tidbits from the Fresno Times

The January 28, 1865, edition of the *Fresno Times* was the first newspaper ever published in Fresno County. It saw the light of day in the gold mining camp and county seat of Millerton. The editor, Samuel J. Garrison, held pro-Southern secessionist views that were reflected in his paper. After publishing ten issues, the paper ceased to exist.

The advertisements within its pages give us a picture of life at Millerton. The ads do not contain addresses because they were not needed. The town had only one main street.

At the top of one column of ads were three words, "Cash! Cash! Cash!" Underneath was a plea from general store owner George Grierson to all his customers with unpaid bills. The words, "Please call [on us] immediately and settle [your] bills," completed the ad. Since Grierson's store carried everything from whiskey to shoes, it's easy to assume that most Millerton residents owed him money.

Ira McCray, owner of the Oak Hotel, invited the traveler to his hostelry where he would find "a well-supplied Table, good beds, a well stocked bar, a fine billiard table, and a commodious Stable, abundantly furnished with Hay and Grain." McCray also advertised his stage line that made two trips a week and could take parties to the placer mines of the upper Kings River.

Stephen Gaster invited the public to visit his first class saloon that had been "fitted up with taste and neatness" and offered the best wines, liquors, and choice Havana cigars. "Plain and fancy drinks to suit all tastes," the ad continued, "Unbelievers are requested to call and try their quality."

In the midst of ads touting saloons, stage lines, and blacksmiths, one stands out. Mrs. L. C. Winchell's private school announced the beginning of the spring term. Reasonable rates were asked for the six-month session. Mrs. Winchell was doing her best to provide education and manners for the young people of this rough gold mining area. It can't have been an easy business.

Basso Profundo

For many who grew up in the Central Valley, a program of Gospel music on KMJ Radio was a popular daily show. It started in 1947 and featured a quartet called The Gospelaires. In 1968, the program became a Sunday-only event, but it remained an important part of the lives of many valley residents.

Those who listened to the beautiful voices of the four men who comprised The Gospelaires will long remember one voice that stood apart from the rest—the booming bass that not only set the tempo for the group, but also had a depth of richness that pierced to the core of one's soul. That memorable bass voice belongs to Don Smith, the founder of the Gospelaires.

Growing up on a dairy farm in Lubbock, Texas, Smith remembers milking twenty-five cows every morning and evening. Becoming a singer was not on the agenda. However, one morning during services at the Central Baptist Church, the minister heard Don's voice. Although he was only fourteen, his voice had changed and the deep, rich quality was unmistakable. He was asked to sing a solo the following Sunday. The congregation responded so warmly that his solos became regular events. He studied music in high school and, at age seventeen, joined the Echols Singers. It was the beginning of his career in Gospel music.

Don Smith came west to San Diego in 1947. He joined a quartet called the Blackwood Brothers and met and married a young lady named Peggy Shepherd. The quartet moved to Iowa, but, after a year, Don and Peggy grew homesick for California. They returned to San Diego and, shortly after, Bob Jones, an old friend and gifted radio emcee, invited Don to move to Fresno and join him in forming a new quartet. They came to Fresno. The new group became The Gospelaires and included A. V. Wall, tenor; Art Haynes, lead; Don Smith, bass; and Billy Clanton, pianist.

As the years unfolded, Don Smith also founded Gospel Music and Supply, a successful music store that offered musical instruments, television sets, and stereos. But, it is for his voice that he will be remembered—that deep, rich basso voice that, for many KMJ listeners, was an important part of every Sunday morning and will long be remembered in the legends of our valley.

The Rambunctious Judge

David Smith Terry, one of the most colorful attorneys ever to grace the halls of the old Fresno Courthouse, was born in Kentucky in 1823. After his parents divorced, he and his three brothers were raised in Texas by their mother. Terry left school at age thirteen and embarked on the turbulent journey that would be his life. Steeped in the traditions of the old South, he strongly believed in the code of honor that made a duel the proper way to settle an insult to one's name.

While serving in the Mexican War, Terry became proficient with a Bowie knife. He carried this weapon with him for the rest of his life. After studying law in a Houston law office, he was admitted to the bar in 1845. He came to California in 1849 and practiced law for a time in Stockton, but, after several displays of unruly conduct, went back to Texas, married childhood sweetheart Cornelia Runnels and returned to California. He was elected to the California Supreme Court, but, after slashing a San Francisco vigilante's throat with his Bowie knife during a brawl, was thrown in jail. The man recovered. Terry was released and banished from San Francisco. He continued to serve his term on the California Supreme Court and became chief justice in 1857. His unruly temper combined with his unpopular opinions caused his colleague, Stephen J. Field, to engage him in loud, public arguments.

In the 1859 primary election, Terry ran for re-election on the Democratic ticket. William Gwin and Senator David Broderick were running for governor. Terry and Broderick argued violently over the issue of whether or not Kansas should enter the Union as a free or a slave state. Broderick questioned Terry's honesty. Terry challenged him to a duel. The men met on September 13, 1859, south of San Francisco. Broderick was nervous and fired his pistol too soon. The bullet hit the ground. Terry's bullet struck Broderick in the chest, killing him. Terry was charged with murder, but was acquitted.

Justice Terry left California and headed to the Southern states. The Civil War was underway. Terry formed a regiment to fight for the Southern cause. He was wounded, but eventually became a brigadier general. He was bitter when the South lost the war. He headed for Mexico to try his hand—unsuccessfully—at homesteading.

Terry returned to California and set up a law practice in Stockton. He soon became embroiled in a case that involved the fabulously wealthy Senator William Sharon of Nevada and his mistress, Sarah Hill. Terry represented Miss Hill, who claimed that Sharon had married her and that she had a certificate to prove the marriage had been legal. Terry lost the initial case, but Miss Hill won an appeal in federal court. Senator Sharon died. Now Miss Hill would inherit his wealth if she won her case. Complicating matters still further, Terry, who was now a widower, and Sarah Hill fell deeply in love and were married. Add to this mix that a new Supreme Court judge on circuit in California would hear the case, none other than Terry's old nemesis Stephen Field.

The trial opened. Proceedings were going against Sarah. She stood up, interrupted Justice Field and argued with him. Field ordered the marshal to take her out of the courtroom. Terry drew his Bowie knife and became violent. Field sentenced him to six months in prison. Terry served his term and, upon his release, he and Sarah moved to Fresno where his nephew, Real Terry, was the district attorney. Terry joined the law practice of W. D. Grady and H. Z. Austin. He purchased several pieces of property including the entire block that is now the site of the Cesar Chavez Adult School.

David and Sarah Terry settled into a somewhat peaceful life in Fresno. He practiced law; she took care of their home. Then tragedy struck. His law office, in the Donahoo Building, was hit by fire, destroying not only Terry's extensive law library, but also the piece of paper that was Sarah's alleged marriage contract to the deceased Senator William Sharon.

On August 14, 1889, the Terrys boarded a train for San Francisco to appear again in federal court before Justice Stephen Field. The couple did not realize that Field and his bodyguard, Dave Neagle, were on the same train. Terry, who possessed a violent nature and an often-used Bowie knife, had been making very public threats against Field who, because of this, had hired Neagle to protect him against the Terrys.

When the train reached Lathrop, the Terrys, Field and Neagle all disembarked and headed for the station's restaurant. Terry, seeing Field sitting at a table, came up behind him and struck him on the side of the head. Neagle jumped up and ordered him to stop. Terry started to put his hand in his inside coat pocket. Neagle, thinking he was reaching for the infamous Bowie knife, pulled his gun and shot Terry. Sarah screamed and threw herself on her husband. It was too late. Terry was dead and his coat pocket was empty. For once, he had left his weapon at home.

Neagle, who had honed his gun fighting skills in Tombstone during the days of the Earp brothers, was charged with murder. He was acquitted. The statute that resulted from the case was called *in re Neagle*. It holds "that a Federal officer can not be prosecuted in a state court for an act arising out of his discharge of a Federal duty."

And thus ended the life of one of Fresno's most colorful and tempestuous lawyers.

One of the earliest sheepmen of Fresno County was born in Marysville, Kentucky, on April 7, 1829. He was the eighth of ten children. His grandfather was one of the first to volunteer to fight in the Revolutionary War and his father served in the War of 1812. Patriotism ran strong in his veins.

His parents died when he was only fourteen years old. He was forced to find his own way in the world. On his twenty-first birthday, he and his brother were making their way across the plains with a team of oxen bound for California. The Gold Rush was well underway and, on their arrival, the brothers tried their luck at mining in Placerville. After two years in the gold fields, he decided that it would be more profitable to supply food for the rapidly expanding population of the new state rather than mining for gold. He returned to the East, bought sheep and cattle and made his way back to California driving his stock before him. Coming with him was another sheepman, Jesse Hildreth. The party arrived in Los Angeles in November 1852. They journeyed north. Hildreth established a ranch near what is known as Bates Station. The other gentleman located his ranch halfway between Raymond and Madera. In 1854, he married Hildreth's daughter, Mary Jane.

It was in this manner that Henry Clay Daulton arrived in Fresno County. He was not only one of the first sheepmen, but also served for fifteen years as a member of the board of supervisors. He purchased land on the valley floor that became known as the Santa Rita Ranch. He was chairman of the commission that successfully worked to establish Madera County in 1893. He served as the first chairman of the Madera County Board of Supervisors— a position he held until his death on October 28, 1893.

The history of the great Central Valley would not be complete without remembering the contributions of one of her most honored pioneers—Henry Clay Daulton—by any standard a true legend of our valley.

Hedge Row Vineyard

When one thinks of the beginnings of agriculture in Fresno County, one usually thinks of the hard physical work involved—work that was usually undertaken by men. Although it is true that many of the pioneers were men, there were several women who played major roles in the development of agriculture in our county. The stories of four of these women must be told together because their accomplishments were a joint effort.

In 1876, four women—all schoolteachers in San Francisco—saw an advertisement for the Central California Colony that was being developed by Bernhard Marks and William Chapman. Intrigued by the opportunity to buy inexpensive, fertile farmland, they decided that one of their number—Minnie Austin—should visit the colony. She brought back a glowing report—so enthusiastic was she that they decided to join together in a cooperative effort to purchase a hundred acres. They formed an operating company. Julia Short and E. A. Cleveland each bought twenty acres. Lucy Hatch and Minnie Austin were in partnership with the remaining sixty acres. The major portion of their acreage was planted in vineyards; the rest in fruit bearing trees and shrubs. They named their farm Hedge Row for the hedges of pomegranates, oranges, and cypress that defined the boundaries of their property that fronted on Elm Avenue.

The Misses Hatch and Austin built a large home and outbuildings on their portion of land. They moved permanently from San Francisco to run the operation. The challenges were great. The untamed land was visited by coyotes, jackrabbits, and wild horses that trampled and ate the young vines. They persevered, however, and in the first harvest, in 1878, Miss Austin packed thirty boxes of raisins. The next year, three hundred boxes were shipped to market—the first time packaged raisins had been shipped from Fresno.

By 1885, Hedge Row vineyards was producing twenty thousand pounds of raisins annually—a major accomplishment made even more significant by the knowledge that this record was achieved by four women who took up a challenge, learned as they worked, and made a significant contribution to the history of agriculture in Fresno County that will never be forgotten.

One of the premier pioneers in the history of Fresno County agriculture is a woman who began her life off the eastern shores of the United States—on the island of Nantucket. After completing her higher education at Bridgewater Normal School, Minnie Austin obtained a teaching position in Chicago. She excelled as an educator and, seven years later, was promoted to the position of principal.

In 1864, she traveled west to San Francisco and was hired as a teacher in a local high school. Minnie Austin then became the principal of Clark Institute—a position she would hold for seven years. During her tenure at Clark, she met three other teachers: Lucy Hatch, E. A. Cleveland, and Julia Short.

About this time, promotional literature about a colony development south of the newly emerging town of Fresno was circulating in San Francisco. The advertisements, written by M. Theo Kearney, were especially enticing to women—offering them the alternative of farming to the drudgery of 8-to-5 jobs. "When the year's work is done," the ad said, "and no special disaster has interfered with success, two or three thousand dollars clear profit feels much more satisfactory in the pocket than the savings of weekly earnings behind the counter, the case, the desk, or sewing machine." Austin and her friends probably read this literature. She visited the colony, returned to San Francisco with a good report, and the four women decided to buy land in the colony.

Minnie Austin resigned her teaching position and moved to the teachers' Hedge Row Vineyard in 1878. Their operation became a great success—due in large part to Austin's innate ability and hard work. Her lists of "firsts" include: first to ship raisins from the colony, first to discover the proper way to sulfur Gordo Blanco Muscat vines, first to build a raisin dryer, and first to create novel ways of packaging raisins, thus creating greater consumer appeal. Her "Austin" brand of raisins became widely known throughout California.

Minnie Austin died in 1889 leaving behind a rich legacy in the agricultural history of our valley.

Lucy Hatch

The other half of the successful partnership that managed Hedge Row Vineyard in the Central California Colony was Lucy Hatch. Born in Rockland, Maine, in 1834, Lucy Hatch received her college education at Mount Holyoke Seminary in Massachusetts. She entered the teaching profession in Kansas, but after a visit to California in 1870 decided to make San Francisco her home in 1875. For the next four years she taught at Clark Institute.

The story of how she and three other teachers combined their assets to establish Hedge Row Vineyard has been told. Two of the ladies were silent partners in the venture, but Lucy Hatch and Minnie Austin gave up their teaching positions, built a home on their land, and moved there. The eventual success of their endeavor was due to their hard work and to Miss Austin's talent for farming and merchandising.

After Miss Austin's death in 1889, Lucy Hatch continued to run the vineyard. In 1893, she was one of ten people named to a design committee for the Fresno County exhibit at the Columbian Exhibition in Chicago. She was pleased to have the chance to share the story of Fresno County's developing agriculture and the success of the colony experiment.

Soon after this, she sold Hedge Row. When she offered the property for sale, she had the following comment to make in the *Fresno Morning Republican*, "We paid ($5,000) for this land, with the water rights, and we are now offering the place for sale for $60,000."

Lucy Hatch had interests other than agriculture. She donated land for the Central California Colony Union Church and helped to organize the Parlor Lecture Club and the Leisure Hour Club. The story of agriculture in Fresno County would be incomplete without sharing the life and contributions of Lucy Hatch.

K Street (Van Ness Avenue) looking south from Tuolumne Street toward Courthouse Park in 1920. Note the white-columned Parlor Lecture Club building on the left. Lucy Hatch was one of the original organizers of the popular club. *R. W. Riggs photo. Author's collection.*

The No-Cow Law

In the earliest years of Fresno, it was perfectly acceptable for every homeowner to have a horse, some chickens, and possibly a cow in his backyard. The horse provided transportation, the chickens kept the larder supplied with fresh eggs, and who could not want the family cow close at hand to provide fresh milk? It was, after all, one of life's necessities.

As the town grew and became a bona fide city in 1885, laws had to be enacted to keep the animals in backyards and off the city's streets. That worked out rather well. The city continued to grow and, by 1906, had spread well beyond the original townsite laid out by the Central Pacific Railroad. The city limits now went well beyond the downtown area. Old habits, however, are often hard to break. Many people were beginning to trade their horses for cars, but chickens and cows still graced the yards of many a Fresnan.

The board of health decided it was time to do something about this situation. On May 15, 1906, it made a formal recommendation to Fresno's board of trustees stating that citizens who lived with the area bounded by Stanislaus, G, Kern and Q streets could no longer keep cows on their property. Other residents of Fresno who lived within the city limits, but not in the specified area, would be allowed to maintain one cow only at their residence. Furthermore, that one cow could not be kept within fifty feet of any other dwelling. In other words, cows could no longer graze right next to the backyard fence.

The "No-Cow Law" became another step along Fresno's path of transition from a pioneer town to a major city. Unlike the "No-fence Law" of the 1870s that required cattle ranchers to fence in their herds, this law didn't engender any hostilities. It would be many years before chickens were banned from the city's backyards—that would have to wait for another time.

Farmer, Businessman & Entrepreneur

One of Fresno's early entrepreneurs was Truman Calvin White. A man of enthusiasm and vision for the new community, he came to Fresno at the age of twenty-seven from his home state of Vermont for health reasons. His brother, Ray White, who had come earlier and was a farmer in the Central California Colony, had invited his brother to join him. When T. C. White arrived, he purchased a colony parcel that fronted on Cherry Avenue.

The year was 1877. He met and married Augusta Fink, one of the owners of another colony parcel—the Raisina Vineyard, the same year. They had one child, Harry. The couple's success in raisin farming enabled them to not only purchase other tracts of land within the colony, but also led to his involvement in raisin associations. White served as president of the Producers Packing Company, the first raisin cooperative in the state.

T. C. White's interests extended beyond farming. He became involved in real estate and purchased a large parcel of land at the corner of Merced and I (Broadway) streets. Here, in 1910, he built the four-story, 1,500-seat White Theater that, at the time of its completion, was one of the most modern in the state. The theater would, in its heyday, play host to many of the important actors and musicians of the time and was long remembered as a venue for vaudeville. In 1913, White built the Hotel Fresno—one of the most luxurious in the city. Erected at a cost of $350,000, it boasted a pipe organ in the lobby and an elegant dining room.

T. C. White was a great booster of Fresno. His commitment to the community manifested itself not only in his building projects that helped to develop the downtown area, but also in his service on the board of supervisors from 1887 to 1892, his presidency of the chamber of commerce and his role in helping to organize the National Bank of Fresno. White performed another public service as well. When the old mill ditch on Fresno Street became a public nuisance and the city trustees did nothing about it, he gave orders to have it filled in above Fresno Street outside of the city. This happened on a Sunday and stopped the water from Fancher Creek from flowing into the ditch. The people of Fresno seized their opportunity and, after dark, filled in the rest of the ditch. It was a glorious moment in the city's history and was provided courtesy of Truman Calvin White.

Jesse Clayton Forkner

Jesse Clayton Forkner's arrival in Fresno in 1910 was well timed. The right man had come at the right time. Forkner, who was born in Kentucky, studied theology at Drake University and later became a member of the first law class at the University of Kansas. He graduated in 1893 and spent several years in private law practice. He decided to leave the field and go into real estate. In later years he would say that training for the ministry and the law gave him the necessary background for a career in real estate. This, combined with his "gift of gab," made him an outstanding promoter. His first ventures in the new field were in Southern California. Then he moved to the Tulare Lake area where he studied colony settlements and irrigation methods. The year 1910 brought him to Fresno.

Forkner became interested in developing the huge area of northwest Fresno that was owned by the Bullard family. Much of the area had not been farmed. It was called "hog wallow" land because the area was covered with mounds about fifty feet in diameter. Many people thought it was unfit for farming—indeed, it was land in which only hogs could wallow. It also contained an underlying layer of hardpan that was impenetrable. The land flooded in winter and, in summer, the sun baked it until it became as hard as a rock.

It was certainly a challenge and Forkner was determined to conquer it. He took a one-year option to buy on six thousand acres of Bullard's land. For the next year, Forkner hiked over his land making calculations, bringing in experts, and being very mysterious about his intentions. People in Fresno were amazed—how could anyone tame the unfit "hog wallow" lands? Forkner's movements were closely watched. When he announced that he was not only going to develop the land, but also plant it in figs, the locals thought the newcomer was crazy.

What they didn't know was that Forkner had received some good advice from George Roeding and Henry Markarian. Markarian, who had successfully grown Smyrna figs, was hired by Forkner as a full-time consultant. From these two men, Forkner learned the necessary components of fig production. Markarian

This map of the Forkner Fig Gardens appeared in the *Fresno Morning Republican* on November 15, 1917.

showed Forkner that, by using dynamite to blast holes in the earth, the hardpan could be broken up and the land could be cultivated.

Some varieties of figs were being produced in the Fresno area. Markarian felt that a superior variety, the Smyrna fig, would produce well on the Bullard lands. They were ideally suited to the environment. They required only one deep, heavy watering in the winter and needed no fertilizers or pesticides. Markarian also showed Forkner the importance of planting the trees thirty feet apart to give them the ideal situation for growing. The Smyrna figs had one other important feature—there would be no competition. Outside of Markarian's ranch and Smyrna (in Turkey), the Smyrna fig was grown nowhere else in the world. The figs from these trees would be called Calimyrna, a name coined by Roeding who dropped the 'S' from Smyrna and added 'Cali' for California to the front of the word.

In 1912, J. C. Forkner purchased the Bullard lands. At the same time, a right-of-way was granted to the Fresno Traction Company so it could build a streetcar line from Fresno to the San Joaquin River. Today, the path of that line is Forkner Avenue.

Forkner set to work. He would eventually spend eight million dollars developing the land. First, the land had to be leveled. Not just leveled, but contoured so that water from the canals that were also being created could reach the future trees. He started with Fresno Scrapers. However, he soon added another six thousand acres to his holdings—too much area to be covered by this slow method. So, he purchased forty-eight of Henry Ford's first Fordson tractors to come off the assembly line. He attached smaller scrapers and disk tillers to the huge tractors. This worked so well that he purchased more tractors. Henry Ford, learning of this use of his tractors, drove up from Los Angeles in his Model T coupe just to observe the process. What he saw, as he stood with Forkner watching the tractors at work, was the beginning of the creation of the largest fig orchard in the world.

The next step was to dynamite holes for the trees. Over the next three years, Forkner's workers would use 660,000 pounds of dynamite in this process. Then they planted 600,000 fig trees. Other trees were planted, too. Sixty thousand ornamental and shade trees were planted along eight miles of Van Ness Boulevard stretching from what is today the Fresno High School neighborhood all the way to the river. Included in these ornamental trees were the deodar cedars and eucalyptus trees that line these streets today. It is the two miles of deodars in the Old Fig Garden area that become Christmas Tree Lane each December.

B y 1920, five hundred families were living on small fig farms of about sixteen acres each in J. C. Forkner's fig garden development in northwest Fresno. There was a high school and, in the little town of Fig Garden, there were Santa Fe and Southern Pacific stations as well as a fig packing plant, Forkner's offices, a grocery store, and a post office. The town was located on Bullard Avenue and the Santa Fe tracks.

In 1912, Forkner had married a local girl, Lewella Swift, the daughter of Ella Swift and the late Lewis P. Swift, a lumberman, who with Charles Shaver had developed Shaver Lake. A year later the Forkners moved into their two-story Craftsman style home at Bullard and Van Ness Extension. It was called Northfield because it was situated in the north field of the development. It had large sleeping porches and numerous bedrooms as well as a large kitchen. It made a fine setting for entertaining prospective buyers and, on one very special occasion, was the scene of a dinner party that included Governor Hiram Johnson of California. The Forkner family eventually grew to include a daughter and four sons. During the years the children were growing up, the Forkners moved to a home at Swift and Wilson avenues. Later, they would return to Northfield. Although Lewella Forkner always credited her husband with the vision and the accomplishment, she was an important part of the success of the fig gardens. She entertained her husband's clients, raised her family, and provided her husband with steadfast faith in his vision and the constant support of a loving partner.

Despite severe financial problems during the Great Depression, Forkner was able to weather the crisis. By the time of his death at Northfield in August 1969, his fig gardens had become the best address in town.

Forkner's contributions to Fresno go beyond his real estate interests. He served as head of the state Water Resources Investigation Commission which surveyed and mapped the Friant Dam project. He also was involved in many civic endeavors.

A marker sits on a triangle of ground where Van Ness Boulevard runs into Palm Avenue. It honors Jesse Clayton Forkner, a

This ad ran in the *Fresno Morning Republican* on November 13, 1917. It was placed there by W. W. Stanforth, the selling agent for Forkner lands. The ad shows a cross section of the soil in northwest Fresno and how, once the layer of hardpan is blasted through with dynamite, the roots of the fig tree can go deep into the earth.

man of vision, who said "there [is] no such thing as poor land; that God in His wisdom intended all the earth for some good purpose, no matter how poor the quality of the soil might appear to the casual observer." It honors the man who with vision and hard work turned the hog wallow land into a Garden of Eden.

Exterior of Harpain's Dairy at Dakota and Cedar avenues. Note the sign advertising ice cream and the parking lot filled with cars of the late 1940s and 1950s.
Courtesy of Walter Harpain.

The northeast corner of Cedar and Dakota avenues was a special place—a treasured spot not only for the premium milk and cream that were produced, bottled, and sold there, but also for the Victorian farmhouse, shade trees, and petting zoo that made every visit a cherished memory. It was on this land that Harpain's Dairy once stood.

Rudolph Frederick Harpain was born in Schmachtagen, Germany, on May 12, 1890. He came to the United States when he was twenty, settling first in Texas, then Butte, Montana, and, finally, coming west to San Francisco. He worked for a time in a sausage kitchen before coming to Fresno. He opened a meat market downtown and eventually leased space for his Beef Shop in the Liberty Market on Van Ness Avenue just south of Tulare Street. Soon after he arrived in Fresno he met and married Alma Catherine Meisetschlager. In 1926, he purchased land on Lincoln Avenue between Cherry and Elm avenues in Easton and started a dairy.

In 1931, Rudolph Harpain purchased a forty-acre parcel of land

Rudolph Frederick Harpain's Beef Shop in the Liberty Market in the early 1920s.
Courtesy of Walter Harpain.

at Cedar and Dakota avenues. The land was mostly vineyard, but had a large horse barn which he converted to house cows. There were other buildings on the property—a tray barn, a two-story tank house, and a home for his family that now included eight children. Two years later, a fire started in the lumber shed. A wind came up and blew embers toward the house, engulfing it in flames. The family home and outbuildings were gone. Rudolph and Alma had to begin again. They moved a small house onto the property; then a larger Victorian home from the Belmont and Blackstone area was moved in. They began to work at rebuilding their dairy including a new, modern milk barn.

In September 1939, Harpain's Dairy opened, selling raw, bottled milk to the people of Fresno. They also had a milk delivery service for those who found that more convenient.

In June 1946, twenty-year-old Walter Harpain was discharged from the army. He had served for two years in World War II, been seriously wounded in action and was finally home in Fresno. Soon after his homecoming his father took him aside and told him that none of his seven brothers and sisters was interested in staying on

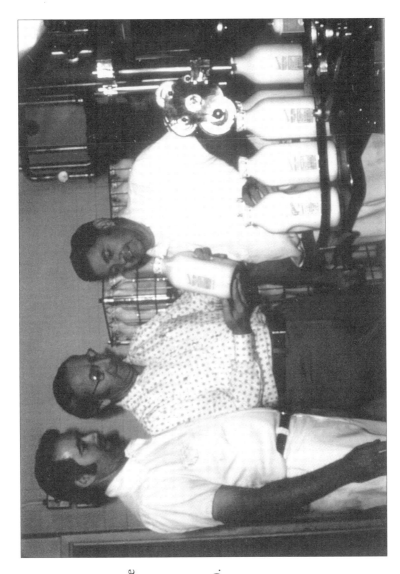

Walter Harpain (center) displays the last bottle of milk to be processed at the dairy to plant manager Larry Byrd (right) and assistant plant manager Larry Huenergardt (left). *Courtesy of Walter Harpain.*

the family dairy. If he would stay and learn the business, his parents would make a permanent arrangement with him later on.

For the next twelve years, Walter Harpain worked for his parents—literally night and day—without salary, only spending money. He learned every aspect of the dairy business. In 1958, his parents transferred one third interest in the dairy to him. Two years later, his parents wanted to retire so Walter purchased the remaining portion at the market price. When he went to the bank manager for a loan, the manager, knowing the cash flow at the dairy, said, "How do you expect to make these payments?" Walter's reply was that he would double the business in two years.

Walter installed a small creamery with a pasteurizer and homogenizer. He knew that he had to reach a larger buying public than the small group of consumers who bought raw milk. In 1963, he put in a more modern high-temperature, short time plate pasteurizer that offered continuous flow pasteurization. He now had one of the most modern small milk processing plants in the state. Harpain's Dairy also featured a small market with cottage cheese, ice cream, butter, bread, eggs, and lunch meats. Harpain's chocolate milk and fruit punch brought customers back again and again.

The dairy also included a petting zoo and picnic tables. Customers came not only to buy Harpain's high quality milk and cream, but also to enjoy the country setting and sense of family that the dairy inspired. Walter's sisters, Bette and Rosemary, worked at the dairy. His brother, August, did too and another brother, Elmer, occasionally helped out. The family appreciated Walter's commitment that had kept their parents' dairy in the family.

In the 1970s, glass bottles were being replaced by paper containers. Walter bought the last run of milk bottles the company made so he could stay in business as long as possible. In October 1977, Harpain's Dairy closed. With its passing, an important chapter in the tales of our valley ended, but the memories held by many Fresnans of the tree-shaded corner of Cedar and Dakota avenues, of Walter's blue ribbon-winning Holstein cows, and the taste of the best chocolate milk in the county will never be forgotten.

A Fine Herd of Holsteins

When Rudolph Harpain began his dairy in the Easton area, he purchased only Jersey and Guernsey cows. These breeds produced milk that was rich in cream. In 1960, when his son, Walter, bought the dairy, people no longer wanted to drink raw milk that had a high fat content. Walter had to change the herd to Holstein cows that produced milk that was lower in fat content. He bought premium Holstein cows and began to study breeding methods and genetics. He decided that he wanted to create the finest herd of cows he could. He analyzed each of his cows and bred them to only selected bulls that exhibited strong features that his cows lacked so the next generation would be more perfect.

By the early 1970s, his herd was winning blue ribbons. In 1972, at the California Holstein Show, one of Harpain's cows—a cow that was born on the dairy—won the blue ribbon for the "Highest Placing Bred by Exhibitor." Also in 1972, Harpain won a blue ribbon at the Western National Holstein Show. As his reputation grew, visitors from twenty-two countries came to view his registered herd. He sold cows and bulls to the governments of Japan and France.

It wasn't only the cows that were winning prizes, but their milk as well. Over the years, Harpain won fifty-six gold medals at the California State Fair and the Los Angeles County Fair at Pomona for his milk, half-and-half, and chocolate non-fat milk. He also won thirty silver medals.

Harpain's Dairy boasted one of the best small milk processing plants in California. The cows were milked by a pipeline milking system. The pipeline carried the milk directly from the cows into the creamery where it was processed, bottled and sealed without ever being touched by human hands.

Walter Harpain had another secret behind his high quality dairy products. He knew that it takes more than modern processing equipment to make a good glass of milk. It takes a staff of dedicated employees, a lot of hard work, and prize-winning Holstein cows.

Harry Lauder, that grand Scots entertainer who was popular in the United States and Europe in the early part of the twentieth century, made his living by singing songs of his own composition. His songs were written in the broad Scots dialect. The melodies were toe-tapping and unforgettable. A few of them like "Roamin' in the Gloamin'" and "I Love a Lassie" became world famous. The songs were interspersed with patter—bits of dialogue that were meant to illuminate the listener's understanding of the lyrics and to poke a bit of fun as well. Lauder always appeared in his kilts with a walking stick that was notable for its crookedness. Lauder appeared often in Fresno, usually at the Kinema Theater. His appearances always filled the house to capacity.

Before one of Lauder's visits to Fresno, J. R. McKay, a Nova Scotia native and a fan of Lauder's work, wrote to him. McKay, the owner of the local Haines car and White truck dealership, knew that Mrs. Lauder always traveled with her husband and offered to be available to show them the local sights in and around Fresno during their visit. The Lauders were delighted. Harry wrote back saying that although he would be busy with rehearsals, Mrs. Lauder would gratefully accept McKay's kind invitation.

On the appointed day, McKay arrived at the Lauders' hotel. After greeting them both, he escorted Mrs. Lauder to his car. The rest of the afternoon was spent driving her in his Haines car all over Fresno. Since he had lived in the city since the late 1880s and had once owned the Dexter Stables on I (now Broadway) Street, McKay knew the history of Fresno well and knew everyone in town. He drove her out Kearney Boulevard and regaled her with stories of the late M. Theo Kearney, the mysterious raisin baron to whom McKay had sold a Locomobile. After a very pleasant afternoon, McKay took Mrs. Lauder back to her hotel.

The Lauders never forgot J. R. McKay's kindness and on future trips to Fresno, they always contacted him. It was a friendship that McKay treasured all his life.

Famed Scots vaudeville star Harry Lauder (right) stands with a group of men including J. R. McKay (second from left). He was appearing in Fresno during one of his several ""farewell"" tours.
Courtesy of Mary Helen McKay.

Our tales of the valley have often mentioned a topographical quirk that appeared most often in the land northwest of Fresno. It caused many people to assume that the land was unfit for farming or even human habitation. Because people thought it was fit only for hogs to wallow in, this topographical oddity was nicknamed a "hog wallow." Scientists prefer to call it a mima mound.

Actually, mima mounds can be found throughout nineteen western states. In our valley, they appear as large mounds on the valley floor. They also are found on the hillside slopes of the foothills. They vary in size from one to five feet in height and from ten to fifty feet across. The mounds have one distinctive feature. Their soil is sandy, loamy, or silty with a layer of dense hardpan not far beneath the surface. They usually appear in rows—an acre of land may have twenty or more. When viewing them, one question begs to be answered, "Where do these mounds come from?"

The answer is that no one knows. However, as one might imagine, many people have put forth fascinating theories. Joseph LeConte, a respected pioneer western naturalist, first saw the mounds in 1874. He said, "Some have supposed that they are Indian burial mounds, veritable cities of the dead. Others [call them] artificial mounds, upon which were built huts of Indian villages. Still others…that they were in fact large fish-nests." Others feel they were created by buffaloes, ants, moles, falling trees, or were the nests of some type of sucker…perhaps even a giant sea snail in prehistoric times. One scientist, George W. Cox, has made solving this puzzle his life's work. Forty years of study has led him to conclude that mima mounds are the work of pocket gophers that staked out their territory by making these nests.

Developers have leveled most of our hog wallow mima mounds today, but some can still be viewed in the foothills near Friant. An oddity for sure, but one has that played an interesting role in the story of our valley.

One of the few places left in our Central Valley where "hog wallows" can still be seen is in the foothills near Friant. *Author's photo.*

A Museum in Clovis

R ight in the heart of Old Town Clovis is a small jewel from days past that might go unnoticed if one didn't take the time to do a little exploring. Amid the antique shops, covered walkways, and small restaurants is a historic building that begs to be entered. Situated at the southeast corner of Fourth and Pollasky streets, this building once housed the Clovis First State Bank and, in 1924, was the scene of a daring robbery. Today, the building has been transformed into the Clovis Big Dry Creek Museum. It contains all manner of historical artifacts that tell the story of Clovis.

On entering the museum, one is struck by the myriad of photos that line the walls. Large class pictures of Clovis High School seniors of years past gaze down on visitors and form a backdrop for the other exhibits. Many of the items are either donated by or on loan from Clovis families. To the right of the front door is a photo of Clovis Cole, for whom the city is named. Another fascinating photo is of the ten daughters of William Cole. They all married local boys and, because so many Clovis families descended from them, they are often called, "The Grandmothers of Clovis."

The second room houses a section of the V-shaped flume that ran from Shaver Lake to the Clovis mill. A third room is called the "Veteran's Room" and contains uniforms and memorabilia from World War I through Desert Storm. The coat, boots, and holster that Ken Curtis wore as "Festus" on the television show "Gunsmoke" proudly grace another exhibit. Items from the Tracy Richard Clark House, which locals believe is haunted, can also be viewed.

Mickey Wells, the first president of the Clovis Big Dry Creek Historical Society, was the founder and driving force behind the establishment of the museum in 1987. Many individuals and organizations joined in the effort to preserve the history of their community.

Next time you're in Clovis on a Friday or Saturday, take a few minutes to step back in time and view some pieces of the past. You'll be glad you did.

Earthquake & Devastation

At 5:16 on the morning of April 18, 1906, the people of San Francisco were awakened from their slumbers by a massive earthquake. Wooden buildings were ripped from their foundations. Multistoried brick structures crumbled—their facades cascading into the streets. Electric power lines shorted out and fell, setting off fires that swept through blocks of the city. Those who survived poured into the streets bringing whatever possessions they could carry with them. The once beautiful city in a matter of minutes took on the appearance and characteristics of a war zone.

Like many Fresnans who had come to San Francisco for the opening of the opera season, Fresno County Coroner Dr. Angus B. Cowan felt the quake. He was staying at the Hamilton Hotel on Ellis Street. At first, the shock was mild. He got out of bed and dressed quickly. Then he said, "The shaking grew violent, increasing as though some unseen power was striking the earth with a mighty battering ram. The walls of my room cracked in all directions and the plaster fell in a shower as I fled down the stairs." Soon afterward, fire destroyed what was left of the building.

Miss Elizabeth Gundelfinger of Fresno attended a private school in San Francisco and related seeing Chinatown ablaze as she and classmates fled to Golden Gate Park where thousands gathered to camp out. Among them were Fresnans Frank Homan and his family, Dr. J. Montgomery Thomas, and Dr. J. D. Davidson. On April 19, W. W. Phillips, O. J. Woodward, Charles Riege, Robert Barton, Maud Helm, and Mr. and Mrs. M. J. Lockhart all arrived safely home in Fresno on the evening train. It was with the greatest relief that they were reunited with their families and friends. They were able to bring reports of other Fresnans who had survived. Also arriving home was M. Theo Kearney. He had been staying at the Saint Francis Hotel and awakened with the first tremors. The frightening experience caused him to suffer a mild heart attack. He was to experience a more devastating and fatal attack five weeks later.

For now, Fresnans were relieved to welcome home their own.

The Telephone—A Modern Necessity

Mr. J. P. Bolton, Fresno's weather observer, had his office and living quarters on the top floor of the Farmer's National Bank building. On the morning of April 18, 1906, he was awake as usual at 5 a.m. and was looking out of his upper story window making his daily weather prognostications when, all at once, the doors of his room began to swing on their hinges, the windows rattled, and the ground began to shake beneath him. The first temblor was followed by a second much more pronounced temblor which lasted for thirty to forty seconds. What Mr. Bolton was experiencing was the massive San Francisco earthquake.

The days of instant communication were far away in 1906. Fresnans had to depend on telegraphed messages at the Southern Pacific and Santa Fe railroad offices and the newspaper. Long-distance telephones calls were placed, but they could not reach San Francisco where the lines were down.

The first thought on everyone's mind was how to help. How could the community be rallied to provide relief to the people of San Francisco? The answer was simple—use the local phone service. And so, for the first time ever, on April 19, 1906, Fresno's telephones were used as a means of general publicity. All the operators went into the main switch room of the telephone company. A bulletin was prepared announcing a citywide meeting at the Barton Opera House. Every home was requested to provide food and provisions that would be picked up at each home by four o'clock that afternoon.

Regular phone service was suspended. The operators went to their switchboards. They began to call every phone subscriber in the city and read them the bulletin. Within two hours and fifteen minutes every subscriber was reached and the message given.

Fresnans responded. The relief effort was a great success. The telephone, a convenient new addition to many homes and businesses, was now a necessity of life—a sign that the twentieth century was well on its journey in the tales of our valley.

Decoration Day 1901

On April 26, 1866, four Southern women went to the Friendship Cemetery where the Battle of Shiloh had taken place. Here, 1,500 Confederate and 100 Union soldiers lay buried. In spite of the hostile feelings still present after the Civil War, the women scattered flowers over the graves of soldiers who had served in both armies. When word of their unselfish tribute reached the north, people were amazed and impressed. A veteran's organization, the Grand Army of the Republic (the G. A .R.), organized a Decoration Day service in Arlington National Cemetery on May 30, 1868. Congress recognized this as an official holiday. Today it is called Memorial Day.

In Fresno, on May 30, 1901, Decoration Day was fittingly observed. At ten in the morning, seventy-five members of the Atlanta Post of the G. A .R. and its ladies auxiliary met at Mountain View Cemetery and held a ritual ceremony over the graves of the departed veterans of the Civil War and the Spanish American War. Among the participating Civil War veterans were W. B. Parker, C. R. Smith, W. T. McKay, Frank Love, W. A. Lyon, and G. W. Brooks. Prayers were said and "America" was sung. Ladies Auxiliary President Mrs. A. V. Parker gave an address in which she paid tribute to the fallen heroes who lay buried in Fresno soil. She also spoke of the need to remember and care for the veterans still among the living and of the importance of keeping the traditions of Decoration Day each year. Mrs. Clara Fuller then gave a recitation. The ladies then proceeded to solemnly decorate all the veterans' graves with flowers. This accomplished, prayers were said and the assembled group went downtown to the G. A .R. Hall in the Edgerly Building, where lunch was served and more speeches were given.

It was apparent to all who were in attendance that day that the number of Fresno's living Civil War veterans was rapidly diminishing. It was a thought that was spoken aloud and cast an even more sobering cloud over the day's events.

Downtown Fresno on Decoration Day 1900. Note the United States flags flying outside the stores. *R.W. Riggs photo. Author's collection.*

Decoration Day 1906

The Decoration Day services planned for May 30, 1906, were scaled down from the usual celebration. Because of the devastating earthquake and fire in San Francisco the month before, it was decided to hold a simpler ceremony.

At 8:00 a.m., people began to gather in Courthouse Park. School children mingled with the citizens of Fresno as they waited for the ceremonies to begin. Promptly at 8:30, the Civil War veterans of the Atlanta Post of the Grand Army of the Republic, the veterans of the Spanish-American War, and Fresno's National Guardsmen, who had just returned from duty in San Francisco, marched through the park to the steps of the Courthouse. The invocation was given by the Reverend Thomas Boyd. A chorus of five hundred schoolchildren led by Professor E. R. Nesbitt sang "Hail Columbia" and the "Red, White and Blue." A series of speeches followed. James E. Hill, who served in the Spanish-American War, spoke on behalf of the younger veterans present and paid tribute to the veterans of the Civil War. The Reverend C. A. Nunn then addressed the children, explaining to them the terrible costs of war, but that it was the duty of each citizen to first serve God and then his country.

After the ceremony, Fresno's remaining Civil War veterans marched quietly to Mountain View Cemetery to pray at the graves of their departed comrades. The group was smaller than in previous years; the number of graves had increased. More gray heads could be seen in the group—their steps were slower, but they still marched proudly—they were still the grand old men who had done their part to preserve the Union. They were joined by the ladies of the General George A. Custer Circle, who decorated the graves with flowers. It was a somber occasion—not only because of the memories evoked, but also because those present knew that the Fresno men who had fought in the Civil War would soon be gone— an era would end; the memories would be gone forever.

Tartans & Bagpipes Galore

In the early days of the twentieth century, Fresno had a very active Scots community. Many of these folks had been born in Scotland or in Nova Scotia; some were the children of immigrants. They all had one thing in common—they felt close ties to the traditions of bonnie Scotland and the keeping of those traditions bound them to each other.

On the evening of May 20, 1906, there was a large, very colorful gathering in Saint Andrews Hall of the Edgerly Building at J (Fulton) and Tulare streets. Horse-drawn carriages and motorcars proceeded through the streets of downtown and, finding parking places nearby, their occupants made their way into the building. Resplendent in Highland dress, the men in dress kilts with the jeweled tops of their dirks showing above the crest of their tartan hose and the women with tartan scarves worn diagonally across their jackets paraded into the hall. They were there for the yearly Gathering of the Clans—the culmination of the social year for the local Saint Andrew's Society.

The drone and skirl of bagpipes welcomed the colorful procession into the hall and set the tone for the evening. Places were found at the gaily-decorated tables. When all were seated, the *ceilidh*, a gathering where everyone participates in song and verse, began in earnest. The Spence brothers—Will and Dave—led off the festivities with songs and piano solos. Undersheriff Cummings addressed the group with a full dollop of dry wit appropriate to the occasion. His remarks were punctuated with a great deal of laughter. The high spirits continued as James Beverage strode to the stage to sing several Scots ballads. Adam Baird followed him, entertaining the group with the songs of Robert Burns.

An elegant supper and a Highland Fling capped off the event. The bagpipes were stilled and the tartans were whisked away as the members of the Saint Andrew's Society went home with happiness in their hearts and, perhaps, a sprig of heather as well—a fitting memento of a festive evening.

The Dean

James Morrow Malloch (left) and his brother Walter Scott Malloch stand in the University of California's Greek Theater in Berkeley, California during the 1918 commencement exercises. James Malloch received his bachelor of arts degree.
Author's collection.

The subject of this story is a man who, in his lifetime, had a major impact on the Fresno community. James Morrow Malloch was born in Oakland, California, on June 12, 1895, to James and Sarah Morrow Malloch. After completing his high school education in San Diego, he enrolled in the College of the Pacific. He later transferred to the University of California at Berkeley, earning a BA degree in 1918 and an MA in 1920. He visited the college group at Berkeley's First Presbyterian Church one Sunday evening. A young lady, Jeanette Belman, saw him and thought, "This is the man I am going to marry." After the meeting, she introduced herself and invited him home for cake and coffee. He accepted. It was truly love at first sight. Courtship followed. They were married on November 22, 1919.

After a varied career in business and teaching, Malloch felt a

"GOODWILL THROUGH UNDERSTANDING"

FORUM OF BETTER UNDERSTANDING

Heard Over KMJ, Fresno, and Other Stations of the California Radio System

RABBI DAVID L. GREENBERG—MONSIGNOR JAMES G. DOWLING—DEAN JAMES M. MALLOCH

This postcard shows Rabbi David L. Greenberg, Monsignor James G. Dowling, and Dean James M. Malloch preparing for their radio broadcast on KMJ in June of 1941. *Author's collection.*

higher calling and entered the Church Divinity School of the Pacific in Berkeley. He graduated in 1933 and was ordained an Episcopal priest in 1934. After a brief teaching stint, he was called to be vicar of Trinity Church in Hayward. In 1937, he was called to Fresno to become dean of Saint James' Cathedral—a post he would hold until he became dean emeritus in 1955.

His years in Fresno were marked not only by service to his congregation which grew to be the largest in Fresno, but also by service to the Fresno community. A man of large physical stature, he also was a man of great intellect and compassion. Noting the prejudice that existed in Fresno against certain ethnic groups, in 1937, he joined with Monsignor James Dowling and Rabbi David L. Greenberg in a KMJ Radio weekly program called the "Radio Forum of Better Understanding." By discussing their beliefs, they dispelled many myths and fears and helped create a greater understanding between peoples. Malloch also served on the Fresno Unified Board of Education, as a director of the Fresno Red Cross Chapter, and headed many other community service committees.

The final work of his life was the compilation of *A Practical Church Dictionary*. The 516-page work is, in Malloch's words, "a practical volume of ready reference for clergy and laity on religious life and thought."

The Very Reverend James M. Malloch died in March 1960. He was a man beloved by his community. Of all the tributes paid to him, perhaps the greatest was witnessed at his funeral. On that day, people of all races and creeds, many with tear-stained cheeks, filled Saint James' Cathedral to capacity to mourn the passing of a man, who by the example of his life, taught tolerance and compassion for all men—regardless of the color of their skin or of their religious beliefs. His influence on the Fresno community was immeasurable.

The Very Reverend James M. Malloch (left) and Rabbi David L. Greenberg enjoy a stroll in downtown Fresno in December 1939.
Author's collection.

Enrich Your Life–Buy a Car!

The pages of the *Fresno Morning Republican* were replete with advertisements not unlike the newspapers of today. However, on November 14, 1917, one advertisement in the *Republican* was of particular note not because of its contents, but because of its appearance. Instead of being encased in a box, this add was written like a news story, byline and all, and took up almost an entire one-inch column of one page of the paper.

The headline to the story ran as follows: "Motor Salesman Says Buy Car Now." Directly underneath was the admonition: "Don't Stint On Life." The article was written by James C. Phelan, who in 1914 built one of the first and certainly one of the most modern automobile showrooms in Fresno.

The United States had entered World War I earlier in the year. Phelan noted that all the factories were up and running to their full capacity producing ammunition and weapons and that there were plenty of jobs for everyone. Agricultural products had their biggest yield in ten years, he continued. That made it possible for anyone to buy one of his Maxwell cars that cost only two dollars a week to operate.

A man who refuses to buy a car is neglecting his family, Phelan felt. If he buys a car then he can provide his family with the healthful benefits derived by long drives in the countryside—bringing his family in closer touch with the earth. "The automobile gives wings not to one selfish individual, but to the whole family," Phelan continued. "It gives youth to the father or mother, strength to the child, too young to walk, above all united pleasure to the family group. Do not…let false economy keep you at home, far from the beautiful world."

Phelan invited the reader to visit his showroom, test drive a Maxwell and, of course, purchase it. The car would enrich the buyer's life. In 1917, life was changing dramatically—the car was replacing the horse, young men were on a foreign shore fighting in a major war, and women would soon be granted voting rights. Fresnans, along with the rest of the country, were on the move and the car was going to help get them where they were going even faster.

A perusal of old high school annuals can be entertaining. Social customs, hairstyles, and clothes can pinpoint an era very dramatically. Occasionally, these books also can yield some good historical information. One case in point is the Sierra Joint Union High School's 1954 *Chieftain*. The yearbook staff provided a page on the history of each mountain community that sends students to the school. It sets the book apart as one that is a valuable addition to a researcher's library.

There were four one-room schoolhouses in the Auberry area about 1900—the Sentinel School, Manzanita School, Auberry School, and Big Sandy School. The education that was provided within their walls was basic, old-fashioned, and substantial. The grueling day followed a strict schedule. Discipline was firm. There were no frills and little time for foolishness.

At 9:00 a.m. all grades studied arithmetic. The next half hour was turned over to reading and spelling for the primary grades. A twenty-minute recess followed. From 11:00 to 12:00 the advanced grades had their reading and history lessons. After lunch, the primary classes studied reading, writing, and spelling. Then everyone had a geography lesson followed by an hour devoted to grammar and spelling. One concession was made to the arts. On Friday afternoons, grammar gave way to drawing. The school day ended at 4:00 p.m.

In 1907, the salary for teachers was $37.50 per month. There were no computers, no adding machines, and no electricity. Teaching may have been done the old-fashioned way with a very basic curriculum, but one thing was certain—when the children completed school they knew how to read, how to spell, and how to construct a grammatically correct sentence. In this case, longing for the good old days might just be in order.

A Cornerstone Is Laid

On May 14, 1906, the citizens of Fresno gathered at the corner of Merced and I (now Broadway) streets to witness an event that was notable in their city. For several years, the building that served as a city hall also was the fire station. Because the board of trustees met in the fireman's dormitory, an ordinance was passed to require the firemen to remain clothed during board meetings. It all smacked of a frontier town. It was time for a real city hall.

The afternoon was warm and sunny as the crowds began to crowd around the site where a foundation had been laid for Fresno's first real city hall. A large granite block sat on the foundation. It was the cornerstone and the centerpiece of the day's festivities. A number of dignitaries, including Mayor W. Parker Lyon and the eight city trustees, were joined by Eugene Mathewson, the architect of the building; ex-mayor L. O. Stephens; and the officers of the Fresno lodge of the Benevolent and Protective Order of Elks, who would preside over the event.

The cornerstone was hoisted into the air as the municipal band played. Then Mayor Lyon strode to the podium. He told the crowd that the custom of consecrating a new public building to the objects and principles for which it is constructed is a noble one. He noted how rapidly Fresno had grown and that the new building was a testament to the maturing of the former pioneer town. Fresno was celebrating its twenty-first birthday—it was coming of age and now would soon have a public building its citizens could look to with pride.

The Reverend Harvey S. Hanson delivered an invocation. Then L. M. Allum, the exalted ruler of the Elks, asked Elks Secretary Eugene Rahill to read the list of documents that would be placed in the cavity under the cornerstone. A "copy of the municipal code, copies of the *Fresno Morning Republican, Evening Democrat, Evening Tribune, San Francisco Chronicle, Examiner, Call,* name of the President of the United States, statistical report of the Fresno County Chamber of Commerce, coins from $1 down, ritual of the day, and a roster of the Elks." The stone was lowered as Exalted Ruler Allum spoke of justice and brotherly love. Then he said, "I hereby declare this cornerstone duly laid according to law, and the building that is to rise upon it devoted to the principles of justice and good government." Rev. Hanson prayed over the stone and the ceremony was complete.

After a long address was delivered by Attorney Lewis H. Smith, the Elks sang an ode, another prayer was said, the band played, and the citizens of Fresno returned to their homes happy in the knowledge that soon they would have a city hall befitting the future of their city.

A Parade on the Fourth

On July 4, 1901, Fresnans awoke to bird song, a cool northwesterly breeze, and the promise of a perfect day. Excitement was evident everywhere because today was a day of celebration of our nation's birthday—it was an event that would last from sunup until midnight.

Seven thousand people poured into Fresno the night before from the mountain communities and from as far away as Visalia and Merced. Every hotel room was taken. By half past seven on the morning of the Fourth, people began to take their picnic baskets to Courthouse Park. Others staked out positions along the sidewalks of downtown. Lemonade and food stands appeared everywhere. Schoolboys held their red, white, and blue barber sticks aloft as they happily found vantage spots from which to view the proceedings. City Marshal John D. Morgan and his corps of mounted police cleared the streets. There was going to be a parade!

The first division to step out was the veterans and militia members. Then Fulton G. Berry, in the white costume of a Spanish Don, rode by on his white horse, closely followed by an elaborate float holding the Goddess of Liberty, Uncle Sam, and a group of costumed men representing the signers of the Declaration of Independence. Chinatown's three floats had scenes depicting Chinese war and religious stories in tableaux. The Native Sons, the firemen of Fresno, local businesses, the Sanger band, and many other bands took part. The parade wound through all the streets of downtown.

In the background could be heard the sound of fireworks. Although they were not supposed to be set off within the city limits, a few people lighted them anyway.

The parade was over. As the crowds began to move toward Courthouse Park, everyone agreed that it had been a spectacular beginning to the day.

July 4, 1901

After the final float had passed through the streets of down-town Fresno, the throngs of parade watchers began to walk toward Courthouse Park. It was July 4, 1901. The morning festivities were over, but more was yet to come.

It was estimated that 22,000 people lined the streets of Fresno that day and most of them now began to seek the shaded lawns of the park. Some folks purchased food from vendors; others opened their picnic baskets. It was time for the next item on the day's agenda to begin—the literary exercises.

A platform, decorated with flags and bunting, was set up beneath the trees. The Fresno Military Band members, fresh from their parade through town, took up their instruments once again and entertained the multitudes with selections of patriotic songs. Roy Hall, president of the day, welcomed city dignitaries, guests, and the assembled crowd. The Reverend J. A. Batchelor of Saint Paul's Methodist Episcopal Church gave the invocation. A hush settled over the park as Miss Mae Jack began to read the Declaration of Independence. Every ear could hear the immortal words of Thomas Jefferson as her commanding voice resounded to the highest treetop. Then the orator of the day, E. C. Farnsworth, also the possessor of a strong voice, strode to the podium. He started to speak. He began with an eloquent and sweeping account of the struggles and growth of the republic, placing special emphasis on the day that Jefferson's inspired document was accepted and signed by the fifty-six representatives of the thirteen colonies—July 4, 1776. The crowd left the park filled with patriotic thoughts.

An afternoon of horse races at the fairground and a carnival with fireworks that night awaited them. The Fourth of July 1901 was truly a day to remember.

The Heat of Summer—1901 Style

In our modern twenty-first century world, weather reporting is a fairly sophisticated business that, among other
things, uses photos of weather patterns photographed by satel-
lites as they circle in their orbits above the earth. We are so accus-
tomed to watching these pictures of storm patterns and temperature projections on television—they have become such a part of
our everyday lives—it is hard to imagine weather forecasting without them. However, for all the modern technology at the
weatherman's fingertips, it still is not an exact science.

One hundred years ago, it was really not much of a science at
all. Fresno's weather observer J. P. Bolton, who was given the job
of reporting on the day's weather, had only one method available
to him—looking out the window. He did this every morning and
every afternoon at five o'clock from his office/rooms on the top
floor of the Farmer's Bank building. He wrote down what he observed and filed his report with the office of the *Fresno Morning
Republican* so it could be published in the newspaper the following
day. That wasn't much help to the residents of Fresno who had
already lived through whatever weather Mother Nature had provided, but, occasionally it made interesting reading.

On Sunday, August 4, 1901, Mr. Bolton noted that he had spent
the previous day sweltering in his rooms—the temperature had
reached 110 degrees. He noted that the past fifteen days had seen
temperatures soar above the 100-degree mark, temperatures that
would "move a salamander to perspiration and tears." "A record
has not been broken," he declared. "We have seen as many as twenty
such days in a row. Hopefully, tomorrow will be a little cooler, but
you will not need your overcoats."

The article went on to note the impact of the heat on men's
starched collars. They were fairly wilting. It was discovered by
many gentlemen that the only solution was to drink a substantial
amount of beer. Evidently, the cooling effect of the liquid on one's
throat cooled the collars. It was noted, however, that too much
beer could have a negative effect on the amount of work one might
accomplish. The iceman was quite thrilled with the increase in his

business. He and the brewer seemed to be the only people in town who were not complaining.

The final word on the weather came from two men on the street who were overheard by a reporter. The first man said, "How hot is it?" The reply came back, "Oh, 'bout a hundred and hell!"

It is late spring—that most beautiful of times in our great Central Valley—when thoughts turn to the end of the school year and that most anticipated of all events in a young person's life—high school graduation.

The first such event in the history of Fresno occurred in 1891. Fresno High School had been organized and opened just two years before. The student body consisted of fifty young people in three grade levels and three teachers, Mrs. Curran, Miss Bartling, and Principal Thomas L. Heaton. There were two courses of study open to the students—a literary course or a business course. Now, after two years, seven students had completed their studies and were ready to receive their diplomas.

On June 5, 1891, Fresnans packed the Barton Opera House to witness this historic event. Four young women, Russie Martin, Mabel Cory, Olive Vogel, and Julia Roff, and three young men, E. Leroy Chaddock, Ed F. Greeley, and DeWitt H. Gray, filed onto the stage. The women were wearing long white dresses and the men were attired in dark suits. After listening to an hour-long speech by the county superintendent of schools and then to another long speech by the chairman of Fresno's board of education, George E. Church, it was the students' turn to shine. Each woman read an essay to the audience; the boys each gave an oration. With this accomplished, diplomas were presented to each young person and they were declared the first graduates of Fresno High School.

On May 29, 2001, just 110 years later, Fresno High School held another graduation. Five hundred and thirteen young people marched into Selland Arena to receive their diplomas. They form part of an unbroken chain of men and women who have made not only incredible contributions to their city for 110 years, but have also retained strong school spirit. As in the words of the school's beloved alma mater:

"Our strong bands will ne'er be broken, formed in Fresno High,
Far surpassing wealth unspoken, sealed by friendship's tie,
Raise the chorus, speed it onward, 'til the hills reply,
Hail to thee, our Alma Mater, Hail to Fresno High.

When in future years we're turning, years of memory,
Then we'll find our hearts returning, Fresno High to thee,
Raise the chorus, speed it onward, 'til the hills reply,
Hail to thee, our Alma Mater, Hail to Fresno High."

On a hot summer morning, August 23, 1901, to be exact, a large party of gentlemen gathered at Fresno's Grand Central Hotel. The group included a number of prominent citizens, namely W. B. Holland, E. F. Bernhard, T. W. Fisher, G. C. Freman, F. M. Chittenden, A. V. Lisenby, William Glass, George H. Monroe, F. M. Helm, J. M. Seropian, Frederick Roeding, and a reporter for the *Fresno Morning Republican* who was charged with writing about the day's events. At precisely 9 a.m. they boarded a large, horse-drawn conveyance and began their journey to Roeding Place, Roeding's home and farm east of Fresno.

When they arrived at their destination, Frederick Roeding escorted them through his Smyrna fig orchard. He showed them the results of his experiments with the successful propagation of this difficult variety of fig and touted the virtues of the tiny Blastophaga wasp—the key component in producing this fruitful fig. As they viewed the ripe fruit, Roeding offered them samples to taste. A spirited contest was waged between the gentlemen to see who could eat the most figs. Judge Holland and George Monroe really got into the spirit of things and ate so many figs that everyone lost count. The judge offered to settle the matter by suggesting that someone measure their waists to determine the winner. Roeding offered other varieties of figs to allow the gentlemen to sample those as well. A great deal of merriment accompanied the tasting.

After walking through Roeding's nursery and listening to the details of his continuing horticultural experiments, the gentlemen retired to the porch of the Roeding home where a sumptuous buffet and cold drinks awaited them. They returned to Fresno around three in the afternoon, happily satiated with figs, food, and fun.

Nuptials at High Noon

One young Fresno couple who decided to begin the twentieth century by embarking on married life were Roy Woodward and Saida Dealey. Woodward, the eldest son of O. J. Woodward, and Miss Dealey both attended Fresno schools. Miss Dealey's parents moved to San Francisco, where she completed her education. Roy Woodward graduated from Fresno High School in the class of 1896, studied electrical engineering at the Lick School in San Francisco and at the University of California at Berkeley. After completing his studies, he returned to Fresno, started a machine shop and purchased the Hopkins Agricultural Works, operating the two businesses alongside each other.

The wedding was scheduled for noon on Thursday, January 3, 1901, at the San Francisco home of the bride's parents. One hundred guests, many from Fresno, were invited. The front parlor of the home was decorated with red and green and the back parlor with green and white. Holly berries, huckleberry vines and a profusion of hyacinths, palms, grasses, ferns, and similax adorned the rooms. White ribbons extended from the front to the back parlor creating an aisle leading to an alcove in a bay window where the ceremony would take place.

The groom, his best man and Fresno High School classmate David Barnwell, and the Reverend Edgar Lyon of Saint Stephens' Episcopal Church, who would perform the ceremony, stepped into the alcove. The bridesmaids, Rova Bowen of Fresno and Genevieve Marvin of San Francisco, wearing white organdy over green taffeta, walked up the aisle to greet the bride and her maid of honor, Clara Rulofon, at the foot of the home's large staircase. The bride, wearing a gown of duchess lace over white taffeta, and her father, preceded by the bridesmaids and maid of honor, walked down the aisle to the alcove. After the vows had been said, the newly wed Roy and Saida Woodard walked back down the aisle to the strains of Mendelssohn's "Wedding March."

After greeting their guests and enjoying a sumptuous wedding dinner, the young couple boarded the train for Fresno. A large delegation of friends greeted them on their arrival. They proceeded to their new home at 811 O Street where they would begin their married life.

The Fig—Then & Now

On November 15, 1917, a map appeared in the *Fresno Morning Republican* (see page 154). It was part of an advertisement, but is noteworthy because the message it was touting has become an important part of our history. On this autumn morning, Fresno readers saw a map of their city with a huge new development, almost as large as Fresno itself, outlined due north of the existing city boundaries. With the exception of one curve at present-day Shaw Avenue, Van Ness Boulevard ran straight through it—all the way from the southern edge of Fresno to the San Joaquin River. Above the map were the words, "The J. C. Forkner Fig Gardens. STUDY THIS MAP! Think About It."

It's safe to assume that many Fresnans were thinking about it. "Let us tell you something," the ad continued. "Six years ago, when these lands were bought, the city of Fresno only went out north as far as Belmont Avenue. Since then the State Normal [school] came to the north of the city…since then came Van Ness Boulevard to the river. Now are coming the J. C. Forkner Fig Gardens…It is a law of the growth of cities. Whether in England, France or America, that most of the high-class growth of any city is toward the prevailing direction of the winds. People build their homes where the air is fresh. In a little while Fresno will stretch itself clear out to the old San Joaquin, and will spread itself all over the J. C. Forkner Fig Gardens…Everybody sees it. Everybody knows it."

Not only did everyone know, everyone was talking about it. By this time, J. C. Forkner had planted thousands of fig trees on his huge acreage. He was urging people to buy. His company would carry the land for ten years. The buyer had to pay only for improvements. Part of this development would be called "The Garden Home Tract," an endeavor that included a partner, Wylie Giffen. This is now called "Old Fig Garden." The rest of the area did develop according to Forkner's plan. It took many years to reach fruition, but today those who live north of Shaw Avenue in the area that stretches clear to the San Joaquin River and is bounded by Blackstone Avenue and Highway 99, live in the Forkner Fig Gardens. The one part of Forkner's dream that didn't last is the fig gardens. As more houses are built, the old fig orchards are leveled. Ironically, figs, the one fruit that could be easily grown in the old hog wallow lands and proved that the land could be developed and productive, are no longer needed. Just like the historic buildings that are considered outdated and torn down, the figs of northwest Fresno have outlived their usefulness and are now becoming a distant memory in the tales of our valley.

On the west side of the San Joaquin River, at a site just after Highway 33 leaves Fresno County and goes into Merced County, is a city that owes its existence to Bernhard Marks and its name to Henry Miller. Before the city was established, the huge Miller & Lux Empire had several large stock ranches in the area including the Poso, Santa Rita, Dos Palos, and the Colony Farm.

In 1893, an enterprising gentleman, who had been a successful developer of the Central California Colony and other colonies near Fresno, traveled northwest and began a new venture on land that was adjacent to a railroad line and rich in agricultural potential. The soil was rich and loamy. Water was available nearby—the San Joaquin River was an inexhaustible source. The developer, Bernhard Marks, along with his son, Frank, began to lay out plans for their Dos Palos Colony. Using horses, mules, and Fresno Scrapers, workmen began to build canals to bring water to the colony. The main street was named Cornelia for Marks' wife. Later, the name was changed to Carmellia. The major cross street was Elgin. On the northwest corner of the juncture of the two streets, a post office was established.

The promotional map of the colony advertises a winning combination of enticements—choice land, a railroad, good neighbors nearby, good schools, churches, a fine climate, and abundant water. "Don't doom your family to needless solitude among farms a mile or more apart…or your children to a poor education…or waiting a lifetime for civilization to come to you…settle on Dos Palos Colony." The advertisements were taken seriously. The colony was a success. The city that grew out of it was called Dos Palos—a name given by Henry Miller who saw two cottonwood trees growing near the site of the future railroad station. In Spanish, *Dos Palos* means two trees.

The historic Brick Block in downtown Dos Palos about 1910.
Courtesy of Dan Sniffin.

The ice cream parlor in the Brick Block was a popular place for Dos Palos residents. Left to right: Charles Foreman, Bert Sniffin, Homer Dye, C. M. Sitton, Bill Boyer, and Bill Johns. Circa 1910–1915.
Courtesy of Dan Sniffin.

The city of Dos Palos was incorporated in 1935. It owes its beginnings to a colony founded by Bernhard Marks in 1893. It can be easily reached from two major highways—Highway 33 through the west side of Fresno County and Highway 152 that goes from Highway 99 west over the Pacheco Pass to the coast. It has a population of five thousand people.

Downtown Dos Palos is small, but with lots of trees and a number of historic structures including one that was built by cattleman Henry Miller. The Dos Palos *Sun*, formerly the *Star*, the city's newspaper, puts out a weekly edition from its downtown office. Dos Palos High School and the local hospital also are located right in the heart of the city. There is a quiet charm to this community that, like so many of our valley towns, makes the visitor nostalgic for the quieter pace of life and friendliness that is often lost in the valley's bigger cities.

The surrounding countryside is filled with farms. Dairy farming is important here. Cotton, sugar beets, barley, melons, tomatoes, and alfalfa are important crops. Dos Palos is host to the only cotton festival on the West Coast. The area's heavy, black, adobe soil is, in the words of one resident, "The best soil in the world!"

To the west of the city are numerous duck clubs covering thousands of acres of marshlands. The Gable, one of the area's oldest and best known, has played host to such Hollywood stars as Bing Crosby, Phil Harris, Bud Abbot, and Lou Costello. The duck-hunting season begins the third week in October and lasts until mid-January. Enthusiasts from all over the state come here to enjoy this sport.

Like other valley communities, Dos Palos has its own unique history and has played its part in the tales of our valley.

The Bank of Dos
Palos was housed in
this building. It was
built by cattleman
Henry Miller.
*Courtesy of Dan
Sniffin.*

B ernhard Marks, who is called the "Father of the Colony System," was born in Germany in 1833. He came to America with his parents when he was two and a half years old and settled in New York City. When he was nineteen, he came west and headed for the minefields in El Dorado County, eventually acquiring interests in several mines including the one called the New York Tunnel. This mine later became involved in litigation that dragged on for a number of years.

Marks married the niece of one his partners in the mine venture, Cornelia Barlow, and decided to go to San Francisco. After scoring second in a competitive examination, he was given a job as principal of a grammar school. During his years in education, he was a member of the state board of examiners. He was given the first "Life Diploma" ever issued in California.

As much as he enjoyed education, Marks' lifelong desire was to be a farmer. He purchased a 1,400-acre grain ranch near Stockton, but it was not a successful venture. Then one evening, in 1875, he attended a meeting and heard professor W. A. Sanders talk about the agricultural potential of Fresno County. As Sanders discussed water rights and available land, an idea occurred to Marks. Why not join with other investors to buy a large parcel of land and water rights, divide the land into small parcels and sell each parcel with a guarantee of water for farming? He met with William Chapman, one of Fresno County's largest landowners. The result was a partnership with William Chapman and William H. Martin in developing the Central California Colony, southwest of Fresno, that became a successful venture in 1877. His next undertaking was to develop the West Park Colony with Moses J. Church. He also founded several smaller colonies in Merced and Kern counties. His final colony development project was the Dos Palos Colony. In this venture his partner was his son, Frank.

Bernhard Marks' valuable legacy to Central California was his successful colony schemes that played an important role in the development of agriculture in our part of California.

The Streets of Downtown Fresno

The new town of Fresno Station was first drawn on a map by the staff of the Central Pacific Railroad in 1872. The main streets ran parallel to the railroad track and were given names of letters...A, B, C and so forth. The cross streets that ran east and west were named for California counties. Hence, we have going south from Divisadero...Amador, San Joaquin, Calaveras, Stanislaus, Tuolumne, Merced, Fresno, Mariposa, Tulare, Kern, Inyo, Mono, and Ventura.

When California became a state in 1850, General Mariano G. Vallejo chose the names of the new California counties. Kern County, named for the Kern River that was named by John C. Fremont to honor his topographer, is the only county with an English name. The rest are Spanish or Indian.

In 1805, Spanish Lieutenant Gabriel Moraga, who was conducting an exploration of our interior valley to see if it would be a good place to build a permanent settlement, discovered and named four of the rivers that would eventually give their names to California counties: the Kings, named for the Holy Kings who brought gifts to the Christ child; the Calaveras—the Spanish word for skulls—was the name given to a river that was lined with skulls left from an Indian battle; the Merced, named for *Nuestra Senora de la Merced*, Our Lady of Mercy; and the San Joaquin, named for Moraga's father and also for the father of the Virgin Mary. Moraga gave the name Mariposa to the great inland valley because, when he first saw it, swarms of yellow butterflies or, in Spanish, *mariposas,* greeted him.

Amador was the name of Spaniard Jose Maria Amador's camp in the gold country. The village that grew around it took his name. Tulare is derived from the Spanish *tule*, a bulrush, and *tular*, the place where tules grow. Ventura takes its name from San Buenaventura Mission, founded in 1782, on the site of the present-day city of Ventura.

The remaining county names all are Indian words or derivatives. Inyo means the dwelling place of a great spirit. Mono is one of the linguistic classifications of California Indians; it is also a popular name given to the Indian tribes living east of the Yokuts.

A battle between Mexicans and a band of Indians led by a mission-educated Indian named Estanislao—most likely named for a Polish saint—occurred near a river that was later called the *Rio Estanislao* and then the Stanislaus River. Tuolumne, originally spelled *Tualumne* in the journal of the first California State Senate, is an Indian word that means a cluster of stone wigwams. It is also the name of an Indian tribe that lived on the banks of the Stanislaus River. It was a branch of the central Miwok.

At the point where Ventura Avenue curves in West Fresno it becomes California Avenue. The Spanish *conquistadores*, possibly Cortez, gave the name California to the land that would become our state. It was the name of an imaginary earthly paradise in a Spanish romance written in 1510.

In 1940, a new park was opened in the mountains east of Fresno. It was named Kings Canyon National Park because it contained the headwaters of the Kings River, which flowed through the park. In 1953, the street that carried travelers to the park was named Kings Canyon Road. Thus, the name of the park and the name of the street are rooted in that day almost two hundred years ago—January 6, 1805—when Lieutenant Gabriel Moraga knelt on the banks of a newly discovered river and named it *El Rio de Los Santos Reyes*, the River of the Holy Kings.

Just over the border of northwestern Fresno County is a small town with a heart full of community pride. One reason is its high school football team—a team that has made valley history.

Dos Palos High School's Frankian Field Hume Stadium has long been the setting for rough-and-tumble football games that draw scores of spectators to the bleachers each week. The whole town turns out to support the Broncos as they continue a tradition that began in 1923. Since then, the Broncos have won forty-two Central Section Titles in Division 4 and thirteen Valley Championships, including winning the Valley Championship title for the last four years. They consistently rank in the top ten in Division 4 in the state. Not bad for a small town team.

Mike Sparks, the Broncos' head football coach for the last thirteen years, has an enviable record of 130–27-1, with four Valley Championships, thirteen North Sequoia League Titles and two No. 1 State Rankings. Since 1923, the Broncos' overall record is 523 wins, 169 losses and 22 tie games.

The success of the Broncos is due not only to good coaching, but to talented and committed players. Certain names are always mentioned when Bronco history is discussed. Earl Austin, who graduated from Dos Palos High in 1969, is usually remembered as the Broncos' greatest running back. His agility, power, and speed are legendary. It was said that he could run over and around the other players, leaving everyone else in his wake. Other celebrated Bronco running backs are Rodney Davis, Bill Sparks, Dalevon Smith, Dave Henderson, Kirk Jimmerson, Willy "The Bull" Lewis, Marque Davis, Juan Nunez, Donnie Antionette, and Dean Collins.

When autumn arrives, Frankian Field becomes the focus of a new Bronco season. Another group of fine athletes, good coaching staff, and rousing community support all work together again to create a winning combination—one of which all the Central Valley can be proud.

The 1936 Valley Championship Dos Palos Broncos football team. Front row (left to right): Ross Sniffin, "Bandy" Bandoni, Lester Mott, Grant Sniffin (over ball), Paul Miller, Hugh Bennett, and Homer Benes. Back row (left to right): coach Checkers Millette, "Bernie" Bernardi, Alex Ardando, Ben Durrer, Lynn Carter, Ed Koda, Don Sande, and John Caropreso. *Courtesy of Dan Sniffin.*

The Dry Road from Millerton

When the results of the election of March 23, 1874, were made public, it was the death knell for the town of Millerton. The decision was now final—Fresno Station would become the new seat of government for Fresno County. No longer would the courthouse at Millerton be the setting for the board of supervisors' meetings. A new courthouse would be built in Fresno. It would be situated in a newly landscaped park rather than next door to a raucous saloon as was the case in Millerton.

Although the last supervisors' meeting at Millerton wouldn't be held until October, by summer most of the residents of Millerton had moved to Fresno. The town was beginning to look empty. Millertonian Bill Wyatt came down to Fresno for a short visit early in July. He had a conversation with a reporter for the *Fresno Expositor* that shed some light on how the locals spent their time.

According to Wyatt, on the day before his arrival in Fresno, William Faymonville, Sam Brown, Dr. Lewis Leach, J. Scott Ashman, Steve Boatwell, Gus Witthouse and Jerry McCarthy were sitting together discussing the finer points of a red wagon that had arrived in Millerton the day before. Enhancing the discussion were several rounds of whiskey that added greatly to the merriment of all. At another saloon he found Henry Curry, Newt Murphy, and Jim McCardle visiting and engaging in libations all round. He paid a call on the village blacksmith, S. W. Henry, who was wrestling with a wagon wheel. His strenuous efforts were rewarded with a shot of whiskey. Wyatt counted seventy-five children sleeping in baby wagons parked on Millerton's main street without any adult supervision. It seemed that the few remaining Millertonians were either drinking or sleeping.

Wyatt had one more comment for the reporter. The road from Millerton was a very long one. Not a drop of either water or whiskey was available to the traveler along the route. A sad situation that was quickly forgotten once Fresno and her many saloons were reached.

This 1864 photo shows the Fresno County Courthouse at Millerton and Court House Exchange saloon next door. Saloons played an important role in the social and political life of both Millerton and Fresno.
Courtesy of Robert M. Wash.

One of Fresno's leading downtown churches was formally established on January 20, 1884. A small group of the faithful had been holding regular worship services at the White School, on the site of the present-day Veterans Memorial Auditorium, since 1882. This nucleus comprised the nine charter members of the First Presbyterian Church of Fresno. They elected A. W. Lyons, J. A. Ewing and J. L. Armstrong to serve as the elders of the first session, the governing body of the congregation.

On March 1, 1884, the Reverend Henry Budge arrived to serve the church until January 1, 1885, when the Reverend I. N. Hurd was installed as the first pastor. Services continued to be held in the White School, but, from time to time, they were also held at the Methodist Episcopal Church South and at Kutner, Nichols, Donahue, and Mission halls. In 1888, the congregation purchased a parcel of land at K (now Van Ness Avenue) and Merced streets for $1,200 in gold coin. Later that year a church building was completed that served the congregation until 1896, when a fire destroyed the building. The church was rebuilt several months later.

In 1904, the congregation sold their building and built a new, larger church to accommodate their growing congregation at a new site at M and Merced streets. In 1922, a new facility, Westminster Hall, was designed and built by Harry W. Shields. The new building not only had classroom space, but a sanctuary and kitchen and dining space in the huge basement. The dream of a proper church building would not be realized until the 1950s, when the present structure was built at the corner of M and Calaveras streets.

During the early 1960s, when many of Fresno's historic churches moved to newer neighborhoods, the members of the First Presbyterian Church made a commitment to remain a downtown church and to provide outreach to the inner city. A registered nurse, who is a church member, makes home visits in the neighborhood. In reinforcing their commitment, a number of church members have moved into the area's Lowell neighborhood. They have bought homes on the local historic register, thus also making a commitment to historic preservation.

The Sunday school classes of the First Presbyterian Church of Fresno stand outside Westminster Hall in the early 1950s. Before the present church structure was built, Westminster Hall was the site of the sanctuary, church offices, classrooms, and such memorable basement rooms as the Ivy Room and the Log Cabin. *Courtesy of Mary Helen McKay.*

In our tales of the valley, we have often spoken of Lieutenant Gabriel Moraga, but who was he and from where did he come?

Gabriel Moraga was born in 1767 at the presidio of Fronteras, Sonora, on the northern frontier of New Spain in present-day Mexico. His father and grandfather were both frontier officers. In 1776, his father, Jose Joaquin Moraga, was the second in command of De Anza's colonizing expedition into California. On September 17, 1776, Jose J. Moraga founded the San Francisco presidio and served as its first comandante.

As a young boy of fourteen, Gabriel Moraga came to California with his mother, Dona Maria Pilar de Leon, on the Rivera expedition. Two years later, he enlisted in the California army as military protector of the frontier. From 1783 to 1806, he was given a number of assignments including serving as a mission guard and the magistrate of the Pueblo of San Jose that had been founded by his father. In 1800, he led a party sent against the Indians in Monterey. The experience established his reputation as one of the most famous Indian fighters in California.

During this period he was given his first assignment to explore California's interior valley. In 1805, he discovered and named the Kings River and the San Joaquin River—a river that his father had seen many years before. From September 21 to November 2, 1806, he led the second expedition into the Central Valley. Fray Pedro Munoz accompanied him and acted as the diarist. A deeply religious man, Moraga was intent on converting as many of the Indians as he could. The diary notes the dialogues he and Munoz had with the Indians and logs the conversions of 141 souls during the trip.

In 1808, Gabriel Moraga led an expedition into the Sacramento Valley and, in the summer of 1812 made the first of three trips to Fort Ross to tell the Russian settlers that they were not wanted and were forbidden to enter Spanish ports.

Gabriel Moraga's first wife, Ana Maria Bernal, whom he married in 1784, died in 1802. He then married Maria Joaquinna Alvarado. Two of his sons, Jose and Domingo, became soldiers.

Another son, Vincente, became a schoolmaster. Moraga died in 1823 and was buried in the cemetery at the Santa Barbara Mission.

A tall, well-built, brave, gentlemanly man, Gabriel Moraga was renowned as the finest soldier in California, but it is for his contributions to the exploration of California's Central Valley that he will be remembered. For it is he who gave the Spanish names to the rivers of our area—names that have become part of the fabric of our valley.

Fresno's Police Department

On July 1, 2001, Fresno's Police Department celebrated its one hundredth birthday. It was a momentous event and, as on all such occasions, invites reflection on our history.

When the city of Fresno was incorporated in the fall of 1885, law enforcement was placed in the hands of an elected city marshal. The policemen who served under him were appointed by members of the board of trustees—the council which governed the city. This political spoils system invited the corruption that grew out of it. The police were undisciplined and owed their loyalty not to the marshal, but to the trustee who appointed them. The wide-open Dodge City flavor of the frontier town Fresno had been was not appropriate for the growing, cosmopolitan city of the 1890s. A better system of law enforcement was needed. It was one of the contributing factors that led the electorate to pass a new city charter in 1899. The charter laid out a new form of government including an appointed police chief who would head a properly run department. The year 1901, when the new slate of city officials was elected, marked the true beginning of the Fresno Police Department. City Marshal John D. Morgan, serving with a salary of $125 a month, was named the first chief of police.

After Morgan's retirement in 1905, his office was filled by John J. White, then R. M. DeVoe and William Shaw, who would serve as chief for five years. By 1914, horses were being replaced by cars. A cop on a motorcycle was assigned to enforce speed limits. In this year a motorized patrol wagon was purchased and a new position was established—the captain of detectives.

The ensuing years would see a long list of names at the head of the police department. The years of prohibition, the Depression, and two world wars would test the skill and resources of the police in many ways. During this time and beyond, the department continued to grow and keep pace while modernizing its law enforcement tools. Of all the men to hold the office of police chief, Henry R. Morton would have the longest tenure in office—from 1950 to 1972.

In 1951, the Fresno Police Academy was founded. In 1960, the department moved from the old City Hall on Broadway and

The Fresno City Police, standing at the foot of the steps of the Fresno County Courthouse, show off their new motor bikes from Wilson's Motorcycles in 1928.
Courtesy of Doug Wilson.

Merced Street to a brand-new building at M and Mariposa streets—a site that continues as its headquarters.

As the police department begins its second hundred years of service to the Fresno community it does so with 701 sworn police officers and a budget of $80.6 million—a far cry from 1903 when the police force consisted of twelve men and was run with a budget of $17,000.

October 11, 1907, was an interesting day at the Carnegie Library in downtown Fresno. It began in a normal way. When the doors first opened, those who wished to peruse the library's books entered in their usual way and proceeded to the stacks to select reading material or, perhaps, to do research for a school paper. Others found a place to sit and read. The almost palpable air of hushed solemnity that always pervaded the Carnegie was very much in place on this particular autumn morning.

All at once there was a clamor at the front door. Skates could be heard scrambling up the library's steps. This was followed by shrieks. All thoughts of leaving their skates at the door forgotten, several children burst through the door and skated into the building. Before the librarians could reach the door and admonish the young people, the door closed and another kind of clamoring began. Such a noise had never before rattled the dignity of the Carnegie, much less its door! It sounded like a herd of elephants was trying to get in. When the librarian reached the door, she pulled it open and looked right into the face of a very large Angora goat which was desperately trying to gain entrance. For a moment both the lady and the goat stood in shocked silence. Then the goat, showing great wisdom, turned and ran down the steps, heading in the general direction of the buildings across I (now Broadway) Street. It was first thought that he belonged to the members of the Odd Fellows Hall for use in their initiation rites, but he was later discovered to be a resident of the boarding house next door.

After the decorum of the Carnegie had been restored, a little boy walked up to the desk and asked the librarian for a copy of God's novels. After some reflection, she handed him a book of Bible stories. He happily went on his way. Yes, indeed, it had been quite a day for all of God's creatures at Fresno's Carnegie Library.

The Clothes Burglar

All was not well in the L and Inyo street neighborhood. It was autumn, 1907. The leaves were turning red and gold, the nights were crisp and cold, the chimneys were spewing smoke into the night sky, and somewhere in the heart of the city was a burglar with a singular obsession—stealing men's clothing.

In our twenty-first century lives, we throw our washed clothes into a dryer, but, in 1907, clothes were hung outside on a clothesline. One Fresno clothesline stretched across two backyards, and each of the housewives hung her wash on the line to dry. That evening, Mrs. F. Mahrone of 2225 Inyo Street was the first to pick up her wash basket and venture out to remove her husband's shirts and linens. She stood transfixed on the porch as she viewed the empty clothesline. Meanwhile, Mrs. A. Alexander, who lived next door, stepped out and saw her husband's shirts were gone. Mrs. J. W. Smith of 807 M Street went out to take in a Turkish couch cover—it, too, was gone. The police were called.

The burglar, not content with pilfering from clotheslines, decided to test his ability to break and enter. He chose the home of John Bartram as his test case. When the family returned from an outing, they found their home in a state of total disarray. When the police were called and an inventory taken, all that was missing was fifteen dollars in cash and all of the clothes of Mr. Bartram and his son. His wife's jewelry and clothing were still in their proper places. The intruder did, however, take a couple of the Bartrams' suitcases along with him—probably to carry the clothes.

The burglar's identity remained a mystery until a tenant of a rooming house nearby was seen a couple of days later boarding a northbound Santa Fe train with the Bartrams' suitcases—one in each hand. He made good his escape, leaving in his wake a number of disgruntled men who had to replenish their wardrobes and a neighborhood full of women who were terrified that he might return.

Shot in the Line of Duty

In the early morning hours of February 21, 1907, twenty-nine-year-old police officer Harry S. Van Meter was patrolling his beat walking south on I (now Broadway) toward Inyo Street. The air was cold; he was glad he had worn his heavy coat over his uniform. As he passed the Boss Dye Works he heard someone sawing and flashed his light around, but he couldn't see anything. He kept walking down I Street and caught up with G. H. Hart of the Fresno Transfer Company. Van Meter told Hart he had heard a suspicious noise and was going to go west on Inyo and into the alley between H and I streets to investigate. He turned into the alley just as a man wearing a white hat pulled down over his eyes came toward him. Van Meter called to the man to wait—thinking he would ask him if he had seen anyone suspicious behind the dye works. The man pulled a revolver from his pocket and fired it. Van Meter reached for his gun, but his heavy coat got in the way. As both men ran toward Inyo, the man in the white hat kept firing his gun. By the time Van Meter got his gun out and began firing at his assailant, he realized he had been hit. The man vanished into the dark night.

Richard McElroy, night watchman at the nearby Crescent Stables, heard the shots and rushed to Van Meter's side. He carried the wounded man into the stable's office and summoned Dr. Davidson and the police. They immediately arrived, applied first aid and took Van Meter by ambulance to the Burnett Sanitarium where he underwent surgery.

An examination of the back door of the Boss Dye Works showed a hole had been sawed next to the lock. Evidently, the burglar was scared away by the approach of Officer Van Meter. While the police searched for the culprit, the life of Van Meter hung in the balance.

While police officer Harry S. Van Meter was undergoing surgery for the serious bullet wounds he sustained while trying to question a possible burglary suspect, police questioned the witnesses to the crime. In so doing they were able to piece together what had occurred in the early morning hours of February 21, 1907. They also captured several suspects including Ernest C. Silvers, a box-maker from Kansas City, Missouri, who moved often from town to town.

At 9 a.m., the police brought Silvers and two other suspects to Van Meter's bedside. Silvers was wearing a white hat just like that of the man who shot Van Meter. Van Meter looked at the three men and then, pointing to Silvers, said without hesitation, "You are the man who shot me full of lead last night." Silvers became agitated. Van Meter repeated his statement. Silvers burst into tears and was led away.

By noon, Van Meter's life was beginning to ebb away. District Attorney Denver S. Church, bringing his official stenographer with him, arrived to take a formal statement from Van Meter. This accomplished, Church left. At 1:30 in the afternoon, with his father, wife, and small daughter at his bedside, Harry S. Van Meter died— the first officer of the Fresno Police Department to die in the line of duty.

On February 24, 1907, the citizens of Fresno witnessed one of the largest funerals in the city's history. After a private service in the family home, a public service was conducted by the Reverend Duncan Wallace in the Cumberland Presbyterian Church. A procession to the internment site in Mountain View Cemetery followed. The funeral cortege consisted of members of the police and fire departments and the Woodmen of the World. The outpouring of grief felt by Fresno's citizens was evident not only in their attendance, but also in the large number of floral tributes and donations to a fund to help his family. The community truly mourned the loss of this brave young man.

The suspect, Ernest Silvers, had an alibi that could not be disproved and was released. The case is still unsolved.

The Tempest over the Red-wheeled Rig

The year was 1907. Early that year, colorful, controversial, ever-cheerful Mayor W. Parker Lyon had enlisted the aid of a traveling evangelist to help him pass the bonds for a much-needed new sewer system for Fresno. Now it was October and it was up to George Hoxie, the city engineer, to implement the plans for the development of the sewer farm and septic tank project. To do this, he needed transportation from his home on Blackstone Avenue to the sewer farm in the country, a number of sites in between and to more far-flung cities in the state. Thereby hangs a tale.

Hoxie had a well-developed sense of humor. When the city rented him a red-wheeled buggy and a white horse, he called it his "white steamer." He termed the assignment his "skeptic tank project," and his trips to Sacramento, Los Angeles, and San Francisco seeking sewer pipes, his "hitting the pipe-line trips."

Unfortunately, one of the livery stable owners in the city did not in share Hoxie's laughter. W. O. White, the secretary of the Livery Keepers Association, was angry because the city rented Hoxie's rig from the association's chairman, R. S. Johnson, owner of the Excelsior Stables, for $2 a day. White, the proprietor of the Arcade Stables, had been charging the city $1.25 to $1.50 for a rig and was incensed when he learned the city had taken its business elsewhere. Hoxie's reply was that the Arcade's rig did not meet his specifications.

So angry was White that he quit his post as association secretary. He stormed into City Hall, announcing that rather than allow Johnson to make that $2 a day, he would furnish a rig for nothing. Hoxie said no, because it made the city look like it was accepting charity. The matter was taken to Mayor Lyon who agreed that charity was not going to be accepted at City Hall. Instead, the mayor ordered the city to purchase Johnson's red-wheeled rig at the price he paid for it. The tempest over the rig ended. The "skeptic" project was allowed to continue with Hoxie and his red-wheeled rig.

Another Hero Laid to Rest

The year 1907 saw three law enforcement officers in Fresno County killed in the line of duty. By an odd coincidence, the tragic death of one of these men took place on his thirty-second birthday and within six miles of the place of his birth.

On March 13, 1907, less than a month after the cold-blooded killing of Fresno police officer Harry S. Van Meter, Temperance Colony rancher J. W. Grayless and Deputy Sheriff Joseph D. Price, armed with a search warrant, headed into the foothills to find a woodcutter named James Richardson. Richardson was suspected of stealing a horse and buggy filled with groceries and a fur coat belonging to Grayless. Price located the buggy, but the horse and the buggy's contents were still missing. Price pulled his rig into the ranch of George Fanabee, Richardson's brother-in-law, near Squaw Valley. Not only was Richardson there, but the contents of the buggy were there also. Price arrested Richardson, who pulled out a revolver and began shooting. The bullets missed and, after a struggle, Richardson threw down the gun. Price tied his hands and made Richardson get in his buggy. Price got in, ordered the horses to start, and began the journey to Fresno with his prisoner. Grayless returned on horseback.

Richardson began complaining of hunger. Price stopped at Will Ockenden's store at Squaw Valley, purchased food and untied Richardson so he could eat on the journey. Several hours later, rancher John Rouse came upon the buggy at Dunnigan's Gap. It contained the body of Joseph Price. It was evident that a bloody stuggle had taken place. There was no sign of Richardson.

The sheriff was notified. The alarm went out. The suspect was thought to have fled to Oat Mountain. Five posses were formed. All the ranchers in the area were deputized. A massive manhunt tried to track down the killer. It was all in vain. Richardson was never found. The case was never solved.

The people of Fresno witnessed another tragic funeral for one of their own who was killed while trying to make their county a safer place. Deputy Sheriff Joseph D. Price's name was added to the ever-growing list of the true heroes of our valley.

Tragedy behind the Barton

In the wee hours of the morning of October 10, 1907, sixty-year-old night watchman Lucius C. Smith was walking his beat in downtown Fresno. He checked on things at the stables of the Grand Central Hotel at Mariposa and J (now Fulton Street) streets and then walked to the alley behind the Barton Opera House located on Fresno Street between J and K (now Van Ness Avenue) streets. As he turned into the alley, Smith saw a man exiting a transom window at the rear of the building. The man dropped to the ground. According to men who were working in the undertaking parlor across the alley, Smith called out to the man, many shots were fired and the sound of someone running echoed down the alleyway. The men ran outside to find Smith lying dead in a pool of blood. He was the third law enforcement officer killed on duty in an eight-month period. Once again, shock and grief filled people's hearts.

Lucius Smith was a familiar figure in Fresno. He was said to be the first uniformed officer and the first street car driver in the city's history. He was well liked by all who knew him. His faithful dog Jim, who walked his beat with him every night, was with him when the shooting took place. According to those present, after the shots were fired, Jim ran to the Central Hotel stables and back to his master's side, refusing to leave even after Smith's body was removed. The next evening he wandered Smith's beat over and over as though in search of his master.

By now, the police and sheriff's department began to wonder if the killer of Smith might not also be the killer of the other two men, Harry S. Van Meter and Joseph D. Price. An all-out effort was made to find the culprit or culprits, but all to no avail. The case, like the others, was never solved and remains a mystery in the tales of our valley.

Biola

Driving west from north Fresno on Shaw Avenue takes the traveler beyond the bustle of the city. A few vineyards and abandoned fig orchards dot the landscape. An oasis of lovely homes clusters around Garfield Avenue. A row of palm trees on the left seem to show that this is the end of any pretense of city and that we are now entering the country. The traveler sees an old farmhouse with its tank house at the back and a large expanse of sky as the flat horizon appears in the distance. After crossing Dickensen Avenue, the land is planted very heavily in vineyards. A water tank appears above a sea of trees to the southwest—the traveler's destination is reached. A turn south on Biola Avenue takes the traveler into the heart of Biola.

In 1912, the community of Biola was founded by William G. Kerckhoff, one of the owners of the San Joaquin Power Company, its name coming from the initial letters of the Bible Institute of Los Angeles. The Fresno Traction Company, now owned by the Southern Pacific Railroad, extended a branch line to the new town in the fall of 1913. It was in use until the 1960s, when, over public opposition, it was discontinued.

The Biola Grammar School District was formed in 1914. The first schoolhouse was a two-room brick building erected at a cost of $7,000. A new, larger school was built in 1922. Today, the Biola area is part of the Central Unified School District.

The business district of Biola is centered around G Street and Biola Avenue. Foster's Pool Hall, which was a popular gathering place, Busick & Stumpf's general store, First National Bank, post office, two barber shops, a library, a movie theater, Wood's Essex car dealership, Soderberg's hardware store, Woodman's Lodge, Diebert Brothers & Schneider packing house, C. S. Pierce Lumber Company, and a Sun-Maid packing house were all part of Biola's central district. Today, few buildings remain. The hardware store, which has been owned by the Belluomini family for many years, is still in operation and is the oldest building in town. The movie theater, built in 1947, is now a mission church. The Mariani Raisin Company, Salwasser Dehydrator, Actegro, a fertilizer manufacturer, Biola Recycling, and Sakatta Packing Company are located in and around Biola. One constant is the Biola Congregational Church on the northwest corner of F and Fifth streets. Built in 1921, the structure still houses an active congregation.

Today, as in 1912, agriculture is the main focus of life in Biola. The town is just a few miles west of Fresno, yet it seems far removed from the bustle of city life. Biola is a quiet place, tucked away among the vineyards and peach, almond, and apple orchards of northern Fresno County.

T he Biola area was settled by a number of German families from the Volga River region of Russia. Surnames like Bitter, Bier, Dauer, Horch, Huber, Meisner, Metzler, Nilmeier, Schneider, and Seibert are part of the fabric of the Biola community. Like most towns, events were held to bring people together. The Raisin Day parades, dances at John's Barn or Foster's Pool Hall, and May Day activities were looked forward to with great anticipation. They all paled by comparison to the most important event of all—a wedding.

The church was booked. The hall was reserved. The band was hired. Beef, hogs, and chickens were killed and prepared; potato salads, coleslaw, and sausage were made. This, alone, could take several days.

On Friday evening, the bride and groom and their parents met at the bride's home for the "Blessings from the house." The bride's father formally gave his permission for the bride to marry. Then they left for the church. When the bride came in view, the church bells began to chime. The bridal party proceeded into the church filled with friends and family and the wedding ceremony took place. After the religious ceremony, the bride and groom were showered with rice as they left the church.

The bride and groom came into the reception hall. As the couple walked around the room, people pinned money on their clothing. The band played polkas, waltzes, and fox trots. Everyone danced, drank beer, and ate from the huge buffet that was set up in an adjoining room. Whoever danced with the bridal couple pinned money on them. Sometime during the evening the newlyweds slipped away, but the reception went on all night. Children were bedded down on the chairs that lined the room. The merriment went on until coffee and kuchen were served Saturday morning. Then everyone went home to freshen up and by noon, they and the bride and groom had returned for another day and night of eating and dancing.

By Sunday morning, the festivities were beginning to come to an end. More coffee was served. About 9 a.m. bowls of steaming hot sauerkraut soup were served. This sobered everyone up and ended the wedding celebration. The three-day wedding was over, but it usually wasn't long until another one was held.

The church has long been the center of social life for the
German people. It was certainly true for the Germans who
lived in the Volga River colonies in Russia. The colonies were small
settlements without the means of communication that we enjoy
today. However, these settlements each had a church and everyone could hear the bells in the tower of that church whether in
their homes or in the fields working. Ringing the bells provided a
way for news to be communicated to everyone within hearing.

When the German settlers of Biola built the Biola Congregational Church, they purchased two bells that were hung in the
church belfry. The thirty-pound north bell swings back and forth
with the clapper free to strike the bell. The thirty-two-pound south
bell has ropes attached to the clapper and remains in place when
rung. The bells were used just as they had been in the old country,
to communicate with the entire village of Biola and the surrounding farms. Just as the bells of the Cross Church in Fresno's Roosian
Town let people know of a birth or death, so, too, did Biola's bells.

The church bells rang out when a bride was in sight and continued until she reached the church. They rang again at the con-
clusion of the wedding ceremony. The bells tolled when a funeral
procession came within sight of the church and continued until
the church was reached.

The small bell rang for thirty minutes to summon people to
worship before church services began; then both bells were rung
at the beginning of the service. At the end of the sermon, both
bells began to ring and continued ringing through the Lord's Prayer.
This was done to let whoever was at home know that the family
would soon be home for Sunday dinner.

On New Year's Eve, both bells were rung from 11:30 p.m.to
12:30 a.m. At one minute before midnight, the bells were silent
for one minute and then began to ring again at midnight.

How did the bells ring? The deacons of the church had this as
their task. Two deacons were needed and had to practice a great
deal to achieve the correct rhythm. The bells were high up in the
belfry and the deacons, standing on the first floor, used the bell's
ropes to ring them. Because they were not in the main sanctuary

and couldn't see the minister during the church service, a small peephole was drilled in the wall. Later, a foot button in the front pew was pressed that rang a doorbell on the first floor and provided the signal to start ringing.

The bells of Biola's Congregational Church were an important part of the community's life. According to the Reverend Edward Veldhuizen, minister of Biola's Congregational Church, the bells still ring on important occasions if the members of the family request it. Their sounds and messages provide a unique reminder of the lives of their ancestors so many years ago in the villages of the Volga region of Russia.

The Good Samaritans

As has often been written in the legends of our valley, life in the pioneer years of our Central Valley communities was often rather rough around the edges. Gold miners came from all over the world—usually without their wives and loved ones—and found freedom from the restraints of polite society. The loggers and some of the early ranchers who followed experienced the same freedom as they made a fresh start in a new land. Saloons and their related businesses flourished. Guns were carried openly. It was a world far different from the established society of the East and South. As women came in greater numbers to the West, they often took it upon themselves to bring moral values to the new towns that were beginning to grow. So it was in Fowler.

In the winter of 1888 and 1889, a few women who followed the teachings of Jesus Christ formed a group called the "King's Daughters." They met often and read the New Testament together, focusing on the life and works of Christ. There were many in need of help in their new community. They decided to try to put their beliefs into action. They changed their name to the Good Samaritans—a name that would include women who might not share their religious beliefs, but who would want to participate in good works. Their motto was, "Keep thy tongue from evil, and thy lips from speaking guile."

They began to work among the less fortunate people in Fowler. An invalid mother found help when these women came to her home, did her mending and sewing and tended to her personal comfort. A family of motherless children was the recipient of their kindness throughout the winter of 1889-1890. The Good Samaritans performed many acts of charity.

The women began to look at other needs in their community—especially how to combat the saloon element. Creating a public park and a library topped their list. They decided to disband, reach out to all the women of Fowler to join their cause and reorganize under another name. Their zeal and commitment led to the founding of the Fowler Improvement Association—a club that is now well over a hundred years old and still going strong.

The Ladies of the F.I.A.

On August 19, 1890, seventeen ladies gathered at the Fowler residence of Mrs. D. W. Parkhurst. This was not a social event; these ladies had a serious purpose in mind. Although it would be eighteen years before their small community achieved city status, their mission was to create a public park and to start a library—beautification and education were the order of business on this hot summer day.

They elected a temporary chairman—Mrs. Antoinette Harris, who had suggested the formation of a group to achieve their goals. She led the group as they began the formal process of organization. They elected officers. Mrs. Parkhurst was chosen to serve as president. A committee was appointed to draft a constitution and bylaws. The name of their group was to be the Fowler Improvement Association.

From that humble, but promising, beginning a group was formed that has more than lived up to its name. In the years since that first meeting, the ladies of the Fowler Improvement Association have created three parks, founded Fowler's library, planted the trees lining many of their city's streets, conducted a fly riddance campaign, assisted in establishing and developing the Fowler cemetery, helped establish Fowler's hospital, held medical clinics for preschool children, started kindergartens in the Fowler schools, spearheaded the hiring of a nurse in the local school, engaged in Red Cross work during World Wars I and II, published a cookbook, and have been involved in many benevolent projects for the less fortunate members of the Fowler community.

The Fowler Improvement Association is the second oldest federated woman's club in California. The members are still actively committed to the mission set out by their founders. Not content with reflecting on their past achievements, they continue to find ways to improve their community.

The family of Amos Harris gather for a photograph in 1900. Seated are Amos Harris and Antoinette Harris. The young girl in the front row is granddaughter Belle Harris Pendergrass. She had a gavel made from the wood of an orange tree that grew on the Harris' ranch and presented it to the Fowler Improvement Association. It is still used today.
Courtesy of Pauline Blayney.

A Craftsman Clubhouse in Fowler

As our traveler drives on Main Street through the city of Fowler, a right turn on South Fifth Street will bring him onto a tree-lined street of older homes. One structure, at 110 South Fifth Street, has the appearance of a home, but a sign out front lets the traveler know that this building has another purpose. It is the clubhouse of the Fowler Improvement Association.

The clubhouse was built in 1910 and is of Craftsman design. The exterior walls are covered with stained redwood shingles. The wide overhanging eaves of the roofline are typical of the period of the structure. The Craftsman details extend to the interior of the building. Solid mahogany doors, wide mahogany baseboards and moldings can be seen throughout the main meeting room, the adjacent coatroom and the reading room to the back. Built-in window seats on either side of the fireplace and in the coatroom evoke the Arts and Crafts era. A clinker brick fireplace is a dominant feature of the main room. It is said that Chinese workers made the bricks.

Typical of Craftsman design, the reading room has a large built-in sideboard. This room also can be accessed from the outside. Above the exterior door can be seen the original "Reading Room" sign that has been restored. The kitchen was enlarged several years ago so that it can now be used by groups who wish to hold luncheons and dinners here.

The Fowler Improvement Association Clubhouse is listed on the Fresno County Landmarks and Records Commission's register and, on January 29, 1991, was given California Historic Landmark status. Its importance to Fowler goes beyond its architecture. For almost a century, it has been home to an organization that has made, and continues to make, enormous contributions to the Fowler community.

Ida Weinberg (left) and Edna Giffin stand by the clinker brick fireplace in the Fowler Improvement Association clubhouse. Photo circa 1940. *Courtesy of Pauline Blayney.*

A Reading Room for Fowler

When the Fowler Improvement Association was organized on August 19, 1890, the members had two goals in mind—to create a park for their town and to erect a reading room within that park. Although both goals would be met, the reading room was started first.

At the club's second meeting, a letter was read from C. L. Walter offering the ladies the room below the Good Templars Hall, free of charge, as a temporary site for their reading room. This building, on Merced Street between Fifth and Sixth streets, is still standing. The offer was accepted. A library board of eight men, who each gave twenty dollars, and of five young men, who gave five dollars annually, was formed. The reading room opened on October 7, 1890. Some of the magazines and periodicals available were *Harper's Magazine, Youth's Companion, Atlantic Monthly, Ladies Home Journal, Century, Current Literature, Art Interchange, San Francisco Chronicle,* and *San Francisco Examiner.* Those who used the room paid a dollar fee annually. Many donated a larger amount. The F.I.A. members held all kinds of events to raise money to buy books for the reading room—they also staffed the room. On September 7, 1891, it was reported that the reading room had 175 books.

The ladies still dreamed of their own building. In February 1895, A. C. Palmer offered the members a building that had housed his chickens. After remodeling, it was moved to a new site and opened as the new reading room in June. The F.I.A. ladies continued to acquire books and, in 1906, joined the California State Library Association.

When the F.I.A. Clubhouse was completed in 1910, it had a room set aside for the reading room. This room was larger and more comfortable. In the same year, the Fresno County Free Library opened a depository library in the Lesher Drug Store. A few months later, it was moved to the F.I.A.'s reading room. In 1913, the Fowler Library, today located on Merced Street, became part of the Fresno County Free Library. The ladies of the Fowler Improvement Association had not only met their goal, they also had been responsible for the creation of a facility that continues to provide enrichment for the citizens of Fowler.

The Greening of Fowler

Those of us who live in this great Central Valley know the importance of trees. Not only do they help to keep the air cleaner, but they also provide shade during the hot summers and they beautify our environment.

The ladies of the Fowler Improvement Association were well aware of the benefits of landscaping. When their group was founded in 1890, their first goals were to create a city park and a library. By 1905, their library was well underway. It was time to tackle a park project. They contacted local businessmen who helped them obtain a lease for lots due north of the railroad station. Here, they planted fifty trees of many varieties including acacia, umbrella, pepper, and eucalyptus. Shrubs and grass completed the landscape. Since the town did not have a water system, a well was sunk and a tank and gas engine installed. In the same year, Fresno's Parlor Lecture Club was planting trees on what is now Golden State Boulevard. The F.I.A. women sponsored the trees that were planted through Fowler.

In 1928, the ladies began to promote the creation of a large park in the heart of the city. Enlisting the support of the Lions Club, they presented their proposal to the Fowler City Council. The council voted to call a special election to give the voters a chance to approve bonds for the project. The bonds passed, a park commission was put in place and tree planting began at a site in the heart of Fowler on Merced Street. The park became a reality.

Since then, the ladies also have planted a small park at the corner of Merced and Sixth streets. Their efforts to beautify their city continue.

Next time you visit Fowler, make it a point to spend some time in the shade of the large trees of Fowler's city park. The park's bandstand and gazebo add a touch of nostalgia evoking an earlier, less hurried time. It is a lovely, quiet spot and a tribute to the ladies of Fowler whose commitment to beauty has given an enduring legacy to their city.

Escape from Dalton Mountain

Our tales of the valley have told of the exploits of the infamous Dalton Gang. There is another tale to tell.

Grat Dalton was serving time in the Tulare County Jail in Visalia for a train robbery committed near present-day Earlimart. Someone smuggled hacksaw blades and a file into his cell. It was an easy matter to cut the bars. On the night of September 20, 1891, Grat escaped, stole a buggy and a team of horses and fled to the Hanford home of Joe Middleton. Middleton took him to a hideout on a mountain which today bears the name Dalton Mountain. It was there that Sheriff John Hensley and his posse spotted Dalton. Deputy Sheriff Ed McCardle and Dalton saw each other at the same moment and fired their guns. Both shots missed their targets. Dalton started running down the mountain ahead of the posse. Seeing Judson Elwood with his team of horses, Dalton pointed his gun at Elwood and ordered him to give him a horse. Elwood complied and Dalton rode off into the night.

It was pouring rain. By the time Dalton reached the Charles Owen Ranch where his brother Lit worked, he was feeling ill. He saw Charles Owen outside and got his attention. Owen gave him shelter in the attic of the house. Dalton developed pneumonia. Charles Owen's young son, Harvey Leroy, climbed the ladder to the attic twice a day to take Dalton food. Every time he knocked on the door, it would open and he would find himself looking down the barrel of a six-shooter. After a week he grew tired of this and complained to Carrie, his mother, who told her husband that Dalton would have to leave.

Charles Owen gave Grat Dalton a horse, a bridle, a saddle, and fifty dollars and told him to leave. Dalton headed for Merced and hid out at the home of W. W. Gray. After he was sufficiently recovered, he headed south and joined up with his brothers Emmett and Bob. They headed to their final confrontation with the law in an alley in Coffeyville, Kansas.

The sons of George W. Owen and their wives. Left to right: John and Jane, Richard Thomas and Amanda, George and Addie, and Charles and Carrie. Charles Owen allowed train robber Grat Dalton to take refuge in the attic of the family home. Carrie was the sister of Clovis Cole. *Courtesy of Byron and Nila Owen Eisner.*

Clovis Cole as a young man.
Courtesy of Byron and Nila Owen Eisner.

In 1873, Clovis Cole, who would later give his name to a valley city, left his home in Vevay, Indiana, to come west to Fresno County with his parents, Mr. and Mrs. Stephen H. Cole. His parents homesteaded a farm near the present-day Balfe Ranch. A few years later the family moved to Fresno. Stephen Cole became Fresno's mayor in 1891.

Clovis Cole went to work on William Heiskel's ranch north and east of present-day Clovis. At age sixteen, he bought a team of mules from Heiskel and started business as a teamster, hauling lumber down from the mountains. Then he homesteaded land on the valley floor and planted wheat. He continued to buy land, including a 480-acre parcel, for which he paid four dollars an acre, that would become the town site of Clovis. He continued buying land and planting wheat. To harvest the wheat, he and his uncle, Jacob Cole, purchased the first combined header and thresher in the district. By 1884, his wheat land comprised forty thousand acres stretching through Fresno and Madera counties. Clovis Cole was known by the sobriquet the "Wheat King of the Nation."

In 1886, the Cole family went into the real estate business forming the company of Cole, Chittenden & Cole. Clovis, his brother Orrel, and Jacob's son, Alvin, took over the ranching operations.

Clovis and Lizzie Cole in 1880 and their home.
Courtesy of Byron and Nila Owen Eisner.

When the Pollasky rail line was built through Clovis, Cole donated the land for the necessary right-of-way and the site for the depot. The depot was given the name Clovis. In 1891, Ingvart Teilman laid out a town site that also was given the name Clovis.

The year 1897-98 was a drought year—a disaster for farmers who depended on rain and runoff for irrigation. Clovis Cole's crop was a complete failure. He quit farming. His wife, Lizzie, started a hotel in Clovis. He opened a machinery repair shop for farmers, specializing in Holt combine harvester repair. His shop was on the northeast corner of the depot at Fourth Street and Clovis Avenue.

At the time of his death on November 14, 1939, Clovis Cole was living in Fresno. All of Fresno County mourned this quiet, soft-spoken man who had helped to write the history of our valley not only by his accomplishments in agriculture, but also by giving his name to one of its cities.

Catherine Morison Rehart

Harvesting wheat on the Clovis Cole ranch. Stephen Cole stands next to the wheel, Clovis Cole is standing next to the smoke stack, and Orrel Cole stands to the right by the steering wheel. Lizzie Cole stands in the background—third from the left.
Courtesy of Byron and Nila Owen Eisner.

Bert Cole & the Prehistoric Man

Not many people know that Clovis Cole had a younger half-brother named Bert. Bert Cole had, according to people who knew him, a Santa Claus physique and an uncanny ability to fix absolutely anything. According to his nephew, Harvey Owen, he was a born mechanic. Present him with an unusual item that needed repairing or with a job that needed a new kind of tool and he would analyze the situation and come up with a solution. A mechanical genius—that was Bert Cole.

Bert Cole, who lived at Manning and Elm avenues, had a rather unusual occupation. He was the owner of a traveling show that featured card tricks and magic. A talented ventriloquist, one of his acts featured two dummies, Dennis and Snow. With one of his sidekicks on each knee, he would entertain his audience. One of their local appearances was at a graduation night at the Manning Street Grammar School.

One day, Bert had an inspired idea. His sideshow needed a new feature to draw more people so he asked a friend to help him. They went into one of the local bordellos and found a man who had had more than one glass of cheap wine and enlisted him in their cause. They took him to Bert's farm and made a plaster of Paris cast of him. After it was set, they filled it with concrete. Using a razor to smooth over the rough edges, they had a "prehistoric man" for their sideshow. After it was finished, they realized the man's mustache didn't look very prehistoric, but hoped the public wouldn't notice.

There is an old Scots saying, "The best laid plans of mice and men don't always work out." Word of the prehistoric man leaked out. Bert was told the police were coming to investigate. The razor was hidden in the bottom of a trunk and the prehistoric man was taken out to Cantua in a two-horse wagon and duly buried. It stayed there until two farmers discovered it and created a sensation. Now the story of its genesis is told for the first time, here, in the legends of our valley.

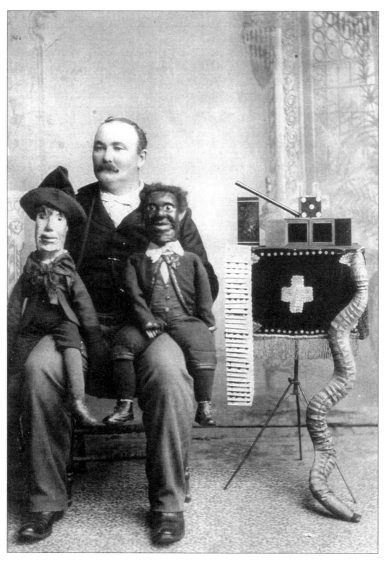

Bert Cole with his vaudeville sidekicks, Dennis and Snow.
Courtesy of Byron and Nila Owen Eisner.

George W. Owen

One of the early pioneers of Fresno County, George W. Owen, was born in Cincinnati, Ohio. As a young man, he worked on a river steamboat before following in his father's footsteps and becoming engaged in farming and stock raising. He married Miss Eleanor Long, also a native of Ohio. During the next few years, they moved a number of times, first to Illinois where he purchased a farm; then to Iowa in 1850; and, finally, to Nebraska.

In 1862, George Owen decided to bring his family, which now included several children, to California. The Owen family joined a hundred other families for the journey west, coming across the plains with wagons and ox-teams. They suffered all the hardships and experienced all the adventures that so many others had as they followed the trails that led to the West.

They arrived safely in Yolo County, where George began to farm and raise livestock. They soon moved to Sonoma County and began a dairy business. In 1868, the family located in Stanislaus County. It was not long before they traveled south again. This time George brought his family to Fresno County and there their long journey ended.

In 1876, George Owen took up government land near the foothills and began to raise livestock. He purchased additional parcels to add to his holdings. On November 27, 1880, he died. His wife, Eleanor, lived for another ten years. Their marriage was blessed with seven children—John, Margaret, Sara Jane, Eliza, Richard, George W., and Charles. The youngest son, Charles Owen, married Carrie Cole, Clovis Cole's sister. He and Clovis Cole were partners in dry wheat farming on land that includes the present-day city of Clovis.

George and Eleanor Owen founded a dynasty—one that has played an important role in the history of our valley.

The family of Richard Thomas Owen. Left to right: George Washington Owen, Mary Weaver Owen, Arminta Ellen, Richard Thomas Owen, and, in front, Sadie Lousie Owen. *Courtesy of Nila Owen Eisner.*

One of the pioneer ranchers of the Clovis area was Richard Thomas Owen. He was born in Freeport, Stephenson County, Illinois, on July 4, 1846. In 1862, he came to California with his parents, George W. and Eleanor Owen. The family settled in Yolo County.

On February 22, 1872, Richard married Mary Amanda Weaver, a native of Missouri, who had come to California with her parents a few years before. They engaged in stock raising and farming before coming to Fresno County in 1882, where Richard's parents had settled six years before. George Owen died in 1880, and Richard, as executor of his estate, had to settle his father's business affairs. During this time, he purchased a section of land that is now part of the city of Clovis.

Richard Owen's brother, Charles, married Carrie Cole, the sister of Clovis Cole. Charles and Clovis both were engaged in dry wheat farming. Charles also raised racehorses. Richard, an expert

A later family photograph shows (left to right) Mary Owen, George Owen, Sadie Owen, Arminta Owen, and, in front, Richard Owen. *Courtesy of Nila Owen Eisner.*

in this area, became his brother's partner in raising livestock and racehorses. A racetrack was part of the Charles Owen ranch at Minnewawa and Nees avenues. In the mid-1890s, one of their racehorses, Flush of Gold, held the mile world's record two years in succession. Richard Owen also grew wheat on his land—a type of farming he would pursue until 1902.

For twenty-five years, Richard Owen devoted his life to raising fine horses. His knowledge was sought after by breeders throughout California.

After the death of his brother Charles in a 1902 train accident, Richard retired. He lived to the grand age of eighty-one years, dying on February 26, 1928. His wife, Mary, had died just thirteen days earlier. They will be remembered for the role they played in laying the foundations of that part of Fresno County that is now the heart of the city of Clovis.

October and November are months that titillate the senses—a whole panoply of colors and autumnal smells bombard us at every turn. The harvest complete, the leaves of the vineyards and orchards wear new colors of red and gold—painted when the temperature dips during the colder fall nights. The wineries spew the remnants of the crush on the ground, filling the air with autumn's most distinctive fragrance. The dimming light of late afternoon only heightens our awareness of the approach of winter when the world of nature becomes quiet and bare. The gold and red leaves will fall and branches will stand stark and naked against the cold, gray winter sky. Soon, Mother Nature will wrap the valley in sporadic cloaks of all-encompassing tule fog, and eerie silence will envelop our lives.

It is in October that we commemorate Christopher Columbus' discovery of the New World. At month's end, mysterious creatures appear on the streets of Fresno. For those of a certain age, October in Fresno evokes memories of sycamore leaves falling on lawns and sidewalks, of the warm glow of piles of burning leaves as the wisps of smoke trailed upward to the very tops of the trees, of the smell of smoldering ashes that lay heavy on the air, and of the happy anticipation of the enchanted night when ghosts, goblins, and all manner of frightening creatures roamed their neighborhoods excitedly seeking treats in the light of the harvest moon. Magic and mystery continue to hold October's spotlight briefly and then are gone.

At November's end, thoughts turn to the celebration of the harvest and to the glorious holidays of winter. Next year October and November will return and, once again, the smells and sights of these most memorable months will stir our senses.

California-Fresno Oil Company

On October 29, 1901, the articles of incorporation of the California-Fresno Oil Company were adopted. Four days later, six men gathered in San Francisco for the purpose of forming the new company. William Spinks, J. J. Hart, W. C. Leavitt, E. N. Atwood, W. H. Sigourney, and C. C. Spinks were meeting as directors. Their first item of business was to elect Mr. William Spinks president of the company.

On March 10, 1903, August C. Ruschhaupt and Karl W. Ruschhaupt became directors in the company and served as president and treasurer, respectively. The company brought crude oil from the Coalinga area to Fresno on mule-drawn tank wagons. Oil was an important commodity in Fresno in the early years of the twentieth century. The California-Fresno Oil Company produced engine distillate to run irrigation pumps, provide residual fuel, and fuel oil to heat Fresno's homes.

In 1917, the topping plant burned down. The owners made a decision not to rebuild the plant, but, instead, to become distributors of gasoline and petroleum products. Road oiling became one important division of the business.

Over the years, quality products, dependability, and service have been the cornerstone of the Ruschhaupt family's business. Ownership is now in its fourth generation with Dolph "Bud" Ruschhaupt, Jr., at the helm. As his great-grandfather did a hundred years ago, Bud distributes petroleum products to both industry and agriculture throughout the San Joaquin Valley. California-Fresno Oil Company is also a major distributor of dust control products for agriculture and industry in the Western United States. A family business over a hundred years old and still going strong— a legendary achievement and source of pride not only for the Ruschhaupts, but also for our Central Valley community.

The Fresno Soap Company

In Germany, the Ruschhaupt family's business was soap making. In 1882, August C. Ruschhaupt came to New York and went to work for Fels-Naptha soap company. A few years later, he moved to Los Angeles and was hired by the Los Angeles Soap Company—eventually becoming superintendent. He heard that there was an opportunity to buy a soap company in Fresno. He sent for his brothers, Karl and Herman, to come to the United States. In 1890, August and Karl came to Fresno and purchased the Fresno Soap Company on F Street from Henry Lang. Herman invested in vineyard property in Dinuba. As the family added to its ranching properties, Herman managed them.

At the time the Ruschhaupt brothers bought the soap company, the staff consisted of five people. Fat and tallow, the white solid fat rendered from cattle and sheep, were the main ingredients used in soap making. At first these were obtained from various butcher shops. Later, the Ruschhaupts built their own reduction plant.

At a time when many housewives spent countless hours making their own soap because good soap had not been readily available, the soap made at the Fresno Soap Company filled a ready market. The company made toilet soaps, laundry soaps, and a washing powder, a true soap to which various chemicals were added, that sold under the name Valley Queen. One of their white soaps was called Solid Gold, but their main laundry soap, which was brown in color, was called Thanksgiving—a fitting title, indeed.

By the beginning of World War I, the company had doubled in size. The reduction plant also made glycerin—a property that was of vital use to the army. The Ruschhaupt brothers discontinued the Fresno Soap Company in 1922 so they could focus their time on the California-Fresno Oil Company that had been started in 1901.

One of the leading citizens of Clovis in the first half of the twentieth century was born in West Virginia on September 4, 1861. His father, John Burke, a native of Ireland, was descended from a distinguished family in that country. His mother, Nancy Calvert, was a direct descendent of Lord Baltimore for whom the city of Baltimore was named.

Young John E. Burke, their son, received his education in the East. He graduated from a coal-mining institute and served as a superintendent for several coal mines in West Virginia.

In 1914, Burke came west to California and purchased ranching property in the Clovis area. He married Alice Good. Their marriage was blessed by the birth of their son, Earl, and daughter, Ruth.

He was elected justice of the peace in 1922—a position to which he would be re-elected five times. He did not retire from the post until just seven months before his death on May 20, 1945.

Burke also operated a bicycle shop in Clovis and, during World War I, filled in for his son, who was serving in the Marine Corps, by taking over his rural mail route.

Burke's many contributions to the Clovis community included an appointment to the city council, serving seventeen years as city clerk and sitting on the board of the Clovis Union High School for eight years.

It is for his fairness as a judge that John E. Burke will be remembered. He was sensitive to the needs of those who were society's less fortunate citizens. He made sure that their rights were defended. Often thought of as the outstanding citizen of Clovis, Judge John E. Burke will long be remembered as a legendary figure in the history of our valley.

A Stage Stop in Centerville

The sun was well up in the sky by the time twenty-seven-year-old Clark Stevens left Fresno on a May morning in 1879. His four-horse team and stage were kicking up dust as the journey took him along the dirt road that led through eastern Fresno County. Although summer was still a few weeks away, it was already getting hot. He could feel the heat rising from the ground, but the air smelled good, so good, in fact, that it made him glad he and his brother, A. T., had left Michigan to begin a new life in the West. There was something about this valley that beckoned to him. He saw the mountains in the distance. Such majesty made him catch his breath. Pulling his hat slightly forward to block the sun, he urged the horses to move faster. He had only recently taken over the stage line from Fresno to Centerville from Jesse Morrow. On this morning he had six passengers who were scheduled to catch the stage that ran from Visalia to Stockton along the foothill route. It was up to him to deliver them to the stage station in Centerville.

Stevens thought about Centerville. It was a growing town. There were hotels, saloons, churches, a newspaper—even a drug store, but, since Fresno was named the county seat five years before, beating out Centerville's chances, he couldn't help but wonder about the town's future. He liked its setting along the Kings River near the mountains. At least now he had a reason to visit often. With this thought, he found himself slowing his horses. As he led his team and stage through the main street of town, in the distance he could see a wooden hotel building with a smaller brick structure next to it. He turned onto Oliver Street and pulled his team into the yard of the brick building. He had safely delivered his six passengers to the stage station. Here they could rest and find refreshment and lodgings until the north-south stage arrived. Stevens watered his horses and began to turn his thoughts to Fresno.

The small brick building that greeted Stevens and his passengers in 1879 still stands at 19 North Oliver Street in Centerville. The bricks, that were made locally, were placed so the walls of the structure are three tiers thick. It was built in 1871 for Mr. Caldwell and his family who owned the hotel next door, making it one of the oldest, if not the oldest, surviving residence in Fresno County. Listed in the Fresno County Landmark & Records Commission's inventory of historic buildings, the Caldwell Home has borne witness to one hundred thirty years of history in eastern Fresno County.

On August 2, 1825, William Temple Cole was born in Cooper County, Missouri. His remarkable family history began with his grandfather's arrival from France. After spending a few years in Virginia, his grandfather traveled with Daniel Boone into the Kentucky wilderness. Later, he followed Boone farther west into Missouri. His son, Samuel, became Boone's errand boy. After Boone's death, Samuel accompanied the widow and her family to a new location where a fort and a town named Boonesville were established. It was here that Samuel met and married Sally Briscoe. Their union would result in nine sons and five daughters. William Temple was the eldest.

There were few opportunities for an education on the frontier. Once, when he was not well enough to work, William attended school for three weeks. That was the extent of his formal education. He was eager to learn and began to acquire books and to educate himself.

Work on the frontier was hard. Cole developed a fine physique as well as tremendous strength and endurance. He could easily walk fifty miles in one day.

When gold was discovered in California, he headed west, arriving in San Francisco on August 10, 1849. He mined for a brief time, then entered the stock raising business. In 1860, he moved to Fresno County. His first farm was wiped out in a flood. He relocated on land one mile above the present site of Academy, eventually owning 680 acres of land on which he raised livestock. In 1854, he had married Jane Sweany. They had ten daughters who all married local boys. They are often called the "Grandmothers of Clovis" because so many Clovis families are descended from them.

William Temple Cole was a generous man whose acts of kindness were never forgotten by those who knew him. His greatest legacy to the area was his role as one of the founders of the Academy, the first secondary school in Fresno County. He served as a director of the school for many years. He saw to it that the children of the foothill country of Fresno County had the opportunity that had not been allowed him—to receive a good education.

Fiesta Days in Madera

Tuesday, September 24, 1901, saw the arrival of hordes of visitors to Madera. They came by train and by wagon, by horseback and on foot. By noon on that day, over two thousand people filled the streets of the city. Excitement filled the air—it was the first day of the much-touted, highly anticipated Madera Fiesta.

Yosemite Avenue was lined with fiesta-goers waiting anxiously for the parade to begin. Suddenly, trumpets could be heard in the distance. Drums set the cadence as the Raisin City Band began to make its way through Madera's downtown. Following close behind were the heroes of the day—Captain Ramos, a much renowned matador, and his two assistants, riding on horseback. Ramos was resplendent in a green suit covered with heavy gold braid. Over this he wore a velvet cape lined in deep red. His assistants were attired in red suits with black beaded braid. All three men wore black rimless hats. Their procession wound through the streets of Madera and ended at the Madera amphitheater where, in a couple of hours, the festivities would begin.

Promptly at three o'clock, members of the fiesta committee walked to the grandstand. The amphitheater was now filled to capacity. Captain Ramos and his two men entered the arena. A bugle sounded. A large bull was released into the arena. He circled around once and turned to face the men. The bullfight was about to begin!

Captain Ramos held out his red cape—the bull charged at him. Fearless, Ramos didn't flinch, but stepped neatly aside. Outraged, the bull charged again, this time running toward one of the assistants who, in his haste to flee, fell onto the ground. The bull barely missed him and was herded out of the ring. The first bullfight had ended. There would be many more to come in the days ahead.

A Bullfight in Madera

The final day of the great Madera Fiesta provided more than just bullfights—it provided a thrill or two and a very funny moment that was enjoyed by the crowd.

The fiesta began on Tuesday, September 24, 1901. By Saturday, September 28, the enthusiasm of the crowds who came to watch the daily bullfights had not diminished. In fact, the number of people filling the stands had swelled to twenty-five hundred people. The sheriff and his deputies were also in attendance. They were standing by to make sure that no blood would be spilled and the bulls would be allowed to return to their home at the Jefferson James Ranch not only intact, but also alive.

There was a moment of panic when the select few who were allowed into the enclosure between the bullring and the outer fence came face to face with one bull that broke into the small space. Speed records were set as men scrambled to safety. This accomplished, the matadors, with stately grace, came into the ring. The bull was released and circled the arena. He was a fighter and a true match for the men. After thirty minutes of charging and dodging by the bull and the men, the head matador, Captain Ramos, called for the banderillas. These were foot-long sticks covered in colored paper with a hook on one end to stick into the bull. The bull, with his head lowered, rushed Ramos. Into the bull's neck went the banderillas. The furious bull charged again.

At this point, one of the matadors, Francisco Patimo, spotted a beautiful lady sitting on an upper tier of the seats. Thinking he might flirt with her, he broke his banderilla in half and signaled to her that he would place the short half in the bull. The bull had other ideas. When Patimo bravely walked toward him, the bull suddenly turned and lunged at him. Patimo took off on a dead run—not stopping until he had scaled the fence of the arena. The laughter of the crowd only added to his humiliation.

About this time Captain Ramos unsheathed his sword to deliver the death blow to the bull. But, it was not to be. The sheriff stepped in and stopped the bullfight. And, thus ended the Madera Fiesta of 1901.

The Death of President McKinley

Two of the most traumatic days in the year 1901 were September 6 and 14. On September 6, President William McKinley was shot by an anarchist while greeting the public following the opening of the Pan-American Exposition in Buffalo, New York. The president underwent surgery and seemed to be recovering, but an infection set in and, on September 14, he died. The nation was plunged into mourning.

Fresnans were deeply shocked at the news of McKinley's death. Mayor L. O. Stephens immediately formed a committee to organize a memorial service for the slain president. The service would be held on the day set aside by California's governor, Henry T. Gage, for these observances. In his proclamation to the citizens of Fresno, Mayor Stephens paid tribute to William McKinley "as a man who was both great and good, and as one whose life was blameless, both in public and private. His name will go down in history as the successful head of a great and successful nation and as one who was loved and honored by his fellow man." Stephens ordered that, on the day of McKinley's funeral, all businesses and schools be closed; that all businesses and residences be draped in mourning; that all flags be lowered to half staff; and that all respect be shown for the solemnities of the day.

On the evening of September 15, a public meeting was held at the Barton Opera House during which the ministers of Fresno paid tribute to the slain president. A fifty-voice choir led by Don Pardee Riggs and accompanied by the Fresno Military Band sang sacred music. Each of the ministers either read scripture or spoke on some aspect of McKinley's life—in his home, his church, his country, the world, and in death. The Barton was filled to overflowing— many were turned away. The outpouring of grief among the citizens of Fresno was evident everywhere.

The Children of Fresno Mourn

An event occurred on the morning of September 19, 1901, that may be unique in the annals of Fresno history. In a service just for them, the schoolchildren of Fresno gathered beneath the trees of Courthouse Park to mourn the death of President William McKinley, who had died just five days before from an anarchist's bullet.

The children assembled in front of a speaker's stand that was draped in black and centered with a picture of the slain president. Their faces represented the richly textured fabric of cultures that is still Fresno's pride and strength. At ten o'clock, City Superintendent of Schools C. L. McLane, who presided over the service, nodded to the director of the Raisin City Band to begin playing "Nearer My God to Thee." McLane briefly addressed the children and then introduced Dr. Chester Rowell.

Dr. Rowell, addressing the children as his "little friends," explained to them in a loving, kindly way what had happened to their president. He told them about President McKinley's great love for children. He talked about how much President McKinley and his wife enjoyed watching the children who came every year to roll Easter eggs on the White House lawn. Rowell, using language they could understand, explained what an anarchist was. He concluded by saying, "The President that is dead was not the ruler, but your friend, the great father. We have laid to rest today one of the best, noblest, grandest of men."

Rowell's talk was followed by remarks by the Reverend Thomas Boyd of the First Presbyterian Church and a prayer given by the Reverend J. A. Batchelor of Saint Paul's Methodist Episcopal Church South. The children of Fresno stood and sang "America" and left Courthouse Park reverently and quietly with a greater understanding of their nation's grief.

A Memorable Day in Fresno's History

Around noon on September 19, 1901, the streets of Fresno quietly filled with people. All businesses were closed— even the saloons. No one could ever recall a day when that had happened, but no one wanted a drink—no one seemed to want to visit either. People were seen nodding to friends, perhaps exchanging a brief smile, but no one was in the mood to visit for this was the day that Fresnans were honoring their slain president, William McKinley.

At 2 p.m., a parade began on H Street. Two thousand men representing every fraternal order in the city, national guardsmen, veterans of the nation's wars overseas, veterans of the Civil War, Fresno's firemen and policemen, and two bands marched through downtown to Courthouse Park. There they joined the thousands of Fresnans who filled the park and overflowed out onto Van Ness Avenue and Fresno and Tulare streets. The memorial service began with Mayor L. O. Stephens presiding.

Mayor Stephens introduced Major Voorhees of the G.A.R., the veterans of the Grand Army of the Republic, who gave the first speech. Major Voorhees spoke of President William McKinley's service in the Union Army during the Civil War, but spoke even more eloquently of his trips to the South after the war and of his efforts to bring the country together. He remembered seeing McKinley at a veterans' encampment in Pacific Grove the previous May. His remarks were followed by the singing of the hymn, "Lead Kindly Light."

The major address was given by the Reverend J. J. N. Kenney, presiding elder of the Methodist Episcopal Church South. He told the silent crowd that there were two principles that guided McKinley's life—love of country and devotion to God. He spoke of the slain president's statesmanship and the legacy of service that he gave to his country.

The benediction was given by the Reverend L. M. Walters, a closing hymn was played, and the gathering dispersed, the people's sadness somewhat lifted.

Banking on Advertising

One of life's small pleasures can be an afternoon at the Fresno County Library's California History Room perusing back copies of early newspapers preserved on microfilm. It's rather like taking a trip back in time—stepping into another world almost—yet a world that played out its daily life on the very streets that we travel today. This is one trip that doesn't require tickets or suitcases, just a little bit of time.

The news stories are revealing, showing not only the events of the day, but also how people worked, what they thought, and how they lived. The advertisements are even more revealing, giving the reader glimpses into local businesses, early medicines, and fashion. One fascinating example of early advertisements is one that appeared regularly in the *Fresno Morning Republican* in 1901. It is a full column advertising local banking houses. Unlike the ads of today that promote the latest interest rate, these ads go to the very heart of these financial institutions and tell it all.

The Farmers' National Bank of Fresno's ad states that this institution has $150,000 in paid up capital and $52,000 in surplus and undivided profits. Adolph Kutner, president, and Alfred Kutner, vice president, of the bank are listed as well as Walter Shoemaker and Joseph M. Smith, cashier and assistant cashier, respectively. The ad further states that this bank buys and sells exchange on all the principal cities of the United States and Europe and has an "absolutely fire and burglar proof safe deposit vault."

The First National Bank of Fresno, with O. J. Woodward as president, advertised $100,000 in paid up capital and touted itself as "the oldest bank in Fresno." Thomas Patterson's Fresno National Bank had $200,000 in paid up capital and listed its directors. Louis Einstein's Bank of Central California had $200,000 in capital stock and advertised that they could not only handle general banking transactions, but they also "issue letters of credit and draw direct on over 1,000 correspondents in all the principal cities of the world."

For the Fresno bank patron of 1901, the bank's stories were clearly told in the pages of the paper right next to the ads for clothes and fine watches. For the reader of today, these ads are another slice of life from an era long gone.

A Scrumptious Banquet in Chinatown

West Fresno's colorful Chinatown was the setting for a spectacular dinner party on the evening of October 30, 1901. The host was one of Chinatown's leading businessmen, Quong Mow Lung, who was about to embark on an extended trip to China. The setting was an upstairs restaurant on the corner of Tulare Street and China Alley.

All the elite of Chinatown came, attired in rich silks and robes. The governmental elite of Fresno was there, too, but not as splendidly garbed. Mayor L. O. Stephens and Police Chief J. D. Morgan came with their families. Police Judge Cosgrave, Chinese businessman Wong On, Constable Puleston, Dante R. Prince, W. P. Thompson and a number of downtown businessmen also were in attendance.

The guests began to gather about 10 p.m. They were entertained by a group of Chinese musicians while they mingled and visited. About 11 p.m., the banquet was served. The Stephens and Morgan parties were honored by being seated with their host, Quong Mow Lung.

The first course of salads, relishes, and pickled eggs was set before the guests. This was followed by stewed duck with dressing, stewed chicken, abalone prepared with chicken, several kinds of stew, and a most special delicacy—birds' nests. A full array of desserts was presented next—stewed nuts, a variety of cakes and puddings, pineapple prepared in China, and, finally, almond soup. The mayor and police chief tried to use chopsticks, but, finally, returned to their knives and forks. Wines of all kinds were served and the party became merry, indeed.

The party ended after midnight. The Stephens-Morgan party thanked their host, and bid him a safe journey. The Cosgrave-Prince party was having such a good time they stayed a while longer, finally leaving laden with cigars and other gifts. A good time was had by all.

A Visit from Saint Nick

The first Christmas Eve of the twentieth century was as close to perfect as possible. The air was crisp and cold; the sky was clear, devoid of fog. No snow was on the ground to hamper Santa Claus' visit and the moonlight was so bright that his reindeer needed no help in finding their destinations.

Many of Fresno's children gathered in local churches for a series of parties and programs. Others hung their stockings with great care and went to bed early, hoping that Santa would remember how good they had been all year.

At the Methodist Episcopal Church on K Street (Van Ness), Santa ushered in the new century by arriving in a very modern automobile. The service had just ended when Santa made his appearance at the east end of the church. He came through the door into the auditorium, bearing gifts and giving a jolly laugh that brightened the faces of everyone.

Santa Claus appeared at Saint Paul's Methodist Church in a more traditional way. A stage set used for a cantata contained a fireplace, giving Santa a delightful way to greet the children gathered to see him. He distributed gifts and stayed to hear the songs and recitations they had planned.

At the Christian Church, Saint Nicholas appeared. The children went wild when they saw him, so happy were they that he come to visit. At the German Lutheran Church, Santa came as Das Christkind. He spoke in German and gave a gift to each of the seventy children present who then gathered around their Christmas tree to sing Christmas carols.

Santa didn't forget the children of the First Baptist and First Congregational churches. He went there, too. And when it was time for Santa Claus, in all his many guises, to go, he did so, leaving great joy in his wake. As his sleigh and reindeer flew through the clear moonlit sky of Fresno, his voice could be heard calling out, "A Merry Christmas to all and to all a good night."

Gambling Dens Are Struck a Blow

The city election of 1901 brought into office the first truly honest administration in Fresno's history. Elected on a platform of reform, Mayor L. O. Stephens was committed to making serious changes. He wanted Fresno to be perceived as a good place in which to raise a family rather than as a wide-open entertainment center for the Central Valley—a reality that businessmen had always supported. Although Stephens would not achieve all he wanted in his four-year term, he did make a good beginning. By autumn of 1901, he was on the attack as far as the gambling parlors were concerned.

On Monday, October 21, the board of trustees met to discuss a proposed gambling ordinance that would severely limit activities of this nature in the city. After much debate, a watered-down version of the original ordinance was passed with only one "no" vote. The new law, when signed by the mayor, would outlaw nickel slot machines, lotteries, poker games played for money, and all games of chance where money was involved. In addition, the trustees passed an ordinance to require all retail saloon owners to pay a business tax of $350 a year. This was a groundbreaking achievement.

As soon as the meeting adjourned, Mayor Stephens took out his pen and signed the new ordinances into law. He did it quietly. It was not until the next morning that Fresnans found out about the new laws.

The first step toward getting rid of the open gambling dens had been taken. Now it was up to the police to take the next step. The law had to be enforced. Was the police department up to the task? Whether they were or not, Fresnans knew that the next week would be an interesting one—most likely, one that people would talk about for a long, long time.

A Police Chief with a Mission

On Monday, October 21, 1901, Mayor L. O. Stephens signed into law an ordinance that outlawed most forms of gambling within the city limits of Fresno. News of the new law spread quickly through the grapevine of the saloons. By noon of the next day, most of the now illegal games were no longer running. However, a few diehards would not give up. In the saloons with back rooms a few poker games were still going on, but the players kept one eye on the door just in case it was necessary to hide the money. Some of the lotteries in Chinatown also had not shut down. But change was definitely in the air.

On the night of October 22, Police Chief J. D. Morgan personally saw to it that the new law was being upheld. He decided to pay a visit to each of the gambling establishments in downtown Fresno. Cigar stores, with gambling rooms in the back, were also on his target list. When he stepped through the door of Degen's Saloon at 1750 Mariposa Street, he saw that Tom Mitchell's poker table was draped in black with a suitably inscribed message. One by one he continued his trek through town. On Mariposa Street he stopped at Metzger's cigar store, L. J. Samuel's cigar store, Dave Bristow Saloon, Fresno Beer Hall, the Mug Saloon, and the Tivoli Saloon. I (Broadway) Street's businesses included E. F. Ball's cigar store, Gilt Edge Saloon, Bohemian Saloon, O.K. Saloon, and the Bowling Alley Saloon. At all these places, he let the owners know that all gaming must cease and that arrests would be made if the law was not upheld.

Then Morgan walked across the tracks to West Fresno. He stopped in the saloons and gave the order to stop the games. He was barred from entering the fan tan parlors by heavy, bolted doors. But he let the owners know his message. Next he visited the parlors where lotteries were held. As he moved from one storefront to the next, the lights of Chinatown went out—one by one.

It was a historic night for Fresno. Chief Morgan was a man with a mission. It was going to be an uphill battle, he knew, but one that he was determined to win.

In 1854, Joseph J. Stephens, like so many others, left Missouri and crossed the plains to seek his fortune in California. Two years later he returned to Missouri to marry Elizabeth Davis. In 1857, the couple made their way back to California and, after raising cattle near Madison for a while, established their home in Woodland, near Sacramento. Eight children were born to the couple. It is of one of these children that our story relates.

On May 31, 1859, Lewis Oliver Stephens was born in Woodland. He attended local schools and graduated from Woodland's Hesperian College. During the years he was growing up, he worked closely with his father on the family's farm. His true interest was in architecture, a course of study he pursued for two years. Then he managed a farm on his own. Finally, he entered the business world, working in a furniture and undertaking establishment. In 1886, Stephens married Bettie Bean in Missouri.

Stephens moved to Fresno in 1891 and became a partner with his brother-in-law, William A. Bean, in the undertaking business. The partnership lasted until Bean's retirement in 1919 when Stephens and his son, J. D. Stephens, took over the business, but kept the name Stephens & Bean intact.

Both W. A. Bean and L. O. Stephens served, at different times, as Fresno County coroner. In 1901, Stephens ran for mayor on the Democrat ticket. He won and served for four years as the first official mayor under the new city charter. He was elected as a reform candidate and signed into law a number of measures that took the first steps needed to move Fresno from a wide-open frontier town to a progressive modern city. He was defeated for re-election in 1905, but continued to serve his city through participation on the board of education and the police commission.

Lewis Oliver Stephens died in 1929. He will always be remembered as the first elected mayor to make Fresnans see a new, better vision for their city and to have the courage to try to make it a reality.

L. O. Stephens

Lewis Oliver Stephens, Fresno's first mayor to officially carry the title, was elected on a reform platform and led Fresno into the twentieth century. Inset: Mrs. Lewis Oliver Stephens, the former Bettie Bean.

A Rousing Gathering in Courthouse Park

An interesting group of people gathered beneath the shade trees of Courthouse Park on a very warm Monday evening in August 1901. It was reported that a band would soon be arriving. A platform was set up with a podium and chairs. Everything was in place for a public meeting.

A number of ladies found seats under trees. Farmers from the colonies around Fresno arrived, tired from a day of working under the hot summer sun. They chose to stand rather than sit down. Other people began to swell the ranks. In the distance, a band could be heard coming closer, ever closer as the drummer rapped off the cadence of a march. The band seemed to be parading through the city streets and, when it soon came into view, a procession of people could be seen behind it. The band and its accompanying marchers, local members of the Retail Clerks Union, came through the park until they reached the platform. The meeting could now begin.

The leaders of the Retail Clerks Union had appealed to the people of Fresno to attend this Courthouse Park meeting. They wanted to have a public discussion centered around their desire to close local stores on Sundays. A number of ministers wanted a chance to speak. W. H. Voorhees of the Federated Trades and Homer C. Katze of the Retail Clerks Union were also on the agenda.

After the band played a song, the Reverend George Fillian of the First Armenian Presbyterian Church offered a prayer. Tim Walton, chairman of the meeting, introduced the first of several speakers, the Reverend J. A. Batchelor. His speech and those that followed dealt with the need for each worker to have a day of rest. This request was not made for religious reasons, but for humanitarian reasons—they felt that each retail clerk should be entitled to one day of rest out of every seven. The logical day, each speaker said, should be Sunday.

The possibility of a boycott of stores who did not agree with their proposal was discussed. The assembled group unanimously adopted a resolution endorsing the request of the Retail Clerks Union for a Sunday closing of retail stores beginning August 18, 1901. Would storeowners agree? Only time would tell.

Will We Remember the Sabbath Day?

At a public meeting in Courthouse Park, on the evening of August 12, 1901, the Retail Clerks Union's proposed resolution requesting the closure of retail stores on Sundays, beginning August 18, was unanimously adopted. The next morning, a committee began canvassing all the businesses in Fresno—circulating the resolution and making personal contact with each business owner to explain their request for Sunday closure. It was an arduous task.

Now, three days later, a second meeting was held to announce the results of their outreach. They reported on which businesses supported their proposal and would agree to close on Sundays. They also announced that a few businesses steadfastly refused to close. A boycott against these retail stores was being considered. It was decided to ask members of the Council of Labor to personally contact each of the owners of these businesses.

The committee was pleased to discover that not only did most of the merchants support the idea of closing on Sunday, but also that a number of them had made the decision to close on Sunday at least fifteen years before and had never wavered from that course. All of the merchants from both these groups readily signed the agreement to close every Sunday beginning August 18. Only three Fresno businesses remained adamant in their refusal to close their doors on Sunday—I. Kinspel's I.X.L. store, H. P. Prettyman's Ideal Clothing Store, and Arkalian Bros. Cyclery.

On Sunday, August 18, 1901, Fresno's retail businesses closed. Since almost everyone complied with this decision, it was found that no one's business suffered as a result. It was a state of affairs that would remain in place until the mid-twentieth century, when the matter surfaced again. This time, Sunday was no longer viewed as a day of rest. The stores opened once again and Sunday shopping became a necessity of life in Fresno.

A Labor Day Parade 1901 Style

September 4, 1901, dawned brightly. The warm sun of late summer was up early to greet the trains bringing celebrants from all over the valley. They were converging on Fresno in happy anticipation of a most interesting celebration in Courthouse Park. Varicolored streamers had been draped on light standards, businesses were decorated appropriately, and Old Glory was flying from every flagpole. Thousands lined the streets, and businesses were going to close between 10 a.m. and 3 p.m. It almost seemed like the Fourth of July, but it wasn't. It was Labor Day—the first one of the twentieth century.

The first order of the day was a parade. Leading the parade was the police chief himself, J. D. Morgan, resplendent in his new double-breasted uniform with brass buttons and a gold trimmed fedora. He led the cordon of mounted policemen who looked most impressive in their official garb. Next came Grand Marshal W. H. Voorhees, resplendent in his blue uniform, yellow sash, and white-plumed hat. A military band ushered in several groups of labor unions. The printer's devils distinguished themselves by dressing in red costumes with horns.

The second division came from Bakersfield and was led off by the band from Oil City. Not only members of the unions were represented, but also many of the union officials who made the trip marched with them.

At 10:30, the Raisin City Band led off the third division. As they stepped onto K (Van Ness) Street, the members of the Retail Clerks Union, the Boot and Shoe Workers' Union, the butchers, and the plasterers readied themselves for the line of march.

The parade ended with a float depicting a restaurant, manned by members of the cooks and waitresses union, and a float representing the Hod Carriers and Mortar Mixers' Union. The parade stretched for more than a quarter of a mile and was one of the largest that Fresno had ever seen. A good time was had by all.

Labor Day Orations, 1901

After the lengthy Labor Day parade through downtown Fresno on September 4, 1901, ended, the public was invited to Courthouse Park, where an afternoon of speeches and music awaited. The day was a warm one and, after marching for so long, many of the parade's participants decided food was more important than Labor Day orations. It was noon and downtown Fresno had a goodly share of fine restaurants—an altogether winning combination.

As a result, the gathering in Courthouse Park was rather small. That did not deter those in charge from forging ahead with their program. After an overture rendered by the band, F. S. Clark, president of the Labor Federation, walked to the podium. After a few words of welcome, he introduced the Reverend A. P. Brown of the First Baptist Church, who gave the invocation. As he concluded his prayer, a fire alarm sounded. This proved irresistible to a large majority of the audience who, as soon as the "Amen" was spoken, were on their feet and running to see the fire. It was quickly decided to adjourn the meeting and to invite everyone to return at 2:30.

At the appointed hour, the park began to fill with a large crowd that was well fed and tired after the excitement of watching the fire. Chairman of the day Homer C. Katze was introduced. His mercifully short address spoke of the history of the work force in this country and the strides that had been made to secure better hours and pay. A poem followed, delivered by the poet himself, G. V. Martin. His Byronesque appearance lent an aspect of romance to the afternoon's festivities and was very much appreciated by the ladies in the audience. Entitled, "The Hand of Toil," his verse lauded the working man.

The major address of the afternoon was delivered by E. J. Emmons. His oration centered on the history of the labor movement in the United States and the legislation that had been passed by Congress. After the closing benediction by Reverend J. A. Batchelor, the gathering dispersed. It had been long day, but a memorable one in the tales of our valley.

Summer Tidbits from 1901

The summer of 1901 was extremely hot. Weatherman J. P. Bolton reported that the average daily temperature from July 17 to August 15 was 104 degrees. No one had air-conditioning, but many had electricity. Electric fans were a great boon to homes and offices. A hundred years later, fans enjoyed renewed popularity—not because they were a new item, but because they became a matter of economy. Many Fresnans spent the summer of 2001 just like their counterparts of a hundred years earlier—sitting in front of a fan with a tall glass of something cold—just trying to get through one more sweltering day.

The ads in the *Fresno Morning Republican* on August 17, 1901, must have drawn a number of customers. The German House was serving cold beer in large mugs. The Fresno Beer Hall was not only serving cold beer, but also pigs' feet, tamales, and all kinds of sandwiches. Ackerman's Beer Garden, which the ad stressed was just 3½ inches inside Fresno's city limits, called itself a "First Class Family Establishment" and touted the fact that it was right next to the Fresno Brewery. Obviously their cold beer did not have far to travel.

Mr. Bolton, in his weather report, cited the peculiar charm of the Fresno climate as the reason that there had been no casualties within the city during the thirty-day hot spell. The human beings seemed to be doing all right, but the animals were having problems.

T. C. White's horse had been left untied on I (now Broadway) Street. Whether it was the heat or something else, the horse decided to run home. In doing so, he ran into a rig containing two young girls. The rig stayed upright, but the girl who was driving it was tossed from the rig. She had lots of spunk and was not about to let go of the reins. She got under the rig and held on tight. She got her horse under control just as some onlookers rushed up to help. White's horse arrived home safe and sound. It was all part of summer in Fresno a hundred years ago.

Two-headed Miss Millie

The pages of the *Fresno Morning Republican* contained not only news, editorials, sports, and advertisements, but also theatrical reviews and listings of upcoming concerts and plays. However, the reader who opened the paper on the morning of January 17, 1880, was probably amazed to see a huge ad for an event that was to be held on January 20 at Magnolia Hall.

The ad, which was four columns wide and stretched from the top to the bottom of the page, carried the headline, "WONDERS OF THE UNIVERSE!!!" For one matinee and one evening performance on January 20, the citizens of Fresno were offered the unique opportunity to see "Miss Millie Christine, the renowned Two-Headed Nightingale." Touted as a human marvel who is the eighth wonder of the world—following the pyramids of Egypt, the walls and hanging gardens of Babylon, the mausoleum erected by Artemesia, the temple of Diana at Ephesus, the colossus of Rhodes, the statute of Jupiter Olympus, and the Pharos, or watch tower of Alexandria—Miss Millie Christine was reputed to be unlike all the other women who had ever lived.

It seems that Miss Millie had two perfect heads and shoulders, but only one body. She had four legs and feet and could walk, dance, or skate on either two or four feet—whichever she preferred. She could speak all languages and converse with two different people at the same time in different languages. Blessed with musical ability, Miss Millie could sing beautifully—one head had a contralto voice; the other was a soprano. It is probably safe to assume that Miss Millie could literally talk to herself and sing duets with herself, too.

This enlightening, if hardly intellectually stimulating, program was offered to the public for the admission fee of fifty cents. Children's tickets cost twenty-five cents. In 1880, this was a hefty price, indeed, even to see the eighth wonder of the world!

Miss Millie Christine as she appeared in the *Fresno Morning Republican* on January 17, 1880.

The Very Reverend James M. Malloch, dean of Saint James' Cathedral, celebrates the Holy Eucharist before the historic cathedral altar.
Author's collection.

The congregation of Saint James' Episcopal Cathedral has a long history in Fresno County. The first Episcopal mission in Fresno was founded by the Reverend William Ingraham Kip in 1874. It faded away, but, in 1879, another mission was founded by the Reverend D. O. Kelley. It was from this mission that Saint James' Episcopal Cathedral eventually developed.

The church met in several locations during those first few years—in the law offices of Walter D. Tupper, then in a room at the Magnolia Saloon, and, finally, in a school. In 1881, a church was completed at the corner of N and Fresno streets. The structure included a parsonage next door. By 1900, a larger building was needed. Architect B. G. McDougall, a member of the church's vestry, was hired to design the new structure.

McDougall envisioned the new church as a simple one, of Tudor-Gothic design. He planned the building to conform to the ritualistic form of the Episcopal service. The entrance was to face N Street and was to be capped by a tower. The baptismal font would be situated in an octagonal bay immediately adjacent to the door, symbolizing baptism as the beginning of Christian life. McDougall chose quiet colors of amber and brown. He pointed out that Episcopalians prefer the interior of their churches to be somewhat dim so there is a feeling of repose when one enters.

Saint' James Cathedral was consecrated on October 27, 1901, and served its congregation until the church moved north in 1960. The old building was torn down and is now the site of the Fresno Chamber of Commerce. Today, Saint James' Cathedral is located on the northwest corner of Dakota and Cedar avenues. When the congregation moved north, two important features of the old church moved with them—the historic altar and pulpit. They remain an integral part of the worship service.

In the late 1990s, another structure was built on the cathedral grounds. At ground-breaking ceremonies in 1997, the Right Reverend Robert Mize, retired bishop of Damaraland (Namibia) and founder of Saint Francis Homes for Boys, declared that this house of prayer would be "dedicated to the glory of God and in honor of the Holy Innocents of Bethlehem." The Chapel of the Holy Innocents was dedicated on May 3, 1998. Two stained glass windows from the 1901 cathedral, in storage since 1960, were restored and installed in the new chapel, providing another important link to the past. The chapel also includes a columbarium that is available to families who have suffered the death of a child, especially by violent means.

Smallpox Comes to Fresno

There is a disease that is rarely spoken of today—one that was dreaded not only because of the illness, but because of the disfigurement often left in its wake. The disease is smallpox. It was, during medieval times, called "the pox." It reached epidemic proportions and was greatly feared. No less a personage than Queen Elizabeth I was said to have fallen prey to its onslaught.

In 1977, the disease was declared eradicated. Now its virus is said to exist only in research laboratories. For most of us, smallpox belongs to a much earlier place in our history. It may be surprising to know that in August 1901 several residents of Fresno contracted the disease and the local health board was forced to take some serious actions.

On August 8, 1901, city and county officials met in the meeting room of the board of supervisors to discuss how an outbreak of smallpox in Fresno could be contained. The meeting was heated because some of the officials were more concerned about who was going to foot the bill than about how to keep the illness from spreading. Dr. Russell, the city health officer, reported that fifteen people in the city were ill with the disease. Most of them lived in west Fresno, but their houses were not close to each other and there was great concern that the disease might become an epidemic. Dr. Russell felt it was imperative to set up some kind of quarantine. Most of the county supervisors and city trustees agreed. Mayor L. O. Stephens felt that the county was as obligated to take care of the ill people within the city as it was those outside of the city. He proposed sending the ill to the county's pesthouse—a place where the ill could be isolated and allowed to recover. The supervisors disagreed. Dr. George Hare, of the health board, proposed setting up a pesthouse within the city. After much discussion the matter was tabled until the following day when the committee met again.

On August 9, 1901, it was decided that the city residents with smallpox would be housed at the county's pesthouse until they recovered. Meanwhile, their homes would be papered to make them airproof and then disinfected with sulphur. That evening the patients were moved and the process of disinfecting began. For now, the scourge had been dealt a blow and, hopefully, eradicated for a long, long time.

Boston seemed a long way from Fresno County in 1901, but for those locals interested in horses and harness-racing, their hearts and minds were definitely in Boston on September 20 of that year. For on that day a race was taking place that matched the blue-blooded horses of the harness racing world with a horse that was born and bred in Fresno County—a ten-year-old chestnut named Toggles.

Toggles was bred at the Fresno County stock-farm of Ed Erlanger. The sire was Strathway; the dam was Fly—both well-known horses locally. Toggles was trained for the trotting track. He became a part of local races and gained some notoriety for his ability to perform extremely well. As his fame increased, he was groomed to be part of the harness-racing circuit.

Toggles' owner Ed Erlander asked Charles E. Clark to take the horse to Los Angeles to sell him. Graham Babcock of Coronado and Joe Chanslor, an oil man, both wanted to buy him. They couldn't come to an agreement about who would become his owner and agreed to let a pair of dice decide Toggles' fate. The dice were thrown and Babcock was the winner. Not long after this Babcock was offered five thousand dollars for Toggles, but turned the offer down.

Babcock began to race Toggles on the national circuit. The horse started winning and gaining nationwide attention. Then came September 20 and the national championship race in Boston. All eyes were on Toggles—would he be able to pull this one off?

Toggles lost the first heat, but easily won the second, third, and fourth. Then came the grand moment everyone had been waiting for—the race for the championship. The gun went off. The horses with their drivers started down the track, but Toggles easily outdistanced them all. Toggles, the horse from Fresno, leaving the bluest of blue blood horses behind, won the ten thousand dollar 2.10 trotting stake—the national harness-racing event, moving the *Chicago Horseman*, one of the great authorities on trotting horses, to pronounce Toggles, the pride of Fresno, the greatest of the 2.10 trotters.

Toggles and his driver prepare for a harness-race in 1901.
Courtesy of Mary Helen McKay.

Many local historians have contibuted to our stories of the Valley. One of them was born in Brooklyn, Iowa, on August 8, 1878. His family moved west to San Jose, California, in 1887, and to Fresno in 1891. He later went to Fresno High School and served as editor of the school's newspaper. He was asked to cover a speech for the *Fresno Morning Republican*. His story so impressed the newspaper's editor, Chester Harvey Rowell, that when our young man graduated from Fresno High in 1899, Rowell offered him a job as a reporter. He served as a member of the editorial staff from 1899 to1932. In 1902, he took a four-year hiatus to attend the University of California at Berkeley, graduating with a bachelor of letters degree in history and earning a Phi Beta Kappa key. When he returned to the newspaper, he became a protégé of Rowell's who named him city editor and, in 1920, the managing editor of the *Republican*. After the newspaper was sold to the *Fresno Bee*, in 1932, he returned to UC Berkeley where he completed a MA degree in history. In 1933, he joined the faculty of Fresno State College as a lecturer in political science and history. One of the classes he taught was Fresno County history.

He was a founding member of the Fresno County Historical Society in 1919 and served as its president for many years. He also wrote the *Fresno County Bluebook* in 1941, the *Fresno Community Book* in 1946, and a pamphlet titled, "1872-1885, A Municipality in the Making." He also edited several local history books and participated in numerous community organizations.

Of all the contributions Ben Randal Walker made to the study of the history of Fresno County, none was more far-reaching than his clipping file. In 1906, Walker started cutting articles from the newspaper and attaching them to file cards. He continued this practice until 1952. The massive collection forms the backbone of the Fresno City and County Historical Society archives. It is an incredible resource that continues to be used by researchers in many fields and represents a great legacy Walker left to his community.

The Ads of W. Parker Lyon

Our tales of the valley have included stories about Fresno's most colorful mayor, W. Parker Lyon, who was elected to office in 1905. He owned a furniture store on I (Broadway) Street and was a very prosperous man.

Lyon was a great booster of Fresno. He believed the city had a great future. He also was blessed with a colorful sense of the ridiculous and lived life with flair—his glass was always half full, perhaps even filled to the brim. He enjoyed every minute he was on this earth. Which brings us to the point of our story. From the moment he opened his store, he bought advertising space in the *Fresno Morning Republican*. His ads did more than promote his business; they also provided a forum for his unique brand of humor—often with his political views thrown in for good measure. Here is a sample or two.

The ad running on July 17, 1901, is headed: "W. Parker Lyon's Fables in Slang Copy Written. IN MEMORIAM. Once upon a Time there lived a woman who was Very beautiful—all except. Her Voice was Falsetto and she had a Falsetto Teeth. One day while in the Park Her Face became Transparent. She took our Her Teeth. She couldn't Remove her Voice, but she could her Teeth and put them in Her Pocket and when She sat down on them They Bit her, they had indeed proven False. She died of Hydrophobia. Moral: Buy your furniture, carpets and wall paper of W. Parker Lyon and you won't get bit."

In 1901, under the reform administration of Mayor L. O. Stephens, a number of laws regulating the saloons and gambling were passed. Lyon had this to say on September 26 of that year: "Whist Club Players Criminals Under New Blue Laws. Society is all aflutter over the passage of these new blue laws, making players of whist for prizes a crime. The poor little blonde who wins a mustache cup as a trophy will have to go to jail in the ice wagon: in fact, no home where swell functions are going on is safe from police raids. Inside of a year we will all have angel's wings and use them as a means of rapid transit. Fresno is getting so good. W. Parker Lyon, Fresno's Furniture King."

The

Glad Hand
Extended
To All!

W. PARKER LYON

The man who is furnishing Ho¹
Air for the New Electric
Car System.

This ad, which appeared in the December 25, 1901, *Fresno Morning Republican*, mixes business with Lyon's unique brand of humor.

Notes

DUTY CALLS
Fresno Bee, August 19, 1943.
A MOUNTAIN JOURNEY ON AN APRIL DAY
Clingan, *Oak to Pine to Timberline*, p. 40.
Based on a drive the author took on April 11, 1998.
TWO HISTORIC PILLARS
Interview with J. Randall McFarland and driving tour of Selma.
Selma Enterprise, August 21, 1941.
THE SOUTHERN MINES
Elliot, *History of Fresno County*, p. 187.
GOOD NIGHT SWEET EMMA
Keeler, "A last alas for a study club unparallel'd."
A CHRONICLER OF HISTORY
Latta, *Handbook of Yokuts Indians*, pg. 764.
Patterson, "Latta, authority on valley Indians, dead at 90."
AN UNRULY LITTLE BUR
Crampton, *Grasses In California*, pp. 158-59.
Robbins, Bellure and Ball, *Weeds of California*, pp. 48-49.
BERMUDA—NOT THE ISLAND
Robbins, Bellure and Ball, *Weeds of California*, pp. 50-51.
THE FALL OF TROY
As told to the author by Eugenie Kinsley McKay.
A CIVIL WAR ROUND TABLE
Clough and Secrest, *Fresno County*, p. 76.
Kubiak, "A History of the San Joaquin Valley Civil War Round Table."
THE BOARDWALK AT SANTA CRUZ
Behind-the-Scenes Facts, Santa Cruz Seaside Company.
AN INTREPID EDITOR
As told to the author by Eugenie Kinsley McKay.
Interview with Schyler Rehart.
Rehart, "Fighting Editor, Chester H. Rowell of *The Fresno Morning Republican*."
Rowell, *A Brief Account of the Life of Chester H. Rowell*.
Vandor, *History of Fresno County*, Vol. I, pp. 936-37.
A MAGICAL PLACE FOR CHILDREN
Interview with Gina Greenwood.
Rotary Kids Country, promotional brochure.
Rotary Storyland and Playland, promotional brochure.
Visit by the author and her daughter and granddaughter, Kate and Courtney Byerly, August 18, 1998.
CHRISTMAS AT THE MEUX HOME
AAUW, *Heritage Fresno: Homes and People*, p. 2.
Author's memories of Christmas at the Meux Home.
Hudelson, *Meux Home News*, Vol. V, No. IV.
A COMPILER OF HISTORY
Fresno Bee, April 5, 1926, obituary.

Notes

THE SPECIAL BELLS OF CHRISTMAS
Interview with Captain Raewyn Aspetitia.
Interview with Frances Dingman.
"The Origin of Christmas Kettles," provided by Captain Raewyn Aspetitia.
THE HOONANIAN HOME
Bursik, Historic Resources Inventory.
THE HOME OF JOHN C. HEWITT
AAUW, *Heritage Fresno: Homes and People*, p. 56.
Patnaude, Historic Resources Inventory.
JESSE MORROW
Clough and Secrest, *Fresno County*, pp. 81, 287-88.
Elliot, *History of Fresno County*, p. 130.
Vandor, *History of Fresno County*, Vol. I, pp. 126-27.
A NEW YEAR—A NEW AUDITORIUM
Fresno Bee, January 1, 1937.
Fresno Bee, "Remember When?" August 4, 1963.
THE ROMANCE OF THE FIG
California Dried Fig Advisory Board, *48 family favorites with California Figs*.
A DIRECT LINK TO HISTORY
Vandor, *History of Fresno County*, Vol. I, pp. 791-97.
A CARTOONIST NAMED BUEL
Fresno Bee, November 11, 1952, obituary, pp. 1A, 3A.
Shelton, "Buel, Veteran Bee Cartoonist, Soon Will Retire, Go Fishing," p. 17.
THE VIKING BELL
First Baptist Church Centennial History, pp. 18, 33.
A LITTLE BOY'S DREAM
Clough and Secrest, *Fresno County*, p. 109.
Smith, *Garden of the Sun*, pp. 193-96.
Vandor, *History of Fresno County*, Vol. I, pp. 254-56.
A MEMORIAL FOR "BLACKHORSE" JONES
Fresno Bee, August 23, 1926.
Kings County: A Pictorial History, p. 62.
Polley, *Another Look At A Second Look*, p. 135.
THE SANGER DEPOT MUSEUM
"A Historical Guide Sanger Depot Museum," brochure, Sanger Historical Society.
Interview with James R. Walton.
THE FESTIVAL OF SAINT ELIA
Hoagland, "The neighborhood is gone, but the memories live on."
Interview with Frank Caglia and Sally Caglia Martinez.
Saint Elia Celebration Committee, program.
JOHN S. EASTWOOD
Clough and Secrest, *Fresno County*, pp. 320-21.
Redinger, *The Story of Big Creek*, pp. 4-5.
Rose, *Reflections of Shaver Lake*, pp. 79-80.

Notes

JOSEPH SANGER, JR.
>   Doucette, editor, *Celebrating the 75th Anniversary of the founding of Sanger*, p. 45.

THE NEW CENTURY
>   *Fresno Morning Republican*, December 31,1899.

A VISION REALIZED
>   Clough et al., *Fresno County in the 20th Century*, pp. 161-62.
>   Redinger, *The Story of Big Creek*, pp. 6-9.
>   Rose, *Reflections of Shaver Lake*, pp. 81-84.

SANGER
>   Clough and Secrest, *Fresno County*, pp. 297-302.
>   Doucette, editor, *Celebrating the 75th Anniversary of the founding of Sanger*, pp. 19, 45, 49, 56, 57.

FREE EVANGELICAL LUTHERAN CROSS CHURCH
>   "80th Anniversary of the Free Evangelical Lutheran Cross Church ," pp. 46, 48, 57, 66, 67, 78.

BERROCKS BY THE THOUSAND
>   Interview with Johnna Meisner.
>   "80th Anniversary of the Free Evangelical Lutheran Cross Church," pp. 78, 81.

TO DARE OR NOT TO DARE
>   Interview with Mary Helen McKay.
>   *Imperial Fresno*, pp. 62, 64.
>   Guinn, *History of the State of California and Biographical Record of the San Joaquin Valley, California*, p. 1024.

THE MC KAY FAMILY OF FRESNO
>   As told to the author by Eugenie Loverne Kinsley McKay.
>   Guinn, *History of the State of California and Biographical Record of the San Joaquin Valley, California*, p. 1024.
>   *Imperial Fresno*, pp. 62, 64.
>   Interview with Mary Helen McKay.
>   Interview witih Oliver Pickford.

SANGER HIGH SCHOOL
>   *Fresno Bee*, July 1, 2000.
>   *Public Schools of Fresno County 1860-1998, Volume One*, pp. 154-57.
>   "Sanger High School's Centennial Celebration," pp. 3-11.

SANGER'S FAVORITE SON
>   Tom Flores, biographical information.
>   Interview with Jim Gonzalez.
>   "Sanger High School's Centennial Celebration," pp. 7, 9.

A FOUNDATION FOR YOUTH
>   Interview witih Jim Gonzalez.
>   "Tom Flores Youth Foundation," informational material.

THE ELECTRIC MOTOR SHOP
>   Electric Motor Shop and Supply Co. promotional brochure.
>   Interview with Frank Caglia and Sally Caglia Martinez.

JULY 4, 1900
>   *Fresno Morning Republican*, July 3, 1900.

Notes

Fresno Morning Republican, July 4, 1900.
Fresno Morning Republican, July 5, 1900.
KING WILLIE I & HIS CARNIVAL PARADE
    Fresno Morning Republican, July 3, 1900.
    Fresno Morning Republican, July 4, 1900.
    Fresno Morning Republican, July 5, 1900.
ALVA E. SNOW
    Clough et al., *Fresno County in the 20th Century*, pp. 47-49, 158.
    Vandor, *History of Fresno County*, Vol. I, pp. 852-53.
THE BURNETT SANITARIUM
    Community Health Systems, "1897-1997 Community: A Century of
    Service," calendar.
LIGHTING UP THE VALLEY
    Interview with Bill Kratt.
    Pollock, "Neon crafters have more to glow about than be glum
    about."
A PARISH FOR SAINT ALPHONSUS
    Interview with Frank Caglia and Sally Caglia Martinez.
    Seventy-fifth Memorial Jubilee Saint Alphonsus Parish, pp. 6-10.
THE SECOND BAPTIST CHURCH OF FRESNO
    First Baptist Church Centennial History, p. 8.
    Centennial Celebration 1888-1988, pp. 13-16.
SAM'S
    Interview with Harold Samuelian.
    Interview with Morris and Richard Samuelian.
LYON'S BERIBBONED GAVEL
    Fresno Morning Republican, September 2, 1905.
    Fresno Morning Republican, September 6, 1905.
THE FLY-SWATTING CAMPAIGN OF 1914
    Fresno Morning Republican, April 18, 1914.
    Fresno Morning Republican, April 19, 1914.
A HORSEWHIPPING IN HANFORD
    Fresno Morning Republican, April 10, 1914.
A CRUSADE COMES TO TOWN
    Darling, "Organization, Planning Bring Graham Crowds."
    Fresno Bee, July 12, 1958.
    Fresno Bee, July 13, 1958.
    Fresno Bee, July 14, 1958.
BILLY GRAHAM RETURNS
    Strentz, "25,000 Are Expected at Graham Crusade."
    Fresno Bee, July 8, 1962.
    Fresno Bee, July 14, 1962.
    Fresno Bee, July 16, 1962.
    Fresno Bee, July 20, 1962.
    Fresno Bee, July 23, 1962.
    Interview and meeting with Bud Richter, Richard Griffin, and Cliff
    Ruby.

Notes

THE BURGLAR WITH NINE LIVES
Fresno Morning Republican, September 9, 1905.
THE GREEN BUSH SPRING REVISITED
Interview with Harold Samuelian.
THE BELLS OF THE CROSS CHURCH
Letter from Johnna Meisner.
"80th Anniversary of the Free Evangelical Lutheran Cross Church,"
pp. 59, 66.
THE CASE OF THE MISSING LIGHT GLOBES
Fresno Morning Republican, December 16, 1900.
HOLIDAY SHOPPING 100 YEARS AGO
Fresno Morning Republican, December 14, 1900.
Fresno Morning Republican, December 16, 1900.
Fresno Morning Republican, December 23, 1900.
THE CHRISTMAS THAT USHERED IN A NEW CENTURY
Fresno Morning Republican, December 16, 1900.
Fresno Morning Republican, December 23, 1900.
Fresno Morning Republican, December 26, 1900.
Fresno Morning Republican, December 27, 1900.
A NEW CENTURY BEGINS
Centennial Celebration 1888-1988, p. 11.
Fresno Morning Republican, December 29, 1900.
A SECRET CHRISTMAS WEDDING
Fresno Morning Republican, December 26, 1900.
NEW YEAR'S EVE 1900
Fresno Morning Republican, January 1, 1901.
THE HONEYMOON CAPER
Fresno Morning Republican, December 23, 1900.
SIDNEY L. CRUFF
Eulogy at funeral of Sidney L. Cruff by Robert M. Wash.
Fresno Bee, "Sidney Cruff Funeral Is Set."
A TOWN HALL FORUM FOR THE VALLEY
Interview with Carol Cowin and Phyllis Wilson.
San Joaquin Valley Town Hall Forum, 50th Anniversary Celebration
program.
Tondel, "Remembering Town Hall's founder."
WILLIAM RUFUS NUTTING
Clough et al., *Fresno County in the 20th Century*, pp. 172-73.
Vandor, *History of Fresno County*, Vol. II, pp. 1997-2002.
THE VOLGA GERMANS
Frodsham, *A Study of the Russian-Germans in Fresno County*, pp. 32, 33.
"The History of the Volga Germans from Russia to America."
Klassen, "The Volga Germans in Fresno County."
Spomer, "German Influence in the History of Fresno County," pp. 11-
13.
FRESNO'S GERMAN MUSEUM
Tours of American Historical Society of Germans from Russia
Genealogy Library & Museum.

Notes

A GERMAN NEIGHBORHOOD IN WEST FRESNO
Bell, "One Hundred and Ten Years of Volga Germans in Fresno," pp. 40-46.
Interviews and discussions with Diana Bell, Elsie De Pierri, Bernice Dixon, Molly Henderson, Vera Hills, Joan Kincade, June King, Marie Lehr, Johnna Meisner, Denny Ohlberg, Helen Pfister, Ray Spomer, Irene Ulrich and Paul Wasemiller.
Klassen, "The Volga Germans in Fresno County."

AN ANNUAL BANQUET
Carillon, *San Joaquin Power Club 1921-1968*.
Interview with Jack Brase.

SAN JOAQUIN POWER CLUB
Carillon, *San Joaquin Power Club 1921-1968*.
Interview with Jack Brase.

NEW YEAR'S DAY IN THE MORNING
Fresno Morning Republican, January 1, 1901.

DAVID COWAN SAMPLE
Clough and Secrest, *Fresno County*, p. 94.
Vandor, *History of Fresno County*, Vol. I, pp. 651-52.

JOHN GREENUP SIMPSON
Clough and Secrest, *Fresno County*, p. 94.
Elliot, *History of Fresno County*, p. 230.
Morison, *The Oxford History of the American People*, pp. 298, 299, 365, 476, 477, 543-46.
Vandor, *History of Fresno County*, Vol. II, pp. 2008-2012.

PUNDITS & PROGNOSTICATORS
Rowell, "Prophets and Prophecies."
Rowell, "The Twentieth Century Must Develop Character."

MISS ROGERS CHARMS FRESNO
Interview with Robert A. Schoettler.

LAURA ALSIP WINCHELL
AAUW, *Heritage Fresno: Women and Their Contributions*, p. 105.
Vandor, *History of Fresno County*, Vol. I, pp. 638-40.

SCHOETTLER TIRE INC.
Interview with Dave and Tom Schoettler.

ROBERT A. SCHOETTLER
Clough et al., *Fresno County in the 20th Century*, p. 70.
Interview with Robert A. Schoettler.

TIDBITS FROM JANUARY 1901
Fresno Morning Republican, "Local Brevities," January 12, 1901.

THE BIOLA CONGREGATIONAL CHURCH
Hullender, editor, *75th Anniversary of the Biola Congregational United Church of Christ*, pp. 1, 2.

MR. SMITH'S EAR GOES TO COURT
Fresno County Centennial Committee, *Fresno County Centennial Almanac*.
Fresno Morning Republican, January 12, 1901.

Notes

BIBB HALL
    Carillon, *San Joaquin Power Club 1921-1968*.
    Interview with Jack Brase.
IT STARTED WITH A NICKEL
    Clough et al., *Fresno County in the 20th Century*, p. 216.
    Eaton, *Vintage Fresno*, pp. 74-75.
    Fresno Morning Republican, May 9, 1906.
CONEY ISLAND RED HOTS
    Fresno Bee, June 21, 1989, George Callas obituary.
    Fresno Bee, October 3, 2000.
    Interview with Koula Skofis.
    Laughnan, "Hot Dogs Are Still King On Tulare Street."
    McEwen, "Baseball, hot dogs don't mix in Fresno."
    Nax, "Dog Gone Wild."
    Nax, "Landmark downtown Fresno hot-dog stand to reopen today."
MOTORCYCLES BY THE DOZEN
    Interview with Doug Wilson.
EARLY AFRICAN-AMERICAN PIONEERS
    Beasley, *The Negro Trail Blazers of California*, pp. 151-53.
A MOST UNTACTFUL TACK
    Fresno Morning Republican, January 4, 1906.
LILBOURNE ALSIP WINCHELL
    Vandor, *History of Fresno County*, Vol. I, pp. 674-78.
A LADY OF LETTERS
    AAUW, *Heritage Fresno: Women and Their Contributions*, p. 104.
    Vandor, *History of Fresno County*, Vol. I, p. 677.
A LIFE WELL LIVED
    Heritage Fresno: Women and Their Contributions, p. 21.
THE CONEY ISLAND'S COMEBACK
    Fresno Bee, October 3, 2000.
    Interview with Koula Skofis.
    McEwen, "Baseball, hot dogs don't mix in Fresno."
    Nax, "Dog Gone Wild."
    Nax, "Landmark downtown Fresno hot-dog stand to reopen today."
THE DAY THE LIGHTS WENT OUT
    Fresno Morning Republican, May 3, 1898.
BLOSSOMS BY THE MILLIONS
    Fresno Chamber of Commerce, *Fresno County Blossom Trail*, promotional brochure.
    Interview with Brian Ziegler.
THE DAY WENDELL WILLKIE CAME TO TOWN
    Fresno Bee, September 20, 1940.
MR. ROEDING'S STREETS
    Eaton, *Vintage Fresno*, pp. 13-15.
    Fresno Bee, 1952. Exact date unavailable.
    Interview with Ken Hohmann.

Notes

TIDBITS FROM THE FRESNO TIMES
   Fresno Times, January 28, 1865.
BASSO PROFUNDO
   Henry, *Give the World a Smile: the Life Story of Don Smith*.
THE RAMBUNCTIOUS JUDGE
   Clough and Secrest, *Fresno County*, p. 251.
   Jarvise, "Justice David S. Terry—Another View," pp. 1-3, 7.
   Secrest, "Judge David S. Terry: The Final, Fresno Years," pp. 8,9.
   Wash, "Colorful, Tempestuous Lawyer David Terry Was His Own Man."
HENRY CLAY DAULTON
   Clough, *Madera*, p. 31.
   Vandor, *History of Fresno County*, Vol. I, pp. 611-12.
HEDGE ROW VINEYARD
   AAUW, *Heritage Fresno: Women and Their Contributions*, pp. 7, 56.
   California Homes and Industries, pp. 27-28.
MINNIE F. AUSTIN
   AAUW, *Heritage Fresno: Women and Their Contributions*, pp. 7, 56.
   California Homes and Industries, pp. 27-28.
   Panter, "Central California: 'Marvel of the Desert,'" pp. 6-8.
LUCY HATCH
   AAUW, *Heritage Fresno: Women and Their Contributions*, p. 56.
   California Homes and Industries, pp. 27-28.
   Panter, "Central California: 'Marvel of the Desert,'" pp. 6-8.
THE NO-COW LAW
   Fresno Morning Republican, May 15, 1906.
FARMER, BUSINESSMAN & ENTREPRENEUR
   Fresno Evening Expositor, May 14, 1890.
   Panter, "Central California: 'Marvel of the Desert,'" pp. 8, 9.
   Vandor, *History of Fresno County*, Vol. II, pp. 1430-31.
JESSE CLAYTON FORKNER
   Rehart, "J.C. Forkner Turned Fresno's 'Hog Wallows' Into 'Garden of Eden,'" pp. 1-6.
   Walker, *The Fresno County Bluebook*, p. 154.
FIG FARMS BY THE SCORE
   Rehart, "J.C. Forkner Turned Fresno's 'Hog Wallows' Into 'Garden of Eden,'" pp. 6-7.
HARPAIN'S DAIRY
   Interview with Walter Harpain.
A FINE HERD OF HOLSTEINS
   Interview with Walter Harpain.
ROAMIN' IN FRESNO
   Interview with Mary Helen McKay.
MIMA MOUNDS
   Clough and Secrest, *Fresno County*, p. 3.
   Cox, "Mounds of Mystery," pp. 36-45.
A MUSEUM IN CLOVIS
   Interview with Peg Bos.

Notes

Interview with Ron Sundquist and tour of Big Dry Creek Museum.
EARTHQUAKE & DEVASTATION
Fresno Morning Republican, April 20, 1906.
Rehart and Patterson, *M. Theo Kearney Prince of Fresno*, pp. 40-41.
Rolle, *California A History*, p. 414.
THE TELEPHONE—A MODERN NECESSITY
Fresno Morning Republican, April 20, 1906.
DECORATION DAY – 1901
Fresno Morning Republican, May 31, 1901.
Miziuk, "On the Occasion of Memorial Day."
DECORATION DAY – 1906
Fresno Morning Republican, May 6, 1906.
Fresno Morning Republican, May 31, 1906.
TARTANS & BAGPIPES GALORE
Fresno Morning Republican, May 21, 1906.
THE DEAN
Author's memories of conversations with James M. Malloch and
Jeanette Bellman Malloch.
Malloch, *A Practical Church Dictionary*, p. vii and cover biography.
Rehart, *The Valley's Legends & Legacies I*, p. 290.
Walker, *Fresno Community Book*, pp. 389-90.
ENRICH YOUR LIFE—BUY A CAR!
Fresno Morning Republican, November 14, 1917.
READIN', WRITIN' & 'RITHMETIC
Sierra Joint Union High School, *Chieftain*, p. 66.
A CORNERSTONE IS LAID
Fresno Morning Republican, May 15, 1906.
A PARADE ON THE FOURTH
Fresno Morning Republican, July 5, 1901.
JULY 4, 1901
Fresno Morning Republican, July 5, 1901.
THE HEAT OF SUMMER—1901 STYLE
Fresno Morning Republican, August 4, 1901.
110 GRADUATIONS
Chaddock, *120° in the Shade*, pp. 19-21.
Interview with Jeannie Adkins.
Stuart and Fowler, eds., *Fresno High School Centennial*, pp. 8-11.
A FIG SOCIAL
Fresno Morning Republican, August 23, 1901.
NUPTIALS AT HIGH NOON
Fresno Morning Republican, January 5, 1901.
THE FIG – THEN & NOW
Fresno Morning Republican, November 15, 1917.
DOS PALOS COLONY
Atlas of Dos Palos, pp. 1-3, 15.
Durham, *California's Geographic Names*, pg. 767.
Interview with Dan Sniffen.
Interview with Betty and Bud Wooten.

Notes

DOS PALOS
>Interview with Dan Sniffen and tour of Dos Palos.
>Interview with Betty and Bud Wooten.

BERNHARD MARKS
>*Atlas of Dos Palos,* p. 15.
>Clough and Secrest, *Fresno County,* pp. 143-44.
>Guinn, *History of the State of California and Biographical Record of the San Joaquin Valley, California,* p. 773.

THE STREETS OF DOWNTOWN FRESNO
>Durham, *California's Geographic Names,* pp. 799, 833, 839, 1055, 1173, 1185.
>Latta, *Handbook of Yokuts Indians,* p. 25.
>Rolle, *California: A History,* pp. 25, 115.

THE DOS PALOS BRONCOS
>Borboa, "Riding the 'Big Horse' To Victory," pp. 17-19.
>*Star and Journal,* "Football Special," October 24, 1974.

THE DRY ROAD FROM MILLERTON
>*Fresno Expositor,* July 7, 1874.

FIRST PRESBYTERIAN CHURCH
>Taylor, "A Brief History of the First Presbyterian Church, Fresno, California," pp. 5-6.

THE SPANISH LIEUTENANT & EXPLORER
>Bancroft, *The Works of Hubert Howe Bancroft,* p. 571.
>Cook, *Expeditions to the Interior of California.*
>Cutter, translator and editor, *The Diary of Ensign Gabriel Moraga's Expedition of Discovery in the Sacramento Valley,* pp. 1-10.

FRESNO'S POLICE DEPARTMENT
>Clough et al., *Fresno County in the 20th Century,* pp. 39-41, 68.
>Frazier, "History of the Fresno Police Department."
>Interview with Detective Todd Frazier.
>Interview with Lieutenant John Fries.

ALL GOD'S CREATURES
>*Fresno Morning Republican,* October 12, 1907.

THE CLOTHES BURGLAR
>*Fresno Morning Republican,* October 8, 1907.

SHOT IN THE LINE OF DUTY
>*Fresno Morning Republican,* February 21, 1907.

A LIFE HANGS IN THE BALANCE
>*Fresno Morning Republican,* February 21, 1907.
>*Fresno Morning Republican,* February 22, 1907.
>*Fresno Morning Republican,* February 23, 1907.
>*Fresno Morning Republican,* February 24, 1907.

THE TEMPEST OVER THE RED-WHEELED RIG
>*Fresno Morning Republican,* October 6, 1907.

ANOTHER HERO LAID TO REST
>*Fresno Morning Republican,* March 14, 1907.
>*Fresno Morning Republican,* March 15, 1907.

Notes

TRAGEDY BEHIND THE BARTON
  Fresno Morning Republican, October 10, 1907.
  Fresno Morning Republican, October 11, 1907.
BIOLA
  Bergman, "The Ending of an Era."
  Clough et al., *Fresno County in the 20th Century*, pp. 249-50.
  Fresno County Centennial Almanac, p. 84.
  Interviews with Claudine Scheidt Bergman, Alice Dauer, Byron
  Eisner, Nila Owen Eisner, Jack Isheim, Eldora Lutz, Adam Meisner,
  Johanna Meisner, Molly Meisner, Eileen Schneider, George Schneider,
  Lydia Schneider.
  Interview with Mabel Seibert Belluomini.
  Kean, *Wide Places in California Roads*, pp. 29-30.
  Rehart, *The Heartland's Heritage*, p. 91.
THE THREE-DAY WEDDING—GERMAN STYLE
  Interviews with Claudine Scheidt Bergman, Alice Dauer, Byron
  Eisner, Nila Owen Eisner, Jack Isheim, Eldora Lutz, Adam Meisner,
  Johanna Meisner, Molly Meisner, Eileen Schneider, George Schneider,
  Lydia Schneider.
BIOLA'S CHURCH BELLS
  Hullender, editor, *75th Anniversary of the Biola Congregational United
  Church of Christ*, p. 2.
  Interview with the Reverend Edward Veldhuizen.
THE GOOD SAMARITANS
  Harris, "History of the F.I.A."
THE LADIES OF THE F.I.A.
  Clifton, "The F.I.A. at 95."
  Colwell and Carter, "History of F.I.A."
  Feaver, "Fowler Improvement Association."
  Giffen and Smith, "Six Decades of F.I.A. Accomplishments."
  Henshaw and Wilson, "Fowler Improvement Association."
  Interview with Pauline Blayney.
  Interview with Jean Pereira.
  Manley, "A Brief View of F.I.A. Early History."
A CRAFTSMAN CLUBHOUSE IN FOWLER
  Henshaw and Wilson, "Fowler Improvement Association."
  Interview with Pauline Blayney.
  Interview with Jean Pereira.
A READING ROOM FOR FOWLER
  Fowler Ensign, March 28, 1940, pp. 1, 8.
  Manley, "A Brief View of F.I.A. Early History."
THE GREENING OF FOWLER
  Fowler Ensign, March 28, 1940, pp. 1, 8.
  Tour of Fowler with Jean Pereira.
ESCAPE FROM DALTON MOUNTAIN
  Interview with Harvey Owen.
  Wash, "The Dalton Gang."

Notes

A MAN NAMED CLOVIS
   Clovis Independent, November 16, 1939, Clovis Cole obituary.
   Fresno Bee, November 15, 1939, Clovis Cole obituary.
   Interview with Harvey Owen.
   Zylka, Greenberg and Thun, *Images of An Age: Clovis*, pp. 121-22.
BERT COLE & THE PREHISTORIC MAN
   Interview with Harvey Owen.
GEORGE W. OWEN
   Vandor, *History of Fresno County*, Vol. I, p. 707.
RICHARD THOMAS OWEN
   Interview with Harvey Owen.
   Vandor, *History of Fresno County*, Vol. I, p. 707.
OCTOBER & NOVEMBER
   Author's memories of the autumns of her childhood growing up in
   Fresno.
CALIFORNIA-FRESNO OIL COMPANY
   "The History of California-Fresno Oil Company." Information
   provided by Dolph "Bud" Ruschhaupt.
   Interview with Dolph "Bud" Ruschhaupt.
   Interview with Ted Rusmore.
   Walker, *The Fresno County Bluebook*, p. 500.
THE FRESNO SOAP COMPANY
   August A. Ruschhaupt, taped interview with his son, Dolph.
   "The History of California-Fresno Oil Company." Information
   provided by Dolph "Bud" Ruschhaupt.
   Interview with Dolph "Bud" Ruschhaupt.
   Interview with Ted Rusmore.
   Walker, *The Fresno County Bluebook*, p. 500.
CLOVIS' DISTINGUISHED JUDGE
   Fresno Bee, May 21, 1945, obituary.
   Walker, *Fresno Community Book*, p. 367.
A STAGE STOP IN CENTERVILLE
   Clough and Secrest, *Fresno County*, p. 268.
   AAUW, *Heritage Fresno: Homes and People*, p. 83.
WILLIAM TEMPLE COLE
   Guinn, *History of the State of California and Biographical Record of the
   San Joaquin Valley, California*, pp. 1483-85.
FIESTA DAYS IN MADERA
   Fresno Morning Republican, September 25, 1901.
A BULLFIGHT IN MADERA
   Fresno Morning Republican, September 29, 1901.
THE DEATH OF PRESIDENT MC KINLEY
   Fresno Morning Republican, September 15, 1901.
   Fresno Morning Republican, September 17, 1901.
   Morison, *The Oxford History of the American People*, p. 810.
THE CHILDREN OF FRESNO MOURN
   Fresno Morning Republican, September 20, 1901.

Notes

A MEMORABLE DAY IN FRESNO'S HISTORY
  Fresno Morning Republican, September 17, 1901.
  Fresno Morning Republican, September 20, 1901.
BANKING ON ADVERTISING
  Fresno Morning Republican, September 21, 1901.
A SCRUMPTIOUS BANQUET IN CHINATOWN
  Fresno Morning Republican, October 31, 1901.
A VISIT FROM SAINT NICK
  Fresno Morning Republican, December 25, 1901.
GAMBLING DENS ARE STRUCK A BLOW
  Clough and Secrest, *Fresno County*, p. 41.
  Fresno Morning Republican, October 22, 1901.
  Fresno Morning Republican, October 23, 1901.
A POLICE CHIEF WITH A MISSION
  Fresno Morning Republican, October 23, 1901.
LEWIS OLIVER STEPHENS
  Fresno Weekly Democrat, May 15, 1901.
  Vandor, *History of Fresno County*, Vol. I, pp. 846-51.
  Walker, *The Fresno County Bluebook*, p. 140.
  Walker, *Fresno Community Book*, p. 313.
A ROUSING GATHERING IN COURTHOUSE PARK
  Fresno Morning Republican, August 13, 1901.
WILL WE REMEMBER THE SABBATH DAY?
  Fresno Morning Republican, August 17, 1901.
A LABOR DAY PARADE 1901 STYLE
  Fresno Weekly Democrat, September 4, 1901.
LABOR DAY ORATIONS, 1901
  Fresno Weekly Democrat, September 4, 1901.
SUMMER TIDBITS FROM 1901
  Fresno Morning Republican, August 17, 1901.
TWO-HEADED MISS MILLIE
  Fresno Morning Republican, January 17, 1880.
SAINT JAMES' EPISCOPAL CATHEDRAL
  Clough and Secrest, *Fresno County*, p. 135.
  Fresno Morning Republican, October 27, 1901.
  "Ground Broken for Chapel of the Holy Innocents."
SMALLPOX COMES TO FRESNO
  New Encyclopaedia Britannica, 15th Edition, vol. IX, p. 280.
  Fresno Morning Republican, August 8, 1901.
  Fresno Morning Republican, August 9, 1901.
TOGGLES—FRESNO'S PRIDE & JOY
  Fresno Morning Republican, September 21, 1901.
BEN RANDAL WALKER
  Fresno Bee, April 29, 1954, obituary.
  Walker, *Fresno Community Book*, pp. 391-92.
THE ADS OF W. PARKER LYON
  Fresno Morning Republican, July 18, 1901.
  Fresno Morning Republican, September 26, 1901.

"A Historical Guide Sanger Depot Museum," brochure, Sanger Historical Society.

Adkins, Jeannie. Fresno High School registrar. Interview, March 29, 2001.

American Association of University Women (AAUW). *Heritage Fresno: Homes and People*. Fresno: Pioneer Publishing Company, 1975.

_____. *Heritage Fresno: Women and Their Contributions*. Fresno: Pioneer Publishing Company, 1987.

_____. *Public Schools of Fresno County 1860-1998, Volume One*. Clovis: Word Dancer Press, 1999.

American Historical Society of Germans From Russia. "The History of the Volga Germans from Russia to America."

Aspetitia, Captain Raewyn. Salvation Army. Fresno Corps. Interview, December 2, 1998.

Atlas of Dos Palos. Facsimile reproduction of original 1899 edition. Dos Palos: Dos Palos Historical Society, 1982.

Bancroft, Hubert Howe. *The Works of Hubert Howe Bancroft*. Santa Barbara: Wallace Hebberd, 1966.

Beasley, Delilah L. *The Negro Trail Blazers of California*. San Francisco: R and E Research Associates, 1919.

Behind-the-Scenes Facts. Brochure. Santa Cruz Seaside Company.

Bell, Diana, Elsie De Pierri, Bernice Dixon, Molly Henderson, Vera Hills, Joan Kincade, June King, Marie Lehr, Johnna Meisner, Denny Ohlberg, Helen Pfister, Ray Spomer, Irene Ulrich and Paul Wasemiller. Interviews and discussions at American Historical Society of Germans from Russia Genealogy Library & Museum, May 18, 2000.

Bell, Diana. "One Hundred and Ten Years of Volga Germans in Fresno." *AHSGR Journal*. Fresno, Fall 1997.

_____. Tour of American Historical Society of Germans from Russia Genealogy Library & Museum, August 28, 2000.

Belluomini, Mabel Seibert. Interview, April 26, 2001.

Bergman, Claudine Scheidt, Alice Dauer, Byron Eisner, Nila Owen Eisner, Jack Isheim, Eldora Lutz, Adam Meisner, Johanna Meisner, Molly Meisner, Eileen Schneider, George Schneider, Lydia Schneider. Interviews at American Historical Society of Germans from Russia Genealogy Library and Museum, April 23, 2001.

Bergman, Claudine Scheidt. "The Ending of an Era." Unpublished manuscript.

Blayney, Pauline. Past-president of Fowler Improvement Association and great-granddaughter of Antoinette Harris. Interview and tour of clubhouse, May 2, 2001.

Borboa, David. "Riding the 'Big Horse' To Victory." *The Dos Palos Sun*. Dos Palos High School 2000 Football supplement.

Bos, Peg. President of Clovis Big Dry Creek Historical Society. Interview, March 10, 2001.

Brase, Jack. Interview, August 23, 2000.

Bursik, George. Historic Resources Inventory. City of Fresno. The Hoonanian Home. 1993.

Caglia, Frank and Sally Caglia Martinez. Interview, May 11, 2000.

California Dried Fig Advisory Board. *48 family favorites with California Figs.*

California Homes and Industries. San Francisco: The Elliot Publishing Company, 1891. Reprinted edition by the Fresno City and County Historical Society, Fresno, 1982.

Carillon, Earl V. *San Joaquin Power Club 1921-1968.* An unpublished history.

Centennial Celebration 1888-1988. Fresno: Second Baptist Church, Souvenir Book Committee, 1988.

Chaddock, E. L. *120° in the Shade.* Fresno: Lifelines, 1989.

Clifton, Corinne. "The F.I.A. at 95." *The Selma Enterprise.* November 7, 1985.

Clingan, Helen and Forest. *Oak to Pine to Timberline.* Clovis: Word Dancer Press, 1985.

Clough, Charles W. and William B. Secrest, Jr. *Fresno County : The Pioneer Years.* Fresno: Panorama West Books, 1984.

Clough, Charles W. et al. *Fresno County in the 20th Century*, Panorama West Books, Fresno, 1986.

Clough, Charles W. *Madera.* Madera: Madera County Historical Society, 1968.

Colwell, Kathryn and Kenny Carter. "History of F.I.A." Undated. Unpublished manuscript.

Community Health Systems. "1897-1997 Community: A Century of Service." Calendar.

Cook, Sherburne F. *Expeditions to the Interior of California.* Anthropological Records. Vol. 16. No. 6. Berkeley: University of California Press, 1960.

Cowin, Carol, and Phyllis Wilson. Interview, August 15, 2000.

Cox, George W. "Mounds of Mystery." *Natural History*, Vol. 93, No. 6, June 1894.

Crampton, Bucher. *Grasses In California.* Berkeley and Los Angeles: University of California Press, 1974.

Cutter, Donald C., translator and editor. *The Diary of Ensign Gabriel Moraga's Expedition of Discovery in the Sacramento Valley 1808.* Glen Dawson, 1957.

Dingman, Frances. The Salvation Army Western Territory Museum. Interview, December 2, 1998.

Doucette, Forrest E. Editor. *Celebrating the 75th Anniversary of the founding of Sanger (1888-1963).* Sanger: *Sanger Herald*, 1963.

Durham, David L. *California's Geographic Names.* Clovis: Quill Driver Books/Word Dancer Press, 1998.

Eaton, Edwin M. *Vintage Fresno.* Fresno: The Huntington Press, 1965.

Electric Motor Shop and Supply Co. Promotional brochure.

Elliot, Wallace W. *History of Fresno County.* Reprinted by Valley Publishers, Fresno, 1973.

Feaver, Mrs. Ronald. "Fowler Improvement Association." February 1975. Unpublished manuscript.

First Baptist Church of Fresno Centennial Committee. *First Baptist Church Centennial History.* Fresno: First Baptist Church, 1982.

Flores, Tom. Biographical information. Courtesy of Tom Flores.

Frazier, Detective Todd. "History of the Fresno Police Department." Unpublished manuscript.

_____. Fresno Police Department. Interview, April 17, 2001.

Fresno Chamber of Commerce. "Fresno County Blossom Trail." Promotional brochure.

Fresno County Centennial Committee. *Fresno County Centennial Almanac.* Fresno, 1956.

Fresno City and County Historical Society. *Imperial Fresno.* Facsimile reproduction. Fresno: Pioneer Publishing Company, 1979.

Fries, Lieutenant John. Fresno Police Department. Interview, April 17, 2001.

Frodsham, Noel. *A Study of the Russian-Germans in Fresno County, California.* Redlands: University of Redlands, 1949.

Giffen, Edna J. and Pearl E. Smith. "Six Decades of F.I.A. Accomplishments." Undated. Unpublished manuscript.

Gonzalez, Jim. Interview, June 25, 2000.

_____. Interview, July 12, 2000.

Greenwood, Gina. Director of marketing & public relations for Storyland. Interview, August 27, 1998.

"Ground Broken for Chapel of the Holy Innocents." *San Joaquin Star*, Vol. 34, No. 6, November/December 1997.

Guinn, J. M. *History of the State of California and Biographical Record of the San Joaquin Valley, California.* Chicago: Chapman Publishing Company, 1905.

Harpain, Walter. Interview, March 6, 2001.

Harris, Antoinette. "History of the F.I.A." *Fowler Ensign*, January 7, 1899.

Henry, Herb. *Give the World a Smile: The Life Story of Don Smith.* 1995.

Henshaw, Shelley and M. Wilson. "Fowler Improvement Association."

Historic Resources Inventory. Fresno County Landmarks Commission, November 30, 1990.

"The History of the Volga Germans from Russia to America." Fresno: American Historical Society of Germans from Russia.

Hoagland, Doug. "The neighborhood is gone, but the memories live on." *Fresno Bee*, September 6, 1985.

Hohmann, Ken. Interview, February 15, 2001.

Hudelson, Nancy. *Meux Home News,* Vol. V, No. IV.

Hullender, Beth. Editor. *75th Anniversary of the Biola Congregational United Church of Christ*. Fresno: Pyramid Printing, 1996.

Imperial Fresno. Facsimile reproduction. Fresno: Fresno City and County Historical Society and Pioneer Publishing Company, 1979.

Jarvise, Robert. "Justice David S. Terry—Another View." *The California Supreme Court Historical Society Newsletter*. Vol. 3, No. 2, Fall 1994.

Kean, David W. *Wide Places in California Roads*. Sunnyvale: The Concord Press, 1996.

Keeler, Guy. "A last alas for a study club unparallel'd." *Fresno Bee,* May 27, 1983.

Kings County Centennial Committee, *Kings County: A Pictorial History*. Hanford, 1992.

Klassen, Peter J., Ph.D. "The Volga Germans in Fresno County" *Fresno Past & Present*. Fresno City and County Historical Society quarterly journal. Vol. 22, No. 4, Winter 1980.

Kratt, Bill. President of Fresno Neon Sign Company, Inc. Interview, July 13, 2000.

Kubiak, Rick. "A History of the San Joaquin Valley Civil War Round Table."

Latta, Frank F. *Handbook of Yokuts Indians*. 50th Anniversary Commemorative Issue. Salinas: Coyote Press, 1999.

Laughnan, Woody. "Hot Dogs Are Still King On Tulare Street." *Fresno Bee*, June 5, 1978.

Malloch, James M. *A Practical Church Dictionary*. Kay Smallzried, editor. New York: Morehouse-Barlow Co., 1964.

Manley, Mrs. J. S. "A Brief View of F.I.A. Early History." 1933. Unpublished manuscript.

McEwen, Bill. "Baseball, hot dogs don't mix in Fresno." *Fresno Bee*, September 28, 2000.

McFarland, J. Randall. Interview and driving tour of Selma, May 7, 1998.

McKay, Mary Helen. Interview, June 16, 2000.

_____. Interview, March 10, 2001.

Meisner, Johnna. Tour of American Historical Society of Germans from Russia Genealogy Library & Museum, May 18, 2000.

_____. Interview and tour of berrock making session, May 31, 2000.

_____. Letter, July 14, 2000.

Miziuk, George A. New Jersey state commander of the Ukranian American Veterans. "On the Occasion of Memorial Day." http://www.geocities.com/uavets.geo/press/95memorial.htm. Originally published in *Ukrainian Weekly*, May 28, 1995.

Morison, Samuel Eliot. *The Oxford History of the American People*. New York: Oxford University Press, 1965.

Nax, Sanford. "Dog Gone Wild." *Fresno Bee*, September 30, 2000.

_____. "Landmark downtown Fresno hot-dog stand to reopen today." *Fresno Bee*, October 4, 2000.

New Encyclopaedia Britannica, 15th edition, vol. IX. Chicago: University of Chicago, 1984.

Owen, Harvey. Grandson of Charles Owen. Interview, May 5, 2001.

Panter, John. "Central California: 'Marvel of the Desert.'" *Fresno Past & Present*, Fresno City and County Historical Society quarterly journal. Vol. 36, No. 2, Summer 1994.

Patnaude, William. Historic Resources Inventory. City of Fresno. The Hewitt Home. June 26, 1978.

Patterson, William K. "Latta, authority on valley Indians, dead at 90." *Fresno Bee*, May 17, 1983.

Pereira, Jean. Past president of Fowler Improvement Association. Interview and tour of clubhouse and of Fowler, May 2, 2001.

Pickford, Oliver. Interview, June 8, 2000.

Polley, Doris Robertson. *Another Look At A Second Look*. Hanford Carnegie Museum, April, 1997.

Pollock, Dennis. "Neon crafters have more to glow about than be glum about." *Fresno Bee*, February 9. 1986.

Redinger, David H. *The Story of Big Creek*. Los Angeles: Angelus Press, 1949.

Rehart, Catherine Morison. *The Valley's Legends & Legacies*. Clovis: Word Dancer Press, 1996.

Rehart, Schyler. "Fighting Editor, Chester H. Rowell of The Fresno Morning Republican." Fresno Past & Present. Fresno City and County Historical Society quarterly journal, Vol. 18, No. 4, Winter 1977.

_____. Interview, August 7, 1998.

_____. "J.C. Forkner Turned Fresno's 'Hog Wallows' Into 'Garden of Eden.'" *Fresno Past & Present*. Fresno City and County Historical Society quarterly journal, Vol. 19, No. 3, Fall 1977.

_____ and William K. Patterson. *M. Theo Kearney Prince of Fresno*. Fresno: Fresno City and County Historical Society, 1988.

Robbins, Wilfred William, Margaret K. Bellure and Walter S. Ball. *Weeds of California*. Sacramento: State Department of Agriculture, 1941.

Rolle, Andrew F. *California: A History*. Arlington Heights, Illinois: AHM⋅ Publishing Corporation, 1978.

Rose, Gene. *Reflections of Shaver Lake*. Clovis: Word Dancer Press, 1987.

Rotary Kids Country. Promotional brochure.

Rotary Storyland and Playland. Promotional brochure.

Rowell, Chester H. *A Brief Account of the Life of Chester H. Rowell*. Unpublished manuscript.

_____. "The Twentieth Century Must Develop Character." *Fresno Morning Republican*, January 1, 1901.

_____. "Prophets and Prophecies." *Fresno Morning Republican*, January 2, 1901.

Ruschhaupt, August A. Taped interview with his son, Dolph, February 3, 1982. Provided by Dolph "Bud" Ruschhaupt.

Ruschhaupt, Dolph "Bud." Interview, September 12, 2000.

Saint Elia Celebration Committee. Program, September 7, 1941.

Samuelian, Harold. Interview, August 11, 2000.

Samuelian, Morris and Richard Samuelian. Interview, August 1, 2000.

Sanger High School Centennial Celebration Committee. "Sanger High School's Centennial Celebration." Sanger, 1999.

San Joaquin Valley Town Hall Forum. 50th anniversary celebration program, May 3, 1987.

Schoettler, Dave and Tom Schoettler. Interview and tour of Schoettler Tire Inc. retreading plant, November 16, 2000.

Schoettler, Robert A. Interview, November 2, 2000.

Secrest, William B., Sr. "Judge David S. Terry: The Final, Fresno Years." *Fresno Past & Present*. Fresno City and County Historical Society quarterly journal. Vol. 32. No. 1. Spring 1990.

Seventy-fifth Memorial Jubilee Saint Alphonsus Parish. Commemorative booklet. Fresno, 1983.

Shelton, G.M. "Buel, Veteran Bee Cartoonist, Soon Will Retire, Go Fishing." *Fresno Bee*, June 27, 1948.

Sierra Joint Union High School. *Chieftain*. Senior class, Auberry, 1954.

Skofis, Koula. Interview, November 14, 2000.

Smith, Wallace. *Garden of the Sun*. Los Angeles: Lymanhouse, 1939.

Sniffen, Dan. Interview and tour of Dos Palos, March 27, 2001.

Spomer, Roy W. "German Influence in the History of Fresno County." 1989.

Star and Journal, "Football Special," Section Two, October 24, 1974.

Stuart, Dorothy Williams and Jack Fowler, editors. *Fresno High School Centennial 1889-1989*. Fresno: Fresno High School Centennial Yearbook Committee, 1989.

Sundquist, Ron. Curator of Clovis Big Dry Creek Museum. Interview and tour of museum, March 10, 2001.

Taylor, Roger "A Brief History of the First Presbyterian Church, Fresno, California, 1882 through 1984." *Centennial Directory, First Presbyterian Church of Fresno*. Fresno: First Presbyterian Church, 1984.

"The History of California-Fresno Oil Company." Information provided by Dolph "Bud" Ruschhaupt.

"The Origin of Christmas Kettles." Provided by Captain Raewyn Aspetitia, the Salvation Army, Fresno Citadel.

The Souvenir Book Committee. *Centennial Celebration 1888-1988*. Fresno: Second Baptist Church, 1988.

"Tom Flores Youth Foundation." Informational material.

Bibliography

Tondel, Healey. "Remembering Town Hall's founder." *Fresno Bee*, Letters to the Editor, November 23, 1986.

Vandor, Paul. *History of Fresno County*. Vols. I & II. Los Angeles: Historic Record Company, 1919.

Veldhuizen, Reverend Edward. Minister of Biola Congregational Church. Interview, June 8, 2001.

Walker, Ben R. *Fresno Community Book*. Fresno: Arthur H. Crawston, publisher, 1946.

_____. *The Fresno County Bluebook*. Fresno: Arthur H. Cawston, 1941.

Walton, James R., president of Sanger Historical Society. Interview and tour of Sanger Depot Museum, May 1, 2000.

Wash, Robert M. "Colorful, Tempestuous Lawyer David Terry Was His Own Man." *Bar Bulletin*. September-October 1984.

_____. Eulogy given at funeral of Sidney L. Cruff. May 13, 1972.

_____. "The Dalton Gang." Unpublished paper presented to the Fowler Friday Evening Club. Date unavailable.

Wilson, Doug. Interview, December 8, 2000.

Wooten, Betty and Bud Wooten. Interview, March 27, 2001.

Ziegler, Brian. Director of Tourism, Film & mMedia Relations. Fresno City & County Convention & Visitors Bureau. Interview, February 7, 2001.

Zylka, Claire Baird, Ken Greenberg and Jessie Myers Thun. *Images of An Age: Clovis*. Fresno: Pacific Printing Press, 1984.

"80th Anniversary of the Free Evangelical Lutheran Cross Church 1892-1972." Fresno: Free Evangelical Lutheran Cross Church, 1972.

Clovis Independent. November 16, 1939. Clovis Cole obituary.

Fowler Ensign. March 28, 1940.

Fresno Bee. April 5, 1926. Obituary.

_____. August 23, 1926.

_____. January 1, 1937.

_____. November 15, 1939. Clovis Cole obituary.

_____. September 20, 1940.

_____. August 19, 1943.

_____. May 21, 1945. Obituary

_____. 1952. Exact date unavailable.

_____. November 11, 1952. Obituary.

_____. April 29, 1954. Obituary.

_____. "Remember When?" August 4, 1963.

_____. June 21, 1989. George Callas obituary.

_____. October 3, 2000.

_____. July 1, 2000.

_____. "Sidney Cruff Funeral Is Set," no date available.

Fresno Evening Expositor. May 14, 1890.

Bibliography

Fresno Expositor. July 7, 1874.

Fresno Morning Republican. January 17, 1880.

_____. May 3, 1898.

_____. July 3, 1900.

_____. July 4, 1900.

_____. July 5, 1900.

_____. December 14, 1900.

_____. December 16, 1900.

_____. December 23, 1900.

_____. December 26, 1900.

_____. December 27, 1900.

_____. December 29, 1900.

_____. January 1, 1901.

_____. January 5, 1901.

_____. January 12, 1901. "Local Brevities."

_____. May 31, 1901.

_____. July 5, 1901.

_____. August 4, 1901.

_____. August 8, 1901.

_____. August 9, 1901.

_____. August 13, 1901.

_____. August 17, 1901.

_____. August 23, 1901.

_____. December 25, 1901.

_____. July 18, 1901.

_____. October 22, 1901.

_____. October 23, 1901.

_____. October 27, 1901.

_____. October 31, 1901.

_____. September 15, 1901.

_____. September 17, 1901.

_____. September 20, 1901.

_____. September 21, 1901.

_____. September 25, 1901.

_____. September 26, 1901.

_____. September 29, 1901.

_____. September 2, 1905.

_____. September 6, 1905.

_____. September 9, 1905.

_____. January 4, 1906.

_____. May 9, 1906.

_____. April 20, 1906.

_____. May 6, 1906.

_____. May 15, 1906.

_____. May 21, 1906.

_____. May 31, 1906.

_____. February 21, 1907.

_____. February 22, 1907.

_____. February 23, 1907.

_____. February 24, 1907.

_____. March 14, 1907.

_____. March 15, 1907.

_____. October 6, 1907.

_____. October 8, 1907.

_____. October 10, 1907.

_____. October 11, 1907.

_____. October 12, 1907.

_____. April 10, 1914.

_____. April 18, 1914.

_____. April 19, 1914.

_____. November 14, 1917.

_____. November 15, 1917.

Fresno Times. January 28, 1865.

Fresno Weekly Democrat. May 15, 1901.

_____. September 4, 1901.

Selma Enterprise. August 21, 1941.

Index

Index

Index

Index

Index

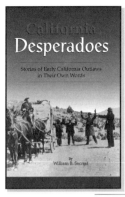
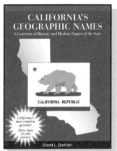

About the Author

Cathy Rehart's mother's family arrived in Fresno Station in 1873, the year after the town was founded. She was born in the Sample Sanitarium on Fulton Street, is a third generation graduate of Fresno High School and a second generation graduate of Fresno State College with a BA in English and history. She is the mother of three grown children.

During the years her children were in school, her involvement in their activities resulted in service on several PTA boards, the Fresno High School Site Council and the Cub Scouts. Later she served as first vice-chairwoman for the Historic Preservation Commission for the City of Fresno; as a member of the board of directors of the Fresno City and County Historical Society; as chair of the Preservation Committee of the FCCHS; and a president of the La Paloma Guild, the FCCH's auxiliary.

From 1986 to 1994, she held the position of education/information director for the FCCHS.

Her work as a freelance writer includes writing the KMJ Radio scripts for "The Valley's Legends and Legacies" —from which this book is derived—and other writing projects on local history.